D1611888

CHRISTIAN LOVE AND JUST WAR

CHRISTIAN LOVE AND JUST WAR

Moral Paradox
and Political Life in St. Augustine
and His Modern Interpreters

William R. Stevenson, Jr.

Mercer
University Press

ISBN 0-86554-272-4

BT
736.2
.S65
1987

Christian Love and Just War
Copyright ©1987
Mercer University Press,
Macon GA 31207
All rights reserved
Printed in the United States of America

The paper used in this publication meets
the minimum requirements of American National Standard
for Information Sciences—Permanence of Paper
for Printed Library Materials, ANSI Z39.48-1984.

Library of Congress Cataloging-in-Publication Data
Stevenson, William R., Jr.
Christian love and just war.
Bibliography: p. 153.
1. Augustine, Saint, Bishop of Hippo—Contributions
in just war doctrine. 2. Just war doctrine—History
of doctrines—Early church, ca. 30-600. 3. Ramsey,
Paul. 4. Niebuhr, Reinhold, 1892-1971. I. Title.
BT736.2.S65   1987   241'.6242   87-15376
ISBN 0-86554-272-4 (alk. paper)

CONTENTS

TO
ROSEMARY
certe adeodatae

FOREWORD

Politics is about getting, keeping, and using power. All of those activities pose moral issues that have intrigued and puzzled and bedeviled thinking people throughout human history. Morality has to do with means: How should power be secured, increased, defended, and put to use? What means are impermissible, and what are justified only by stern necessity? Morality also has to to with ends: What are the appropriate purposes of getting and keeping power, and for what ends should it be used? What is the relationship, if any, between the moral dignity of ends and the moral acceptability of means? Theorists sometimes postulate a "pure" politics to which morality is utterly irrelevant, and cynical observers on occasion purport to discover the total exclusion of moral considerations from political practice. In actual practice, however, statespersons and peoples alike subject political behavior to moral judgment and agonize over the moral aspects of political issues. They may not attain either clarity or agreement about what constitutes justice in political life, and they may not treat the rules of political morality as inviolate, but neither do they regard these precepts as inapplicable.

Some of the most enduring and troublesome problems of political morality arise in the sphere of international relations, that political context in which the sense of community is weakest, consensus on the rules of the game is minimal, formal institutions are least adequate, and raw power in the form of military violence therefore figures most prominently. Chief among those problems are those relating to war among states: Under what circumstances, and for what purposes, is resort to war justified and perhaps even required? People have rarely believed that war requires no justification, or that it can never deserve approval, but they have never found it easy to formulate and agree upon guidelines for distinguishing between proper and improper engagement in hostilities. How should war be conducted? What restraints are morally obligatory, even for belligerents whose resort to arms deserves approbation? As the destructive potential of war has burgeoned, the imposition of effective limitations upon its conduct has become at once more urgent and more difficult. The temptation of resignation to the grim reality expressed by General William Tecumseh Sherman, that war is hell, is recurrently powerful, but humankind never really abandons the hope of restricting the violence of war and the conviction that even fragile limitations are better than none at all. How should war be ended? What are the obligations of the victors to the vanquished? How can military triumph be translated into a just and lasting peace, a settlement that can endure, at least in part because it deserves to endure? The moral issues posed by war—its beginning, its conduct, and its ending—are at the center of humanity's longstanding discourse about justice and decency in the relations of states with each other.

Dr. Stevenson's book deals with these central questions, primarily by examining their treatment in the works of that seminal Christian thinker of the fourth and fifth centuries, Saint Augustine, and the interpretations of their treatment by two prominent theological and political scholars of our own time, Reinhold Niebuhr and Paul Ramsey. Analyzing the theological underpinnings of Augustine's views about morality in the political realm, the author makes it clear that the good bishop bequeathed to posterity no systematic theory or tidy formula for just war, but rather some basic principles and an appreciation of the perplexities and uncertainties that accompany their application to the struggles of states in the real world. For students of political science and of Christian ethics, this volume provides a valuable entree into some of the most profoundly important and excruciatingly difficult questions that a human being can grapple with. It does not purport to give the answers, but thoughtful readers will be rewarded by the stimulus that it provides for their own search for answers.

Inis L. Claude, Jr.
Edward R. Stettinius, Jr., Professor
of Government and Foreign Affairs
University of Virginia

ACKNOWLEDGMENTS

Intellectual debts can never be acknowledged adequately, and yet, to quote out of context a renowned line from the *Confessions*, "Woe to them that say nothing, since even the loquacious are as mutes!" This project has been a long time coming, and is the result of several years of encouragement by many other people to read, think, and converse further about Augustine and about Christian social responsibilities. I can only trust that those to whom I am in debt but who are unnamed here will sense my gratitude and not think less of me for omitting their names.

For sound, precise, timely, and constructive criticism, I am indebted to James F. Childress, Kenneth W. Thompson, Inis L. Claude, Jr., James W. Skillen, Alan Pino, Alberto R. Coll, Glenn Tinder, and the two outside readers consulted by Mercer University Press. For skillful copyediting and attentive shepherding of the manuscript, I am indebted to Marvin Bergman, recently of Mercer University Press, as well as to Susan Carini, currently of the Press. For critical financial assistance, I am indebted to Barry Howard, and Dr. and Mrs. Charles B. Howard of the Howard Christian Education Fund.

For spiritual comradeship and encouragment, I am indebted to those already mentioned as well as to Tinsley E. Yarbrough, John P. East (1931-1986), Elmer L. Puryear, Philip E. Kennedy, Edward S. Twardy, William B. Stillerman, M. L. Fisher, Jr., Farhang Rajee, and James F. Pontuso. For indispensable love, support, and patience, I am indebted to my parents, William R. Stevenson, Sr. (1911-1981) and Margaret R. Stevenson; my parents-in-law, Sawyer A. and Ruth H. Cooler; my children, Rachael Claudia Stevenson and Clark Sawyer Stevenson; and, most important, my wife and our mom, Rosemary Cooler Stevenson.

A NOTE ON SOURCES AND TRANSLATIONS

In examining the works of Augustine, I have concentrated primarily on the *Confessions* (*Confessiones*), trans. William Watts, 2 vols. (Cambridge: Harvard University Press, 1912) and *The City of God* (*De Civitate Dei*), trans. William M. Green et al., 7 vols. (Cambridge: Harvard University Press, 1968). A great many of Augustine's other works touch upon the subject of warfare, of course. Yet the two cited above demand the closest scrutiny. *The City of God* was Augustine's magnum opus, his defense of the Christian faith against the charge by some of his pagan compatriots that such discipleship debilitated political institutions. The *Confessions* was perhaps Augustine's only work of pure literature, the one work that arose from no particular issue or occasion in his ministry. *The City of God* thus gives us the best glimpse of Augustine's views on politics, while his *Confessions* provides our best view of his understanding of human nature and of God.

In looking at each of these works I found the English translations cited above helpful starting points. However, I frequently found it necessary, especially regarding the Watts version of the *Confessions,* to put Augustine's Latin prose in my own words. By great and good fortune, neither of these works is particularly hostile to such translations.

In seeking out Augustine's other works revelant to my topic, I relied on the following English editions: J. H. Baxter, ed. and trans., *Select Letters of St. Augustine* (London: William Heineman, 1930); John H. S. Burleigh, ed. and trans., *Augustine: Earlier Writings*, The Library of Christian Classics, vol. 6 (Philadelphia: Westminster Press, 1953); John Burnaby, ed. and trans., *Augustine: Later Works*, The Library of Christian Classics, vol. 8 (Philadelphia: Westminster Press, 1955); *The Fathers of the Church* (New York: Fathers of the Church, Inc., 1951-6); and, most heavily, Philip Schaff, ed., *A*

Select Library of the Nicene and Post-Nicene Fathers of the Church, vols. 1-8 (New York: Charles Scribner's Sons, 1887), abbreviated within as *NPNFC*.

When checking particular translations I consulted the following standard editions of Augustine's works: *Corpus Christianorum, Series Latina* (Turnholti: Typographi Brepols editores Pontificii, 1961); *Corpus Scriptorum Ecclesiasticorum Latinorum* (Vienna: Academy of Letters, 1866-); and, in certain cases, J. P. Migne, *Patrologiae cursus completus . . . series Latina,* 221 vols. (Paris: N.P., 1844-1865).

In citing particular works, I have used the following list of abbreviations:

Conf.	*Confessions* *(Confessiones)*
Con. Faus.	*Reply to Faustus the Manichee* *(Contra Faustum Manicheum)*
Con. Mend.	*Against Lying* *(Contra Mendacium)*
De Agone Christ.	*On Christian Agony* *(de Agone Christiano)*
De Bapt.	*On Baptism, Against the Donatists* *(De Baptismo contra Donatistas)*
De Bono Coniug.	*On the Good of Marriage* *(De Bono Coniugali)*
DCD	*The City of God* *(De Civitate Dei)*
De Cat. Rud.	*On Catechising the Uninstructed* *(De Catechizandis Rudibus)*
De Correp.	*On Rebuke and Grace* *(De Correptione et Gratia)*
De Div. Quaest. ad Simplic.	*On Diverse Questions to Simplicianus* *(De Diversis Quaestionibus ad Simplicianum)*
De Div. Quaest. LXXXIII	*On Eighty-Three Diverse Questions* *(De Diversis Quaestionibus LXXXIII)*
De Doctr. Christ.	*On Christian Doctrine* *(De Doctrina Christiana)*
De Gen. ad Lit.	*Literal Commentary on Genesis* *(De Genesi ad Literam)*
De Grat. et Lib.	*On Grace and Free Will* *(De Gratia et Libero Arbitrio)*

De Lib. Arb.	*On the Free Choice of the Will* *(De Libero Arbitrio)*
De Mor. Eccl. Cath.	*On the Morals of the Catholic Church* *(De Moribus Ecclesiae Catholicae)*
De Nat. et Grat.	*On Nature and Grace* *(De Natura et Gratia)*
De Peccat. Meritis	*On the Merits and Remission of Sins,* *and on the Baptism of Infants* *(De Peccatorum Meritis et Remissione,* *et de Baptismo Parvulorum)*
De Perf.	*On Human Perfection in Righteousness* *(De Perfectione Iustitiae Hominis)*
De Serm. Dom.	*On the Lord's Sermon on the Mount* *(De Sermone Domini in Monte)*
De Vera Rel.	*On True Religion* *(De Vera Religione)*
De Trin.	*On the Trinity* *(De Trinitate)*
En. in Ps.	*Expositions on the Psalms* *(Enarrationes in Psalmos)*
Ep.	*Letters* *(Epistulae)*
In Epist. Ioann.	*Homilies on the First Letter of John* *(In Epistolam Ioannis ad Parthos Tractatus)*
In Ioann. Evang.	*Homilies on the Gospel of John* *(In Ioannis Evangelium Tractatus CXXIV)*
QH	*Of Questions on the Heptateuch* *(Quaestionum in Heptateuchum)*
Retr.	*Retractions* *(Retractationes)*
Serm.	*Sermons* *(Sermones)*

INTRODUCTION

"Judging," says Michael Walzer in his essay *Just and Unjust Wars*, "is as common a human activity as loving or fighting."[1] The American bishops' pastoral letter, "The Challenge of Peace," issued just seven months before that fateful Orwellian symbolism began to manifest itself as history, has capped a century marked by overwhelming empirical verification of Walzer's insight. In the past twenty-five years, ever since the publication of Paul Ramsey's *War and the Christian Conscience*, Americans have been confronted with a veritable "media blitz" exhibiting the engagement of both individuals and institutions in attempts either to rejoin these three activities in holy matrimony or to annul once and for all their traditional marriage. Does war annul love? Or might love include war? Might we judge war to be obligatory? Or ought we to judge war at all? Is war in fact judicable?

We are confronted simultaneously by bombastic declamations for peace and love, and by coolly reasoned arguments that war is a kind of love; by demonstrated need for moral sterility in describing war, and by condemnation of the destructive sterility of academic evaluation of war; by war for principle and by war only for interest; by judgments of reason and by judgments of faith; by "principled theory" and by "prudential statecraft." How are we to deal with this profusion of propositions? How do we sift through the harvested bundles of intellectual discourse to discover the grain? Or is any grain to be found? In short, how ought we to think about war? Where can we find some solid intellectual pillars from which to begin our discourse?

Persons in search of answers to these questions may find themselves looking back to the writings of the great fifth-century bishop

---

[1]Michael Walzer, *Just and Unjust Wars* (New York: Basic Books, 1977) 3.

of Hippo, Saint Augustine. We find in Saint Augustine the man who, almost alone among Western political thinkers, appears to have set the ground rules for the moral discourse about war. He appears to have first announced to the Christian West a middle ground between absolute pacifism on the one hand and uninhibited, because uncontrolled, combat on the other.

Contemporary academic investigations into the historical connections between Walzer's three "most common" human activities are almost unanimous in pointing to Saint Augustine. "The just war tradition begins with . . . St. Augustine," says William V. O'Brien. Augustine was "the acknowledged well-spring of the Catholic just war tradition," echoes Alan Keyes. Augustine was "the great co-ordinator of Christian doctrine upon peace and war," asserts John Eppstein. The idea of just war "delineated" by Augustine "is of extreme importance because it continues to this day in all essentials to be the ethic of the Roman Catholic Church and of the major Protestant bodies," affirms Roland Bainton. "The die for the Medieval just war was cast by St. Augustine," Frederick Russell joins in saying. Augustine's place is "at the head of a long line of theologians, natural law philosophers, and international lawyers . . . who set forth criteria according to which the justness of resort to war should be determined," adds Inis Claude. Augustine's authority, suggests Richard S. Hartigan, had "great influence . . . in shaping the traditional 'just war' doctrine." In sum, offers Paul Ramsey, Augustine "was the first great formulator of the theory that war might be 'just,' which thereafter has mainly directed the course of Western thinking about the problem of war."[2]

---

[2]William V. O'Brien, *The Conduct of Just and Limited War* (New York: Praeger, 1981) 4; Alan L. Keyes, "The Morality of Deterrence," *Catholicism in Crisis* 1 (1 April 1983): 41; John Eppstein, *The Catholic Tradition of the Law of Nations* (London: Burns, Oates and Washbourne, 1935) 65; Roland H. Bainton, *Christian Attitudes Toward War and Peace: A Historical Survey and Critical Re-evaluation* (Nashville: Abingdon Press, 1960) 99; Frederick H. Russell, *The Just War in the Middle Ages* (Cambridge: Cambridge University Press, 1975) 16; Inis L. Claude, Jr., "Just Wars: Doctrines and Institutions," *Political Science Quarterly* 95 (Spring 1980): 87; Richard S. Hartigan, "Saint Augustine on War and Killing: The Problem of the Innocent," *Journal of the History of Ideas* 27 (1966): 195; Paul Ramsey, *War and the Christian Conscience: How Shall Modern War Be Conducted Justly?* (Durham NC: Duke University Press, 1961) 15. See also James Turner Johnson, *Can Modern War Be Just?* (New Haven: Yale University Press, 1984) 1; Michael Novak, "Moral Clarity in the Nuclear Age," *Catholicism in Crisis* 1 (March 1983): 8; National Conference of

Although one can point to clear differences of interpretation among these contemporary scholars regarding Augustine's specific pronouncements, one can recognize a significant common ground upon which they rest their various analyses. All agree that Augustine's pronouncements about the relationship of war to justice have formed the backdrop against which all subsequent judging of, and theorizing about, war by Christian thinkers has taken place. All credit Augustine with having promulgated an idea of "just war," a recognizable body of propositions that Christian thinkers can use in approaching an ethical evaluation of specific instances of organized interpolity conflict.

Few contemporary scholars have gone further to ascribe to Augustine a just war "theory"; few, that is, have ascribed to him a *systematic* body of propositions concerning the relationship of war to justice.[3] One must look to earlier twentieth-century interpretations by such scholars as Robert Regout and Joachim von Elbe to see this more extreme ascription. Even Paul Ramsey, himself a just war

---

Catholic Bishops, *The Challenge of Peace* (Washington DC, 1983) 26; Joachim von Elbe, "The Evolution of the Concept of the Just War in International Law," *American Journal of International Law* 33 (October 1939): 667-68: and Daniel D. Williams, "The Significance of St. Augustine Today," in *A Companion to the Study of St. Augustine,* ed. Roy W. Battenhouse (New York: Oxford University Press, 1955) 3-4.

[3]For discussions of the lack of system in Augustine, see Herbert A. Deane, *The Political and Social Ideas of St. Augustine* (New York: Columbia University Press, 1963) vii-ix, 156, 160-68; Russell, 25; Peter Brown, *Religion and Society in the Age of St. Augustine* (New York: Harper and Row, 1972) 261, 263; Anton C. Pegis, "The Mind of St. Augustine," *Medieval Studies* 6 (1944): 8; Robert E. Meagher, *An Introduction to Augustine* (New York: New York University Press, 1978) 3; and John Neville Figgis, *The Political Aspects of S. Augustine's "City of God"* (London: Longmans, Green, and Co., 1921) 7. In suggesting that a "theory" is by definition "systematic" I am relying on the *Oxford English Dictionary*, as well as on the ways in which Reinhold Niebuhr and Paul Ramsey have used this term. There is, of course, some controversy as to whether "political theory" must be "systematic." Some thinkers justifiably suggest that systematization of political thinking is in fact a kind of betrayal of political theory because political theory deals with phenomena that cannot be systematized. See, for example, Dante Germino, *Machiavelli to Marx* (1972; reprint ed., Chicago: University of Chicago Press, 1979) 343. For a more complete discussion of the meaning of "theory," see Dante Germino, *Beyond Ideology: The Revival of Political Theory* (1967; reprint ed., Chicago: University of Chicago Press, 1976) 7-14.

theorist, finds Augustine to have been not so much a builder of just war theory as its "primary architect."[4]

Clearly, though, contemporary scholars agree that Augustine stood at the beginning of the Christian just war "tradition."[5] Participants in the long and continuing conversation about the relationship of Christian love to justice and war look primarily to Augustine as their intellectual forefather. This tradition includes both systematic "theories" (those of Aquinas, Suarez, and Vitoria, among others) and open-ended "theorizing" (most conspicuously that of Augustine himself). Although the individual theories differ in substance, they have in common a definite form, and it is just this form that the theorists have drawn out of the Augustinian corpus. Just war theorists (and historians) since Augustine have found in him three main "criteria" for evaluating war: "just cause," "legitimate authority," and "right intention."[6] Theorists have modified this format through the years, of course. They have added new criteria, and they have varied their emphasis on the different criteria.[7] None, however, have abandoned any of the original three ascribed to Augustine; they all accept what they view as Augustine's marking off of the field of discourse.

With few exceptions, investigators of Augustine's thoughts on war have denied that a just war format arises spontaneously out of his writings. Most discover instead a complex set of apparently unrelated and perhaps even contradictory ideas. Nevertheless, interpreters have drawn out of Augustine's writings what Herbert Deane

---

[4]Robert Regout, *La doctrine de la guerre juste de saint Augustin a nos jours d'apres les theologiens et les juristes canoniques* (Paris: Pedone, 1935) 44; von Elbe, 667-68; Ramsey, *War and Conscience,* 18.

[5]LeRoy Walters, "Five Classic Just War Theories: A Study in the Thought of Thomas Aquinas, Victoria, Suarez, Gentili, and Grotius" (Ph.D. diss. Yale University, 1971) insists that one speak of the long history of the just war idea as a "tradition" containing many "theories" rather than as a comprehensive "theory." See also James F. Childress, "Just War Theories: The Bases, Interrelations, Priorities, and Functions of Their Criteria," *Theological Studies* 39 (September 1978): 427. Ramsey is wont to speak of the tradition as a "theory." See *War and Conscience,* 18.

[6]See von Elbe, 669; Regout, 44; Russell, 25-26; O'Brien, 17 and *passim;* and Deane, 160-66.

[7]See Childress, "Just War Theories," 428, for a recent statement of those criteria most widely accepted at present. See also Ramsey, *War and Conscience,* xviii, 32; and O'Brien, *passim;* as well as Childress, "Just War Theories," 435 and the references therein.

calls "coherent and consistent patterns [of] views." Both Deane and Frederick Russell exemplify this claim by the way they present Augustine's thoughts on war, organizing their presentations around Augustine's "cluster" criteria for evaluating war.[8]

Perhaps the most interesting investigator of Augustine's thoughts about war is the contemporary Protestant just war theorist, Paul Ramsey. Ramsey claims that the basis for *iustum bellum* in Augustine's writings was Christian love and not natural justice. Thus, Ramsey finds "most later formulations of the *iustum bellum*" to have been "radically unAugustinian." He attacks later natural law formulations, however, only for the purpose of placing just war theory on more solid ground. While natural law formulations have tended to regulate the precept of just conduct in war to disuse, Ramsey forcefully contends that, at its inception in Augustine, the idea of *iustum bellum* turned on the precept of right intention (that is, Christian love) and thus on its concretization, right conduct.[9] Ramsey therefore distinguishes himself both for admirable exegesis of Augustine's writings and for rigorous theory construction in his own right.

One would be tempted to rest content with the conventional labeling of Augustine as progenitor of Christian just war theory, and to confine one's scholarly endeavors in this area to limited exegeses, were it not for the existence of the renowned modern critic of just war theory, Reinhold Niebuhr. Niebuhr claimed to derive from Augustinian premises a "Christian realism" that found just war theory both inappropriate and misleading.[10]

What is the case, then? Did Augustine father just war theory or not? If not, why not? And what are the problems, if any, in just war theorizing? More importantly, what *is* a "just war theory?" What might such a theory encompass?

The potential relevance of the great bishop's writings to our own time and condition depends on our answers to these questions. The road of inquiry is a difficult and seemingly endless one, however,

---

[8]Deane, vii-ix. See also, Deane, 160-66; Russell, 16-26; Ramsey, *War and Conscience*, 15-42; Hartigan, 195-204; and Louis J. Swift, "Augustine on War and Killing: Another View," *Harvard Theological Review* 66 (July 1973): 369-83.

[9]Ramsey, *War and Conscience*, 15, 32-33.

[10]Reinhold Niebuhr, *Christian Realism and Political Problems* (New York: Charles Scribner's Sons, 1953) 2; idem, *The Nature and Destiny of Man*, 2 vols. (New York: Charles Scribner's Sons, 1941-1943) 1:183. (see also 1:157 and 2:137).

because in his complexities and his apparent contradictions Augustine presented no clear picture of himself. His writings were with few exceptions occasional pieces; they were specific answers to specific questions, answers that often lacked clear grounding in a larger framework of thought. Moreover, these writings were so numerous and extensive that one is necessarily constrained to examine only a portion of them.[11]

The inquiry is further complicated by the fact that Niebuhr, who roundly criticized just war theory, did not refer specifically to Augustine in undertaking his criticism. His "Augustinianism" was more implicit than explicit. On certain points of theology he entertained serious questions about Augustinian "doctrine," but he did so on the basis of rather clearly Augustinian premises. For example, in elucidating his political realism, Niebuhr found the human condition to be one of insoluble paradox. He further insisted that no systematic theory could adequately incorporate such paradox. Theories mislead, according to Niebuhr, because they seek to contain the uncontainable—the truth that humans are *simultaneously* rebellious and accommodating. Humans are both children of God and children of pride, said Niebuhr: they are both free from the grasp of animal nature and enslaved by its tentacles; they are both rational and "natural."[12] This simultaneity of apparent opposites, Niebuhr felt, made human attempts to discover rational (systematic) coherence in human social interaction ultimately futile and misleading.[13]

---

[11]According to Brown, *Religion,* 25, "Isidore of Seville once wrote that if anyone told you he had read all the works of Augustine, he was a liar."

[12]Niebuhr, *Nature and Destiny,* 1:1. One possible source of difficulty in Niebuhr's interpretation of Augustine is Niebuhr's "modern" use of *nature* in contrast to Augustine's *classical* use of *nature.* For the classical thinkers, as for Augustine, "nature" meant "full development" or "perfection," whereas for the modern thinkers, beginning perhaps with Marsiglio of Padua, "nature" means "primitive state" or "lowest common denominator." See, for example, Marjorie Reeves, "Marsiglio of Padua and Dante Alighieri," in *Perspectives on Political Philosophy,* vol. 1, *Thucydides through Machiavelli,* ed. James V. Downton, Jr., and David K. Hart (New York: Holt, Rinehart and Winston, 1971) 303. For Niebuhr's "modern" usage, see, for example, Niebuhr, *Nature and Destiny,* 1:1 and 1:3. For Augustine's "classical" usage, see chapter two below, in the section, "Human Nature, Human Perversion." For an example of the difficulty these distinct usages can pose for an evaluation of Niebuhr's critique of Augustine, see chapter three below, in the section, "Grace," and the notes therein.

[13]See, for example, Niebuhr, *Nature and Destiny,* 1:12-13.

Ramsey, on the other hand, finds in Augustine a norm of love that requires the possible. In the conduct of war this love distills itself into a principle, that of noncombatant immunity. For Ramsey, Christian (Augustinian) love requires a primary intent to attack only opposing forces, and not innocent civilians. Ramsey acknowledges that noncombatants may be difficult to discern, that they may be in the line of necessary fire, and that the principle surrounding them with immunity may not be heeded. Nevertheless, he states firmly, the principle remains an obligation and a possibility. Such a principle follows consistently from Augustine's accurate (so says Ramsey) appraisal of the Christian norm of love. Christian love not only allows (or even requires) war in some instances—thus *iustum bellum*— it limits the conduct of war. Moreover, it limits in a way that is both discernible and comprehensible.[14] For Ramsey, then, the just war theory fathered by Augustine revolves consistently (even systematically) around this one central principle. Circumstances shed light on the "whens" and "hows" of application, but the principle itself, rationally coherent as it is, remains inviolable.

So, who is the true Augustinian, Niebuhr with his insoluble paradox or Ramsey with his just war theory? That the discrepancy between Niebuhr and Ramsey on the matter of just war theory is not one of mere semantics is clear if one notes the distinct direction each thinker has taken in regard to foreign policy formulation. For Niebuhr, such formulation must begin with an acute sense of the tragedy and the paradox of moral achievement, and work its way to a prudentially inductive posture drawn from practical and historical experience; it aspires to little more than a long-term vision of national interest. For Ramsey, on the other hand, such formulation must begin with an articulation of moral principle and work its way through necessary practical experience to a deductive posture based primarily on rational distillation of moral obligations; it aspires to exemplary moral vitality in a fallen world. For Ramsey, the Niebuhrian vision is destructively world-compromising. For Niebuhr, the Ramseyan vision is destructively moralistic.

The careful examination of Augustine's writings relating to war that follows attempts to discern either a sense of insoluble paradox or a sense of coherent moralism. Such examination will necessarily be incomplete: the body of relevant material is too great, Augus-

---

[14]See, for example, Ramsey, *War and Conscience,* xx, 59, and passim.

tine's writings on war too diffuse, and the mystery of the man behind the authoring hand too profound. Such incompleteness may not be a liability, however. If the present study initiates a communal inquiry or prolongs its author's own individual search, it will perhaps have served a purpose ultimately more valuable than that served by the mere answering of a most complex question.

In seeking out an answer to the question of just war theory's paternity in Augustine, I organize the bishop's thought according to the three traditionally accepted criteria of the just war: just cause, legitimate authority, and right intention. In so doing I hope to demonstrate a sympathy for the traditional labeling. However, in considering the many paradoxical elements within Augustine's thought on these particular issues, I question the claim of Augustinian paternity in this area, suggesting instead a sonship in Niebuhr's insoluble paradox and consequent prudential statecraft.

The gist of my conclusion is that the just war theory Ramsey derives from Augustinian principles fails to account fully for the many paradoxes that Augustine recognized in the human condition. In other words, although Ramsey recognizes Augustine's "both/and" building blocks, the theory he constructs from those blocks appears to rule out the paradoxical "both/ands" in favor of the more coherent "either/ors." Niebuhr, in contrast, distanced himself from Augustine on one or two points, perhaps failing to recognize the presence of the Augustinian paradox, but fully incorporated into his thinking about war the "both/ands" he recognized in the human social condition. He thus became a true son of Augustine almost in spite of himself.

Hence, Augustine would recognize as his own not so much Ramsey's prudence of principle as Niebuhr's prudence of contingency. The proper human response to the complexities and perplexities of international politics, for Augustine, would not be prudential deduction from principle, whether a principle of ends *or* means, but rather a prudential induction from circumstance. Such induction would try to take full account of the inherent contradictions of human social existence and historical contingency while attempting in prayerful hope to fashion particular and proximate solutions to the insoluble dilemmas of these realms. This response would humbly withhold self-confidence in enduring human achievement and place its hope in a merciful providence. In the nuclear era, such prudence may very well mean, as Niebuhr clearly recognized, that we must prepare for a war that we never intend to fight.

One cannot adequately present or understand Augustine's thoughts on war unless one enters into intimate contact with his thoughts on God. Indeed, Augustine's thoughts on politics generally cannot be divorced from his thoughts on God. For Augustine, one can not begin to understand human politics unless one first endeavors to understand human beings; and one cannot begin to understand human beings unless one first gives some thought to their creator. A person's relationship to God is prior in time and in importance to his or her relationships to others and to human institutions. For these reasons, the serious student of Augustine's political writings is required to explore theological issues in some depth. Both Ramsey and Niebuhr well understood this necessity.

CHAPTER ONE

Earthly Justice and the Two Cities: When Is War Appropriate?

> *"The wise man, they say, will wage just wars. As if he would not all the more, if he remembers his humanity, deplore his being compelled to engage in just wars."*
> The City of God 19.7

FOR AUGUSTINE, the only valid reason for going to war was the restoration of peace. Such a paradox will surprise no student of twentieth-century attempts at collective security. Yet in Augustine's case it illustrated a recognition of the tragic, because insoluble, paradoxes that underlay the choice of war. Augustine knew firsthand both the horrors of organized conflict and the difficulties of determining a time appropriate either to initiate or to join in such conflict. Hence, although he used the phrase "*iustum bellum*" on several occasions, he did not intend it to imply that "justice" was either obvious or unilateral or that, given certain conditions, war was a positive good.[1] The actualization of even a diluted justice in the world was for him an intensely complicated and in-

---

[1]See, for example, *QH* 4.44, 6.10; *DCD* 4.15, 19.7.

evitably tragic process. Recourse to war, even when appropriate, should, he insisted, be the last resort of a prudent people.

In order to discover more completely what was for Augustine an appropriate reason for going to war, and to discern the underlying paradox of "just cause," it is necessary, first, to determine his understanding of the possible relationship between any political act and true justice. Augustine's metaphor of the "two cities" is critical at this point, for it was within and between the two "cities" that the activity of "politics," for Augustine, had most significance; the "politics" within and among existing cities (kingdom, empires) was much less significant.

THE TWO CITIES

Augustine's thinking on questions of justice in politics rested firmly on his faith in the reality and transcendence of God.[2] For him, God is both the source and center of human existence.[3] Therefore,

---

[2]Such faith has a basis in reason, although of course it recognizes the insufficiency of reason. For the basis in reason, see *DCD* 8.10, 11.4; *De Lib. Arb.* 2.8.12; *Conf.* 6.11, 7.10, 10.6, 11.4, 13.33. See also Reinhold Niebuhr, *The Nature and Destiny of Man*, 2 vols. (New York: Charles Scribner's Sons, 1941-1943) 1:157; Eugene Portalie, S. J., *A Guide to the Thought of St. Augustine*, trans. Ralph J. Bastian, S. J., with introduction by Vernon J. Bourke (Chicago: Henry Regnery, 1960) 109, 125-26; Etienne Gilson, *The Christian Philosophy of St. Augustine*, trans. L. E. M. Lynch (New York: Random House, 1960) 38-43; M. C. D'Arcy, S. J., "The Philosophy of St. Augustine," in *A Monument to St. Augustine*, comp. Thomas F. Burns (New York: The Dial Press, 1930) 155, 160-61; Frederick C. Copleston, *Medieval Philosophy* (New York: Harper Torchboks, 1961) 19; Karl Jaspers, *Plato and Augustine*, ed. Hannah Arendt, trans. Ralph Manheim (New York: Harcourt Brace Jovanovichk, 1962) 83, 104; and John A. Mourant, *Introduction to the Philosophy of Saint Augustine: Selected Readings and Commentaries* (University Park PA: Pennsylvania State University Press, 1964) 11. For the insufficiency of reason, see *DCD* 11.3; *De Lib. Arb.* 2.2; *Conf.* 1.1, 6.5, 10.1, 13.38. See also Niebuhr *Nature and Destiny*, 1:158, 165; Portalie, 107-109, 115-24; Gilson, *Christian Philosophy*, 27-37; D'Arcy, 185; Jaspers, 70; Mourant, 12; Marthinus Versfeld, *A Guide to "The City of God"* (New York: Sheed and Ward, 1958) 3; and Ernest L. Fortin, "The Political Implications of St. Augustine's Theory of Conscience," *Augustinian Studies* 1 (1970): 151. Augustine's favorite scriptural passage on this point, Isa. 7:9, which he quotes as, "unless ye believe, ye shall not understand," can be found in, among other places, *De Lib. Arb.* 2.2; *In Ioann. Evang.* 29.6; *Serm.* 43.9, 118, and 126.1. For arguments that, indeed, for Augustine reason and faith are ultimately inseparable, even analytically, see, Daniel D. Williams, "The Significance of St. Augustine today," in *A Companion to the Study of St. Augustine*, ed. Roy W. Battenhouse (New York: Oxford University

Augustine insisted that a human being's most important decision is the choice between turning toward and turning away from God. The relationship of each human being to God is one's primary relationship; all other choices and relationships are secondary, for Augustine.

Those human beings who turn toward God compose a "city," what Augustine called the *civitas Dei,* or "city of God," while those who turn away, centering their attention on the created world, compose the *civitas terrena,* or "earthly city."[4] These two "cities" of ultimate human allegiance result from "two loves," one "a love of God carried even to the point of contempt of self," and the other "a love of self carried even to the point of contempt for God." Members of the one live "spiritually," the city existing "in the hope placed God," while those of the other live "carnally," the city existing only "in the things of this world."[5]

For Augustine, "the most glorious city of God, the city that knows and worships one God" ("the God of gods"), unquestionably surpasses the earthly city, whose citizens "give preference to their own gods," whose hearts, as Herbert Deane puts it, "are fixed only on material goods and earthly enjoyments." Since Godself, as creator, is the highest good, the various elements of God's creation are by definition of a lower order. So a city whose members attach themselves primarily to God is vastly superior to one whose mem-

---

Press, 1955), 5-6; Charles N. Cochrane, *Christianity and Classical Culture* (London: Oxford University Press, 1944) 400; D'Arcy, 160; and Jaspers, 76-77, 104.

[3]See, for example, *DCD* 11.10, 12.2, 12.26, 14.13, 15.22; *Soliloquies* 1.1.1-1.2.7; *Conf.* 1.2, 1.20, 3.6, 4.16. See also John Neville Figgis, *The Political Aspects of S. Augustine's "City of God"* (London: Longman's, Green, 1921) 39; Etienne Gilson, *God and Philosophy* (New Haven: Yale University Press, 1941) 60-63; F. van der Meer, *Augustine the Bishop,* trans. Brian Battershaw and G. R. Lamb (London: Sheed and Ward, 1961) 28; Herbert A. Deane, *The Political and Social Ideas of St. Augustine* (New York: Columbia University Press, 1963), 13; Portalie, 127, 128, 307; and Jaspers, 69, 71, 82-84.

[4]*DCD* 11.1, 14.1. As many scholars have pointed out, the symbolism of the two cities is not original with Augustine. He probably got it from the Donatist Tyconius. See Christopher Dawson, "St. Augustine and His Age," in Burns, comp., 48, 58; G. G. Willis, *St. Augustine and the Donatist Controversy* (London: SPCK, 1950) 139-40; and Figgis, 46.

[5]*DCD* 14.28, 14.1, 15.21.

bers attach themselves primarily to some part of the created world, and its honors, power, and wealth.[6]

The symbolism of the two cities is more complex than this summary suggests, however. The primary complicating factor is that individuals are not capable of freely making the choice by themselves; they are burdened with the world-centeredness of original sin. To choose God, one must be the beneficiary of God's grace; one must be chosen by God. Thus, as a result of the burden of sin and the necessity of grace, individuals do not themselves truly know what choice they have made (or will make). The decision requires the commitment of one's whole being, and one's whole being is unfathomable. One can have inklings, and can attempt to point oneself in one direction or another, but the ultimate decision, or, rather, the ultimate direction, is always clothed in mystery.

When confronted with that ultimate choice, one will find oneself saying with Augustine, "I am made a question to myself." This "question to myself," emphasizes William Barrett in an interpretation of this point, "is not an adventitious interrogation that may flit through my mind from time to time, but the core of my being. I who ask that question am myself the question I ask." Augustine added, "I cannot comprehend all that I am." As a result of this ignorance, such a radical discontinuity exists in each human being that, Augustine believed, one is simply not capable, on one's own initiative and with one's own efforts, of sustaining one continuous moral intention. "My abilities are concealed . . . in lamentable darkness," wrote Augustine, so that "when my mind questions itself about its powers it does not trust its own report." Thus, "I simply do not know which temptations I can resist and which I cannot." "No one is so well known to himself that he can be sure as to his conduct on the morrow." In sum, said Augustine, "Man is a great mystery [*grande profundum*], O Lord, whose very hairs You number . . . and yet the hairs of his head are more easily numbered than are the affections and movements of his heart."[7]

---

[6]*DCD* 10.25, 11.1; Deane 15, 30. See also *Ep.* 138.2.14; *DCD* 5.17; Conf. 12.15; Stanley Windass, *Christianity versus Violence: A Social and Historical Study of War and Christianity* (London: Sheed and Ward, 1964) 25-26; and Gilson, *Christian Philosophy*, 175.

[7]*Conf.*, 10.33, 8, 22, 5; *Ep.* 130.2.4; *Conf.* 4.14; William Barrett, foreword, in Robert E. Meagher, *An Introduction to Augustine* (New York: New York University Press, 1978) xvi. See also *En in Ps.* 42.12-13, 119.5, 139.16-17; Jaspers, 71, 88;

If individual human beings are ultimately ignorant about themselves, they are so much the more ignorant about other human beings. The hearts of human beings "are hidden from each other," Augustine said. Human communication is thus "one depth calling to another." "For what is so common to man," he added in another place, "as the inability to inspect the heart of man, and therefore, instead of scrutinizing its inmost recesses, to suspect for the most part something very different from what is going on therein?" Only God can offer substantial aid in uncovering either one's own motivations or those of others. For only God can see into the depths of one's soul. Hence, only God can know the ultimate decisions of individual human beings.[8]

The two "cities" are therefore not actual, or at least tangible, cities. They exist, as Augustine said, "mystically" (*mystice*), that is, "allegorically." Although God already knows their content, they will become actual cities only at the end of time, when "justice is turned into judgement." Then, each city will be assembled. Members of the city of God, their bodies resurrected, will be given eternal life and perfect freedom in communion with God and each other; members of the other city will suffer eternal death and punishment absent from God. Then that city will immediately cease to exist, "for when it is condemned to final punishment, it will no longer be a city." At present, however, one can only say that there are two loves and that the two loves imply two cities. The content of those cities, like the content of human hearts, remains a mystery.[9]

Suggesting two "mystical" cities as the repositories of ultimate human allegiance raises an important question. What revelance does such classification have for politics in the conventional sense of the term, the civic interactions of the here and now? Some schol-

---

Portalie, 90-91, 108-109; Peter Brown, *Augustine of Hippo: A Biography* (Berkeley: University of California Press, 1967) 165, 405; idem, *Religion and Society in the Age of St. Augustine* (New York: Harper and Row, 1972) 29; R. A. Markus, *Saeculum: History and Society in the Theology of St. Augustine* (Cambridge: Cambridge University Press, 1970) 103-104.

[8]*DCD* 15.7; *En. in Ps.* 42.12; *In Ioann. Evang.* 90.2; *Conf.* 10.5, 5.1; *De Correp.* 17, 40. See also Brown, *Religion and Society*, 29.

[9]*DCD* 15.1, 1. preface (Ps. 94:15), 15.4. See also *DCD* 5.16, 19.27, 21 (passim), 22.24, and passim; Figgis, 51; Dante Germino, *Poltical Philosophy and the Open Society* (Baton Rouge: Louisiana State University Press, 1982) 109; and Ernest Barker, introduction to *The City of God*, by St. Augustine, trans. John Healy (London: J. M. Dent and Sons, 1931) xxv.

ars have answered this question by deemphasizing the allegorical nature of the two cities and identifying them more directly with existing human institutions. The city of God is thus manifest in the visible church and the earthly city in the visible state.[10] Others have leaned toward a simple identification, at least between the church and the city of God, by proposing that there were at least *three* cities for Augustine. Hans Leisegang called the third the *civitas terrena spiritalis* (the *spiritual* earthly city), distinguishing it from the *civitas caelestis spiritalis* (the spiritual heavenly city) and the *civitas terrena carnalis* (the carnal earthly city). Similarly, Peter Hawkins calls the third city the "earthly City of God."[11] The interpretation of multiple cities is an uncommon one, however; Cranz speaks for most Augustinian scholars, those who take Augustine at his word, when he says, "the fundamental thesis of the *De civitate Dei* [is] that there are in the final analysis not more than two cities.[12]

Although such identification is most tempting, it does not completely square with the thrust of Augustine's thought as a whole. Augustine clearly denied the possibility of knowing one's own or another's ultimate allegiance. Even more problematic for any simple identification of the two cities is the fact that, for Augustine, church and state are two aspects of the same society: members of the church are also members of a state. With this in mind, several scholars stop short of a simple identification, but instead have spoken of church and state as "manifestations," or "organs," or "representatives" of the two cities.[13] Thus one might say, as Figgis did, that the visible institutions represent the invisible cities "rather by symbol than by identification."[14]

---

[10]See, for example, Norman H. Baynes, "The Political Ideas of St. Augustine's *De Civitate Dei*," in Norman H. Baynes, *Byzantine Studies and Other Essays* (London: University of London, 1955) 302, 304; Barker, xxxi; F. Edward Cranz, "*De Civitate Dei*, XV, 2, and Augustine's Idea of the Christian Society," *Speculum* 25 (April 1950): 219.

[11]Hans Leisegang, "Der Ursprung der Lehre Augustins von der Civitas Dei," *Archiv fur Kulturgeschichte* 16 (1925): 127-58 (cited by Cranz, "Christian Society," 216); Peter S. Hawkins, "Polemical Counterpoint in *De Civitate Dei*," *Augustinian Studies* 6 (1975): 106.

[12]Cranz, "Christian Society," 218. Cranz cites *DCD* 12.1, 14.1, and 15.1, all of which support his point.

[13]See, for example, Dawson, 61,72; Rex Martin, "The Two Cities in Augustine's Political Philosohy," *Journal of the History of Ideas* 33 (April 1972): 200.

[14]Figgis, 51.

Nevertheless, these scholars have argued, there is a very definite and obvious connection between the symbol and the reality. For example, the church *is* "the depository and dispenser of grace." Although "the two conceptions of the sacramental visible Church and the *communio sanctorum* cross one another in a way that is often perplexing," Figgis went on, "this difficulty is not decisive. No one is secure of salvation by baptism or even by communion. But they are the conditions *sine qua non*."[15] Dawson echoed this interpretation, noting that the salvation signified by membership in the city of God is "transmitted sacramentally." Thus, as Martin suggests, although there is no "simple identity," there is "an identification at certain points and for certain purposes." Pursuing this kind of tentative, but important, identification, Dawson pointed to Augustine's ambiguous statement in book 20 of *The City of God:* "Accordingly, the Church even now is the kingdom of Christ and the kingdom of heaven." "In spite of all the imperfections of the earthly Church," Dawson explained, "it is nevertheless the most perfect society that this world can know. Indeed, it is the only society which has its source in a spiritual will. The kingdoms of the earth seek after the goods of the earth; the Church, and the Church alone, seeks spiritual goods and a peace which is eternal."[16]

Even this interpretation has some difficulties, however. Herbert Deane, in his study of Augustine's political ideas, is adamant about drawing a sharp distinction, at least between visible institutions and the invisible city of God. According to Deane, Augustine said Christ's statement, "My kingdom is not of this world," made it clear that "no earthly state, city, or association can ever be part or a representative of the city of God"; the eternal city "is not embodied in any human or earthly institution."[17]

---

[15]Figgis, 43. Augustine's view on the need for infant baptism would seem to support this interpretation. See Augustine, *Contra Julianum* 1.7.31 (cited by Brown, *Augustine*, 385).

[16]Dawson, 75; Martin, 200.

[17]Deane, 29. See also 120-21. According to D. J. Macqueen, "The Origin and Dynamics of Society and the State according to Augustine," *Augustinian Studies* 4 (1973): 80, Augustine's purposeful use of *"civitas"* instead of *"res publica"* in naming the "cities" is further evidence that he did not have in mind a simple identification. For it is *civitas* that is used in the critical passages in the *Psalms* to mean the "communion of the saints" beyond time and the world. See also Figgis, 51, where he noted that, at least as far as the earthly city is concerned, *"civitas"* cannot be "state" as *"civitas"* is "not convertible with *res publica*."

Deane's interpretation has the virtue of springing from Augustine's many explicit statements that the members of the two cities are in this life (that is, in the world of space and time) inextricably intertwined. In book 11 of *The City of God,* for example, one reads that the two cities are "interwoven" (*perplexas*) and "blended together [*invicem permixtas*] in this transitory age." In book 18, Augustine wrote, "in this world, as it were in a sea, [members of both cities] swim indiscriminately." And in book 19 he said that the city of God "summons citizens from all peoples, and of all languages, caring naught what difference may be in manners, laws, or institutions." In his short treatise, *On Baptism against the Donatists,* written at least ten years before he began *The City of God,* Augustine emphasized repeatedly the mixture of the two "cities" within the visible church. "Many who seem to be without [the city of God, by virtue of their having no membership in the visible Church] are in reality within, and many who seem to be within yet really are without. [I]t is the position of the heart that we must consider, not that of the body, since all who are within in heart are saved . . . [whereas] all who are in heart without, whether they are also in body without or not, die as enemies of unity." Yet the "true position of the heart" is knowable only by God, and until God's final "winnowing" "there are many ears of corn outside, and many tares within."[18]

Regarding the earthly city, however, Deane says Augustine suggested a more obvious and more positive relationship with visible secular institutions. "On a number of occasions," according to Deane, "Augustine speaks of the states and kingdoms of this world as divisions or parts of the earthly city." Yet even here, Deane states, members of the two cities necessarily intermingle. Citizens of secular states and even some of their rulers "may, as individuals, be members of the city of God."[19]

Seizing upon Augustine's rather clear statements about the intermingling of the citizens of the two cities and upon his tendency to contrast absolutely the two cities as pure types, Deane, echoed by historian R. A. Markus among others, concludes that any kind of identification of a visible human institution with one of the two

---

[18]*DCD* 11.1, 18.49, 19.17; *De Bapt.* 5.27.38, 5.28.39, 4.9.13-14. See also *DCD* 1.35, 18.47; *En. in Ps.* 100.9; *In Ioann. Evang.* 19.18; *In Epist. Ioann.* 5.7, 7.6; and *Con Faus.* 13.16. And see Deane's discussion, 30-31; Barker, xxv; Markus, 63; and Germino, 111.

[19]Deane, 30-31. See, for example, *DCD* 18 and 5.16. See also Markus, 58.

invisible cities is problematic.[20] A primary reason for the difficulty, these critics stress, is Augustine's inconsistency in his use of terms. The "church" could be either the visible, institutional church or the invisible, transcendent city of God.[21] Likewise, the "earthly city" could be either a visible, secular state or the invisible, transcendent unity of those whose primary love is for the created world. As Markus puts the problem, for example, "Augustine's identification of the Roman state with the earthly city is as clear in his writings as is his refusal to abide by this identification."[22]

Finally, however, the argument for no obvious identification is most compelling—logically at least, if in no other way. Markus concludes,

> All [Augustine's] ways of contrasting the two cities imply their mutually exclusive character; and they are manifestly intended to be equivalent ways of stating their fundamental opposition. . . . No identification of either of the two cities with any institution or with any empirically definable body of people can be reconciled with this radical dichotomy. Membership of the two cities is mutually exclusive, and there can be no possible overlap; but membership of either is compatible with belonging to the Roman—or some other—state and with belonging to the Church.

Augustine, he continues, lodged a consistent protest against "the readiness to see within any society the ultimate eschatological conflict prematurely revealed in visible, identifiable form. All we can know is that the two cities are always present in any historical society; but we can never . . . identify the *locus* of either."[23] Markus thus places Augustine squarely, and appropriately, in the middle on a perennial issue in Western political thought: do paradigmatic societies exist, and can they be actualized? For Augustine, the paradigmatic society exists, but only beyond history, never within history.

---

[20]Deane, 31. See his most complete discussion, 28-38.

[21]See, for example, the passages from *De Bapt.* 5.38-39 quoted above, n.18, as well as *DCD* 18.49, where he spoke of the church "preparing for her future high estate." See also Martin, 197-98, where he notes, "Augustine had an essentially tripartite conception of the city of God": as an "eternal city," as an "association of persons who love God," and as a "visible and institutional entity."

[22]Markus, 59.

[23]Ibid., 60-61; 101-102.

One ought to be tentative about announcing a conclusive position on this issue. The bishop's writings are filled with apparently contradictory statements: sometimes he appeared to identify visible institutions and the two cities; other times he insisted on maintaining sharp distinctions. Nevertheless, the strongest evidence indicates that Augustine resisted any simple and obvious identification between the ultimate cities and immanent institutions.[24]

That still leaves another troublesome question: what is the relevance of the two cities metaphor to the world as we confront it day by day, the world in which wars are waged, often for posited "just causes"? Were we to accept the simple identification, the task would be easier. If the church were God's city, a "Christianized" state would by definition have God on its side in any conflict with a non-Christianized state, and there would be little need for elaboration. But Augustine rejected any such identification, and thus the idea of "holy war." In book 5 of *The City of God,* he compared the true "eternal city" with Christian Rome and concluded that the former is "as far removed" from the latter "as heaven is from earth, eternal life from temporal joys, solid glory from hollow praise, the company of angels from that of mortals, and the light of Him who made sun and moon from the light of sun and moon."[25]

---

[24]Even those who connect Augustine's city of God with the later Holy Roman Empire fault him for failing to foresee later misinterpretations of his work, rather than claiming that he made the simple identification himself. See, for example, Niebuhr, *Nature and Destiny,* 1:216, who spoke of Augustine's "identification, however qualified, of the City of God with the historic Church, an identification which was later stripped of all its Augustinian reservations to become the instrument of the spiritual pride of a universal church in its conflict with the political pride of an empire." See also Niebuhr, *Nature and Destiny,* 2:138,144; Germino, Political Philosophy, 112; Cochrane, 377; Eppstein, 67; and Gilson, *Christian Philosophy,* 176.

[25]*DCD* 5.17. As Markus, 54, sums up the Augustinian position, "The Christianization of the Roman Empire is as accidental to the history of salvation as it is reversible." Markus does argue that for a short time Augustine followed Eusebius, Constantine's court theologian, in thinking of Christian Rome as the beginning of "Christian times," with the empire having a special divine sanction. However, Markus quickly points out that such thinking was quite common in the late fourth and and early fifth centuries and that, in fact, Augustine, "almost alone among his contemporaries, managed, in the end, to break the spell." Markus, 40-42, points to *Ep.* 111.2 (written one year *before* Alaric's sack of Rome in 410) as the first in a long line of explicit repudiations by Augustine of the *tempora Christiana* idea. Ernest L. Fortin, "Augustine's *City of God* and the Modern Historical Consciousness," *Review of Politics* 41 (July 1979): 333-34, denies that Augustine ever succumbed to the idea in the first place. See also Dawson, 57; and von Elbe, 668.

What implications for the conduct of domestic and international politics, in the conventional sense, does the metaphor of the two cites have, then, if there is no obvious identification between visible institutions and the invisible cities? The primary implication, which Augustine proceeded to draw out in great detail—if not in systematic fashion—is this: the *saeculum,* the world of space and time, the world as it appears to human senses, the world in which the two cities intermingle, is clearly of secondary importance.[26] The ultimate allegiance of each human being, that is, the city to which one truly belongs, is most important. The *saeculum* will "pass away"; the destiny of every human being lies in eternity, either life and happiness for eternity or death and suffering for eternity. The *saeculum* is merely a way station, a temporary phase in the working out of human destiny. While they are in the *saeculum,* human beings, as potential members of the heavenly city, live as "aliens" (*peregrini*); their true citizenship, potentially at least, lies in a city *beyond* the world. What happens in the world is significant, of course, but it is not *most* significant.[27]

Several further implications flow from this characterization and evaluation of the *saeculum.* First, as the *saeculum* is the site of "civic" intermingling, it is both a place of unresolved tension, of "misery," and an essential stage in the working out of human destiny. Second, since the tension within the *saeculum* is irresolvable, there can be no true justice in this life; justice would resolve the tension in such a way that the world would become ordered and harmonious. Last, because the *saeculum* is an essential stage, it requires, and can attain, if not justice, then some semblance of "peace."[28]

THE SAECULUM AS MISERY AND NECESSITY

As the site of the "temporal life" of the two cities in, as Markus puts it, "their interwoven, perplexed and only eschatologically separable reality," the *saeculum* is a place of great misery and unresolved tension.[29] Augustine's writings abound with graphic

---

[26]See Markus's superb study of the significance of the *saeculum* for Augustine for an elaboration of Augustine's understanding of the term. See also Brown, *Religion,* 37; and Ramsey, *War and Conscience,* 20.

[27]See, for example, *DCD* 5.17; 19.17; *Serm.* 40.7-8. See also Dawson, 38, 48; Brown, *Augustine,* 210, 324; Jaspers, 80; and Bainton, 95.

[28]See, for example, *DCD* 19.7, 2.21, 19.21, and 15.4. See also Markus, 102-103.

[29]Markus, 71.

descriptions of the miseries of this life. Perhaps the most pointed and most convincing of these descriptions occurs in book 19 of *The City of God,* where he attacked the classical understanding of human happiness exemplified by Marcus Varro, a follower of Plato.

Varro, as a representative of the Platonic tradition in philosophy, but also of the philosophic tradition generally, had proposed a final good, attainable in this life, a life of virtue needed to attain this final good, and a happiness resulting from such attainment, such exercise of virtue. Augustine undertook to demolish this kind of thinking. For him the philosophic enterprise, to the extent that it sought happiness in this life, was one the "fraudulence" (*mendacium*) of which was matched only by its "arrogance" (*superbia*). Philosophers such as Varro, because they did not see that the ultimate good could only be "eternal life," as the ultimate evil could only be "eternal death," try "to manufacture for themselves in this life an utterly counterfeit happiness."[30]

Why was their idea of happiness "counterfeit"? Augustine agreed that "only a happy man lives as he chooses," and that "only a righteous man is happy." But, Augustine went on, "even the righteous man himself will not live as he chooses until he arrives where he both is wholly free from death, deception and injury and is assured that he will always so remain." Such true repose in eternity "is what our nature seeks, and [that nature] will not be fully and perfectly happy unless it attains what it seeks." However, "who among us now can live as he chooses when the very matter of living is not in his power? . . . Life therefore will be happy when it is eternal."[31]

Yet the miseries of this life were far from fully catalogued by the mention of human anxiety about death. "Who, no matter how great his torrent of eloquence, can avail to enumerate the miseries of this life? . . . What pain is there, the opposite of pleasure, what turbulence is there, the opposite of repose, that may not assail the wise man's frame?" Augustine went on, eloquently in spite of his

---

[30]*DCD* 19.3-4. Brown notes that Augustine was clearly more sympathetic to the Platonist viewpoint in the years just after his conversion, thinking of this life as in some sense an "ascent." By the time of the completion of the *De Lib. Arb.* in 395, however, a new image had appeared, "that of a long highway, an *iter*" (Brown, *Augustine,* 152; *De Lib. Arb.,* 2.16.41). Life thenceforth became a long journey (*peregrinatio*), from which there was respite but no relief (ibid., 210).

[31]*DCD* 14.25. See also ibid., 4.33, 19.4; and *Conf.* 10.40.

disclaimer, to catalogue only a few of the diseases and corruptions that sap the body and mind of the "wise man," the social evils to which he is inevitably subject, and consequently the never-ending battles that virtue has to fight. All human beings, after all, grow old; at least occasionally they get sick; they suffer physical disability; they grow deaf and blind; they go insane. In short, "who is quite sure that [such] evil cannot befall the wise man in this life?"[32]

In society, into which the person of wisdom is inevitably thrust, as it is only in society that one can gain such wisdom and exercise such virtue as one has in the first place, one fares no better. "The history of man is in every cranny infested with . . . slights, suspicions, enmities and war." The larger the social unit, "the more does its forum teem with lawsuits both civil and criminal." Even if it were free from "the turbulence, or more often the bloodshed, of sedition and civil wars," it would never be free "from the threat of them." What of the "judgements pronounced by men on their fellow men, which are indispensable in cities however deep the peace that reigns in them?" Here perhaps is the real misery of social life, "since those who pronounce [judgments] cannot look into the consciences of those whom they judge." Consequently, they make mistakes and innocent people suffer. Yet the person of wisdom cannot refuse to sit in judgment; he sees it as his duty, to desert which "he counts abominable." Thus, "by ignorance and by office he is constrained to torture and punish the innocent." Here, for Augustine, "is a clear proof of man's miserable lot."[33]

The evils in this life, to which all human beings, even the wise, are subject, are not merely external, Augustine pointed out. In fact, perhaps the most compelling argument for the lack of complete human happiness in this life had to do with the never-ending struggle of human beings with themselves, of the virtues with the vices. "As to virtue itself, . . . what is its activity here but perpetual war with vices, not external vices but internal, not alien but clearly our own." The struggle was summed up well for Augustine by Saint Paul: "For the flesh lusts against the spirit, and the spirit against the flesh." It is precisely this struggle, or better, this tension—per-

---

[32]*DCD* 19.4. See also ibid., 22.22.

[33]*DCD* 19.5, 19.6. See also ibid., 18.2; *Ep.* 15.3; John M. Rist, "Saint Augustine on the Exercise of Power," *Canadian Catholic Review* 4 (November 1986): 374; and Herbert Butterfield, *The Origins of History,* ed. Adam Watson (London: Eyre Methuen, 1981) 183.

sistent, haunting, and ultimately irresolvable in this life—that led Augustine to question the "happiness" of the philosophic tradition and to conclude as he did: "Far be it from us, then, so long as we are engaged in this internal war, to hold it true that we have already attained to that happiness which is the goal that we would gain by victory. And who is so wise that he has no battle at all to wage against his lusts?"[34]

To point out these passages is not to settle the matter once and for all, however. Some scholars have suggested that the overall thrust of Augustine's writing was to point not to a ubiquitous internal struggle but to one that was primarily between members of the one city and those of the other, between good people and evil people. Reinhold Niebuhr claimed that "no Christian theologian has ever arrived at a more convincing statement of the relevance and distance between the human and divine than [Augustine]."[35] Yet in spite of this awareness, said Niebuhr, Augustine fell prey to "one of the most universal of all human ambitions: the ambition to be clear, or to be thought clear, of the ambiguity of all human achievements." As an early builder of the Christian church, Augustine fell prey to the understandable temptation to glorify rather than to criticize that historic institution. Thus although Augustine "was certain that the historic church included both the redeemed and the unredeemed," he tended to exaggerate the effects of the grace that was mediated through the church.[36] In so doing Augustine betrayed in some of his occasional and less thoughtful pieces a tendency to suggest that redemption could be accomplished and made plain within history. In *On Grace and Free Will*, for example, Augustine declared, "It is certain that we can keep the commandments if we so will; but because the will is prepared by the Lord we must ask Him for such force of will as to make us act by willing." The possibility, for Augustine, of historical redemption was thus

---

[34]*DCD* 19.4. The quotation from Paul is Gal. 5:17. See also *De Perf.* 2.1; and *Conf.* 4.5, 10.28.

[35]Niebuhr, *Nature and Destiny,* 1:158. See also ibid., 2:137.

[36]Reinhold Niebuhr, *The Structure of Nations and Empires* (New York: Charles Scribner's Sons, 1959) 102-103; Niebuhr, *Nature and Destiny,* 2:135-36. See also idem, *Man's Nature and His Communities* (New York: Charles Scribner's Sons, 1965) 97-98; idem, *Christian Realism and Political Problems* (New York: Charles Scribner's Sons, 1953) 138; and Kenneth W. Thompson, *The President and the Public Philosophy* (Baton Rouge: Louisiana State University Press, 1981) 31.

clear to Niebuhr; hence the primary struggle within the *saeculum* was between the redeemed and the reprobate: "The historical conflict between self-love and the love of God [for Augustine] is essentially a conflict between the [visible] church and the world."[37]

Similarly, Herbert Deane, after saying that for Augustine "war is not God's doing; it is rooted in the war that rages within every man between flesh and spirit," goes on to conclude,

> In Augustine's vision there are two clearly separated types of man— the minority, who love God and do His will, and the great majority, who love themselves and earthly goods, wealth, power, fame and pleasure. In consequence, there is in his thought [ultimately] no room for the idea that every man is a particular, complex mixture of good and evil impulses, of love and hate, or of egoism and altruism.[38]

Such an interpretation merits close attention, especially in light of Augustine's tendency to speak of the two cities as mutually exclusive categories and of members of the one as "sojourners" in this life and of the other as "at home" in this life.[39] Nevertheless, a number of scholars have preferred to interpret Augustine's intercivic war as taking place primarily within each individual. Peter Brown, for example, says that Augustine "turned the Christian struggle inwards: its amphitheatre was the 'heart'; it was an inner struggle against forces in the soul; the 'Lord of this world' becomes the 'Lord of desires.' " Paul Ramsey, echoing Karl Jaspers, who said Augustine "for the first time laid bare without reserve the struggle of the

---

[37]Niebuhr, *Nature and Destiny*, 2:135 (quoting Augustine, *De Grat. et Lib. Arb.* 17.32), and 139. See also Niebuhr's description of *De Perf.* in *Nature and Destiny* 2:136-37, as well as *Christian Realism*, 138.

[38]Deane, 157, 239-40. Deane does not tie this latter statement to the Augustinian understanding of grace, but such a tie is the clear implication of the statement. See also Baynes, 292, who, after saying. "Between the flesh and the spirit—this is the great opposition which dominates the thought of Augustine," goes on to have Augustine being "freed" from the struggle "by his submission to the authority of the Church." Likewise Dante Germino, *Political Philosophy*, 110, 115: "Augustine grappled heroically with the thorny problem of representing the unity of mankind without either falling into a rigid 'good-evil' characterization or denying the important differences in degree and kind in the responses of individuals to the pull of openness and the counterpull of closure," but he nevertheless ultimately fell victim to the demarcation of human beings "into the two neat categories of saint and sinner."

[39]See, for example, his characterization of Cain and Abel, *DCD*, 15.1.

will with itself," speaks of Augustine's "doctrine of the divided will." "According to Augustine, fratricidal love and brotherly love based on love of God are always commingled in human history. There is no heart, no people, and no public policy so redeemed or so clearly contrary to nature as to be without both. Communities are built over fratricidal love by men with divided hearts."[40]

Perhaps the disagreement in interpretation here is only apparent, however. It is unlikely, as all of these scholars realize, that Augustine meant to point to a readily identifiable location of the intercivic struggle. His primary concern in demonstrating the misery inherent in the *saeculum* was to show that historical existence brings with it inevitable tensions, tensions that can be resolved only by God and only beyond history. Although one may in fact *be* one of the chosen few, one can not know that with certainty as long as one lives within the boundaries of time and space. Historical existence is both existence in ignorance and existence in tension.

For these reasons Niebuhr and Deane, on the one hand, have accurately identified in Augustine's thought the possibility of historical redemption, and have appropriately criticized Augustine for failing to emphasize more consistently the fact that the historical church is essentially a *human* institution subject both to human tensions and temptations and to God's omniscient judgment. As a result of such failure, Augustine left himself open for the specious interpretation later given to his writings by the medieval church. On the other hand, Brown, Jaspers, and Ramsey have accurately recognized in Augustine's writings the ubiquitous tension inherent in historical existence, even for the redeemed, who, because of the barriers of self-love and a finite perspective, live always in tension and ultimate ignorace of their destination.

---

[40]Brown, *Augustine,* 244-45 (quoting from *De Agone Christ* 1.1; 2.2); Jaspers, 88-89 (Jaspers spoke of this struggle as "the cleavage between will and decision"); and Ramsey, *War and Conscience,* 30-31. See also Paul Ramsey, *Basic Christian Ethics* (New York: Charles Scribner's Sons, 1950) 108-109, 131; John Burnaby, "Amor in St. Augustine," in *The Philosophy and Theology of Anders Nygren,* ed. Charles W. Kegley (Carbondale: Southern Illinois University Press, 1970) 185; George Lavere, "The Political Realism of St. Augustine," *Augustinian Studies* 11 (1980): 140; Versfeld, 35; and Brown, *Augustine,* 351. As Brown points out, the existence of this "inner tension" is the basis of Augustine's attacks on the Pelagians.

So one can find in Augustine's writings that most insidious of pronouns, "we," included in his references to the redeemed,[41] as well as the devasting self-indictments so typical of his *Confessions*. Book 10 of this remarkable autobiography contains long and graphic descriptions of tensions Augustine saw still present within himself long after his conversion to Christianity and thus long after his acceptance of the authority of the church. He described, among other things, the lustful thoughts he still had regarding sex, the persistent temptations to overindulge in food and drink, the unremitting need for praise, the "vain and curious itch" seeking trivial gossip, and, above all, the acute awareness of the pride inherent in the very act of self-reproach.[42] All of these things resulted in a heart never at rest, constantly at war with itself.

In the face of evils such as physical and mental disease, social obligation and ignorance, and an internally divided will, therefore, Augustine concluded his attack on the "happiness" sought by philosophers by pronouncing it vain and false. Human existence in the *saeculum* is miserable, as it were, by definition. Its misery derives directly from its being the site of the *mixing* of the two cities. "Good and evil," as George Lavere describes Augustine's thinking, "coexist in human hearts and in human societies in unfathomable combinations. Only God, in the final judgment, can pronounce upon the preponderance of the one over the other." Because human experience consists of just this mixture of faith and pride, of love and lust, of good and evil wills, "the most obvious feature of man's life in the *saeculum* is that it is doomed to remain incomplete." Thus, "no human potentiality can ever reach its fulfillment in [this life]; no human tension can ever be fully resolved."[43]

---

[41]See especially Ep. 189.5: "But as it is necessary in this world that the citizens of the kingdom of heaven should be harassed by temptations among erring and irreverent men so that they may be exercised and tried as gold in the furnace, we ought not before the appointed time to desire to live with the saints and the righteous alone, so that we may deserve to receive this blessedness in its own due time." See also *Ep.* 97.3 and 4, 100.1, 133.1 and 3, 173.1, 3 and 10, and *DCD* 22.30.

[42]*Conf.* 10.30-50. Many scholars have pointed to Augustine's description of his anxiety just before his conversion as evidence of the divided will, but such anxiety proves inconclusive in the face of his subsequent conversion, as Baynes suggests (see note 38, above). For other examples of the tension see *DCD* 19.27; and *En. in Ps.* 137.9.

[43]Lavere, 140; Brown, *Religion*, 38. See also Markus, *Saeculum*, 62-63; and Rist, "Exercise of Power," 371-76.

Although existence in the *saeculum* is miserable, it is also essential to the working out of ultimate human destiny. God has a plan, according to Augustine, and only within the struggles and tensions of the *saeculum* can this plan be worked out. Thus the primary reason for the necessity of the *saeculum* is its function as a "forge" or a "press," which through heat or pressure strengthens and purifies weak or adulterated characters. As Augustine said in speaking of the obvious suffering encountered by the inhabitants of Rome during its sack by Alaric in 410, "Exposed to the same fire gold glows red but chaff smokes." "Just so," he concluded, "one and the same force assailing the good tries, purifies, and purges them clean, but condemns, ruins and destroys the wicked."[44]

The *saeculum* is an essential testing ground. Only in the *saeculum,* in the midst of its temptations and perversions, can individual human beings advance to self-knowledge and thus ultimately to knowledge of God. As Augustine said, "in general there is no other way for the human mind to arrive at self-knowledge except by the trial of its strength in answering, not merely by words but by experience, the questions set by temptation." "Because a man is unknown even to himself," Augustine elaborated, because he "does not know what he can bear, . . . therefore temptation comes like an interrogation, and the man discovers himself." Just as a man can not "be crowned except he shall have conquered, nor can he conquer except he shall have striven, nor can he strive except he shall have experienced an enemy and temptations," just so "a man does not become known to himself unless he is tempted." Thus, it is only in the *saeculum* that the ultimate destinies of human beings become manifest. Life is a constant "trial" (*temptatio*), and salvation is won "by endurance" (*per patientam*).[45]

Yet one can "endure" this life only if one has faith in God's plan and if one through faith seeks God's aid. Augustine was no Stoic; no person can "endure" the world and be ultimately strengthened by such endurance of one's own accord. One needs help. The *saeculum* is thus as much a chance to see who prays for help as it is a chance to see who "endures." God's help, through grace, is always

[44]*DCD* 1.8. See also ibid., 1.9, 1.10, 4.3, 18.14; Deane, 67; and Roy Battenhouse, "The Life of St. Augustine," in Battenhouse, ed., 52.

[45]*DCD* 16.32 (I have translated *experimento* as "experience" here and not "performance"); *En in Ps.* 55.2, 61.2; *Conf.* 10.28; *Con Faus.* 22.78; *DCD* 19.4.

available, but it can only be "helpful" if individuals seek it out and knowingly receive it.[46]

For all its misery, then, the *saeculum* is a place where God is both present and active. In addition to its trials and tribulations it offers a glimpse of a life to come, an awareness of one's proper home and final resting place, a glimpse and an awareness that is offered, first, by God's word as spoken through human beings: the Holy Scriptures.[47] The Hebrew prophesies revealed that, as it had a beginning, the world would have an end. As God created the world, God would let it die. More important, though, the Gospel accounts of the life, death, and resurrection of Christ revealed that God takes an active interest in the Creation as it runs its course, and that God offers the way of Christ to those who would have it; that is, God offers salvation from the world to those who truly seek it.[48]

Second, the glimpse of a life in God is offered by the glories of the Creation itself. One marvels at the wonders and the goodness of Creation if one but stops to notice them. In this way the Creation, when appreciated for what it is, inevitably points to the Creator. "Who but You," Augustine asked plaintively in his *Confessions,* "could be the fabricator of such wonders?"[49]

What are these wonders? Augustine's writings abound with references to them. They include, in addition to the majesty of sky and sea, of mountain views and quiet forests, the wonder of fecundity, that "marvellous power of seed," not only as reflected in animate nature generally but in the continual and constantly new creation of individual human beings. Only human beings have both body and soul, both "corporeal" and "incorporeal" natures, joined, Augustine pointed out, "in wondrous wise" (*miris modis*). They include the power of reason itself, capable as it is "of knowledge and learning, and competent to perceive truth and love the good." Even when it defends "errors and untruth," reason is a wonder to behold in and of itself. They include the wonders of human artistry and artifice, when reason is put to use.

---

[46]See, for example, *DCD* 1.8 and 18.54.

[47]See the oft-quoted line in *Conf.* 1.1; "Our hearts are restless until they rest in Thee."

[48]*DCD* 18.49. See also *Conf.* 7.18 and 10.43.

[49]*Conf.* 9.6. See also ibid., 10.6 and 11.4.

What progress in agriculture and in navigation! What imagination and elaboration [reason] has employed in producing all kinds of vases, and also in the varieties of statues and paintings! . . . What great inventions for capturing, killing and taming irrational animals! . . . And how many drugs and remedies it has discovered to preserve and restore men's health! . . . What ornaments of speech to delight the mind, what abundance of all kinds of poetry! What musical instruments, what modes of song have been devised to soothe the ears! What skill in measuring and reckoning![50]

To Augustine, the wonders of the created world were so clear that he could assert in the *Confessions,* "They are bereft of reason [*Non est sanitas eis*] who find fault with Your creation."[51]

In contemplation of both the Creation and the Holy Scriptures, therefore, one can see—albeit always "through a glass darkly"—one's final and proper resting place; one can see God. This "ultimate optimism" of Augustine, was, as Deane says, "the bedrock that lies beneath his realistic, pessimistic analysis of human nature and human conduct." It was the confidence that the *saeculum,* although by definition miserable, is not directionless. There is a plan unfolding in the *saeculum,* a plan that encompasses all human beings and that is, potentially at least, the source of their salvation. The *saeculum,* though miserable, is also necessary and good.[52]

Two important implications for a discussion of the possibilities of justice appearing in the world and thus of the existence of "just war" flow from this understanding of the *saeculum.* First, because the two cities are "interwoven" in the fabric of the *saeculum,* because of the misery *inherent* in the world, justice here is an insoluble paradox; in its absolute sense, it is simply out of the question. Second, because the *saeculum* serves the necessary functions of both press and preview, some kind of "peace," however temporary and fragile, is a real good. Such peace both moderates the misery and provides an atmosphere for necessary contemplation of God's presence.

---

[50]*DCD* 22.24. See also *Conf.* 1.20, 9.6, 13.24, 13.32; Deane, 64; Figgis, 26; and Theodor E. Mommsen, "St. Augustine and the Christian Idea of Progress," *Journal of the History of Ideas* 12 (June 1951): 374.

[51]*Conf.* 7.14. This translation is that of R. S. Pine-Coffin (Harmondsworth, Middlesex: Penguin Books, 1961) 149. See also Brown, *Augustine,* 325-27.

[52]Deane, 68.

THE PARADOX OF JUSTICE IN THE SAECULUM

In a sense, the possibility of *true* justice in the *saeculum* is ruled out by definition of the relevant Augustinian terms. There has been some controversy about this possibility, however, and it is always dangerous to attempt to simplify the thought of so complex a man as Augustine. Nevertheless, if we accept Augustine's metaphor of the two cities, and the *saeculum* as their place of intermingling, it would seem to follow logically that the *saeculum* can not be home to true justice. For true justice, that ordered harmony of the parts rendering to each its due, is found only in the city of God.[53] Indeed, the city of God is the epitome of justice, whereas the earthly city (as a transcendent unity) is the complete perversion of justice. Therefore, no mixture of the two cities could retain completely any single characteristic of one or the other.

But what, more specifically, is true justice for Augustine and why is it noticeably absent from the *saeculum*? To say that justice is the rendering to each what is due is to say very little. The critical component in Augustine's understanding of justice was the reality and transcendence of God as Creator, Ruler, and Redeemer. Therefore, true justice is, first and foremost, rendering to God God's due. Since only God had created and could redeem humanity, only that order that is directed primarily toward God can be called right or just. Similarly, any order that turns away from God and interferes with God's worship, or that sets up alternative "gods," must be called wrong or unjust. As Augustine put it, "justice for the individual means that God rules and man obeys." This is the primary precept. Of course, justice also means that "the soul rules over the body and reason rules over the vices when they are rebellious . . . and that from God himself we seek to obtain favor for our well-deserving deeds and forgiveness for our sins, and that we offer our service of thanksgiving for the benefits received." But these latter relationships can follow only if the first holds true: "For if a man does not serve God, in no wise can his soul justly command his body or his human reason command his vices." Moreover, these things are true both for the individual human being and for society: "If in . . . a

---

[53]*DCD* 2.21. See also Ernest L. Fortin, "The Patristic Sense of Community," *Augustinian Studies* 4 (1973): 192.

man there is no justice, there can be no doubt that there is no justice in a gathering consisting of such men."[54]

Another way of looking at the notion of true justice for Augustine is to see it as "rightly ordered love." If as individuals and societies human beings love God primarily, then the other objects of their love will each fall into its proper place. Thus it is not necessary to turn away from the world in order to turn toward God, although it is necessary to put the world in its proper perspective. By loving God primarily one comes to love God's creation the way it should be loved, that is, as a reflection of and a pointer to the Creator, and not as an end in itself. Consequently, "a man is just when he seeks to use things only for the end for which God appointed them, and to enjoy God as the end of all, while he enjoys himself and his friend in God and for God." If human beings were rightly ordered toward God, as they should be, they would be rightly oriented toward each other.[55]

Yet it is just this right orientation toward God, fully coherent and obligatory as it is, that is conspicuously absent from the *saeculum*. For Augustine all human beings are tainted by sin; they are divided and discontinuous beings. Hence, although they must, they can not maintain a consistent posture directed toward God. Even those who "persevere" in humble devotion, given strength by constant confession of their own insufficiency and weakness, become fully oriented toward God only *beyond* time and the world.[56]

From this premise of human sin, Augustine launched an attack on the Roman legal notions exemplified by Cicero, according to which the *res publica,* the commonwealth, was a *"societas iuris."*[57] The key term in the Ciceronian understanding, for Augustine, was *"populus"* ("people"). Cicero had seen the *res publica* as a "people's estate" (*res populi*) and a "people" as a "numerous gathering united in fellowship by a common sense of right and a community of interest" (*coetum multitudinis iuris consensu et utilitatis communione sociatum*). But "what he means by a common sense of right he explains

[54]*DCD*, 19.27, 19.21. See also ibid., 5.19; *De Mor. Eccl. Cath.* 15.25; Barker, xxiii; and Anton-Hermann Chroust, "The Philosophy of Law of St. Augustine," *Philosophical Review* 53 (March 1944): 200.

[55]*DCD*, 15.22; *Con. Faus.* 22.78. See also Barker, xxii-xxiii.

[56]*De Perf.* 6.14; 7.17; *De Vera Rel.* 26.48-27.50. See also Deane, 83.

[57]Cicero, *The Republic* (*De Res Publica*), trans. Clinton Walker Keyes (Cambridge: Harvard University Press, 1961) 1.25.39.

by arguing at length that a *res publica* cannot be administered without justice; where there is no true justice [*iustitia*] there can be no right [*ius*]." Yet if justice "is the virtue which assigns to each his due," the lack of full due assignment means that "where there is no true justice there can be no gathering of men united in fellowship by a common sense of right, and therefore no people as defined by Scipio or Cicero; and if no people then no people's estate, . . . [and] no commonwealth."[58]

Clearly there are "peoples" and "commonwealths" in the *saeculum,* but for Augustine they are not signified by the presence of true justice. For the Ciceronian, Augustine offered his own definition of *populus:* "A people is a large gathering of rational beings united in fellowship by their agreement about the objects of their love." Although there are "better" and "worse" objects of love, all such gatherings can be called peoples.[59] Augustine therefore found little to distinguish most earthly kingdoms (*regna*) from "great dens of robbers" (*magna latrocinia*), "justice being absent." He quoted approvingly the reply allegedly made by a captured pirate to Alexander the Great when asked "what he was thinking of, that he should molest the sea . . . : 'the same as you when you molest the world! Since I do this with a little ship I am called a pirate. You do it with a great fleet and are called an emperor.' "[60] Although, as Markus correctly points out, "the critique of a state without true justice was anticipated by Cicero, . . . it is Augustine's translation of it into Christian terms that converts the Ciceronian *ius* into 'righteousness' in the full biblical sense of the word." Consequently, Markus goes on, with *ius* "understood in Augustine's sense, there can be only one *res publica,* and all human kingdoms are in greater or lesser degree 'dens of robbers,' according to the extent of their failure to achieve true justice."[61]

---

[58]*DCD* 19.21. See also ibid., 2.21; Ramsey, *War and Conscience,* 18-19; Deane, 120-21; and Fortin, "Patristic," 193.

[59]*DCD* 19.24. See also *Ep.* 138.2.10; Dawson, 59; and Brown, *Religion,* 42, who notes, "This definition is typical of Augustine. It is deliberately fundamental and all-embracing. Such a definition is so wide that it could include a football crowd on a Saturday afternoon."

[60]*DCD* 4.4.

[61]Markus, *Saeculum,* 64-65. See also Rist, "Exercise of Power," 372-74; Russell, 19; and Fortin, "Patristic," 193. Charles McIlwain, *The Growth of Political Thought in the West,* 154-60, insisted on making a distinction between *res publica* and *regnum*

Augustine did not deny the possibility of greater or lesser *degrees* of proximate "justice" existing in the world, therefore. The true justice of God's city serves as a kind of paradigm against which particular earthly regimes (and particular earthly acts and motivations) can and should be measured. There was in Augustine's understanding some basis for comparison between and among earthly regimes; some political relationships might manifest more "right order" than others. *However,* the primary girder supporting the Augustinian understanding of justice was the basic fact of human sin.

At its most fundamental level, life in the *saeculum* is life in contradiction. Although human beings are obliged to seek justice, the effort tends to subvert the search. Although human beings can and should conceive of justice, they can not detach themselves from personal and selfish interpretations of it. Indeed, the most "just" persons would be the ones least conscious of their own "justice." The consciousness itself is the root of pride, the full turn away from God. Hence, Augustine recognized the acute paradox of justice in the *saeculum.* It is not that individuals and regimes can not fulfill their obligations and so be rightly ordered but that they can not be both rightly ordered and conscious of it; the consciousness undermines the order.

In this way all human evaluations of political orders, acts, or motives, while necessary and proper, are seriously tainted: the sin of the evaluator blinds one to the objectively true situation. Augustine therefore deprecated any grand schemes designed to accomplish, by means of war, a fully just political order. Such schemes require that very self-righteousness that ultimately nullifies "just cause." Proper political, or military, initiatives should be both modest and limited.[62]

---

in Augustine's writings, with only the latter being Augustine's term to refer to those political units founded on force and brigandage, that is, the *"magna latrocinia."* The former term, according to McIlwain, Augustine used to refer to Christian commonwealths. Deane, 120-28, presents a convincing critique of McIlwain's position. See the comparable distinction set up by Barker (xxv-xxviii) and the critique by Paul Ramsey (*War and Conscience*, 18-25). See also Dawson, 61, versus A. J. Carlyle, *A History of Medieval Political Theory in the West*, 2d ed. (Edinburgh and London: Blackwood, 1927) 1:167; as well as Baynes, 294.

[62]See, for example, *DCD* 4.15.

PEACE AS DESIRABLE POSSIBILITY

If true justice is out of the question in the *saeculum*, then, a proximately just peace is not. The final, complete, and permanent peace awaiting the city of God is of course out of the question in the *saeculum*, but there is a kind of "temporal peace" which is both desirable and, on occasion, attainable; indeed, in some form or other it is unavoidable.[63] Augustine's discussion of the phenomenon of peace and its relation to justice and to war is a complex and often confusing one. It even appears contradictory in places. For all of these reasons it is worthy of address.

What is peace, for Augustine? On several occasions he defined peace as the "tranquility of order" (*tranquillitas ordinis*).[64] Order is "the classification of things equal and unequal that assigns to each its proper position." Therefore,

The peace of the body . . . is an ordered proportionment of its components; the peace of the irrational soul is an ordered repose of the appetites; the peace of the rational soul is the ordered agreement of knowledge and action; the peace of body and soul is the ordered life and health of a living creature; peace between mortal man and God is an ordered obedience in the faith under an everlasting law; peace between men is an ordered agreement of mind; domestic peace is an ordered agreement among those who dwell together concerning command and obedience; the peace of the city is an ordered agreement among the citizens concerning command and obedience.[65]

On the surface, this definition of peace sounds a great deal like Augustine's understanding of justice, if justice is "rightly ordered love," or simply "right order." Indeed, some scholars have suggested that Augustine's "break" with Cicero on the possibility of justice in organized communities was not really a break at all, since Augustine simply brought justice into the world through the back door of "peace."[66]

---

[63]*DCD* 19.13, 15.4, 19.12.

[64]For example, *DCD*, 19.13.

[65]Ibid.

[66]See, for example, Martin, 211, 214. See Fortin, "Patristic," 190, for other examples. Augustine's assertion that heavenly peace is the "only peace" (*sola pax*) would seem to support this interpretation (*DCD* 19.17).

If one examines closely both the terms of the definition and the context within which Augustine used it, however, it seems that the interpretation of Augustinian "peace" and "justice" as essentially synonymous terms is a bit simplistic. To begin with, it cannot account for Augustine's use of the phrases "just peace" (*iusta pax*) and "unjust peace" (*iniqua pax*). Nor can it then account for Augustine's assertion that there is peace even among bands of criminals; "Even robbers, in order the more violently and the more safely to attack the peace of other men, choose to maintain peace with their comrades."[67]

What are the differences between the two qualities, then? First, while justice pertains necessarily and primarily to God, so that if God were removed, justice would be removed, peace may or may not pertain to God. In his definition Augustine mentioned a "peace between mortal man and God," but he mentioned as well several other kinds of "peace," none of which did he tie specifically to God's eternal order. Second, while justice is never a matter of "agreement," the order to which it points being always and absolutely "right," peace does seem to be a matter of "agreement." In his description of the various kinds of peace (quoted above), Augustine four times used words that are generally translated by the English word *agreement*.[68] Taking these uses of *agreement* in conjunction with Augustine's use of *peace* to describe a situation existing even among criminals, one can say that peace for Augustine is often simply a "contractual" matter, while justice could never be so. Peace results when the parties concerned agree to work with and not against each other.

To Augustine it was a commonplace that all human beings seek peace, whereas they only rarely seek true justice. Love of peaceful harmony is a part of human nature, as beings made in God's image, and it can not be completely exorcised, no matter how sinful and corrupt one might be. "Peace, of some kind or other, one cannot help loving." Why? Because "no creature's vice is so completely at odds with nature that it destroys the very last traces of nature." In consequence, "so great a good is peace that even where earthly and mortal affairs are in question no other word is heard with more

---

[67]*DCD* 19.12. There could be no "justice" among robbers because the very fact that they were robbers meant that they showed no true love of God *via* love of God's creation.

[68]*Consensio* is used once and *concordia* three times. *DCD* 19.13. See also 19.14 and 19.17.

pleasure, nothing else desired with greater longing, and finally nothing better can be found."[69]

Peace is a good; within the bounds of the *saeculum* it may be the highest good. Peace may very well be unjust; indeed, from God's perspective earthly peace is always unjust. Yet it is also, from the human perspective, very much a good.[70] Peace is good, first, because it means the absence of war. If peace is the great good in the *saeculum,* war is a great evil.[71]

In a sense war is the archetypical misery in the *saeculum.* As in the exercise of human judging, the horrors of war arise from its necessity and from the suffering and pain that such necessity entails. That war is occasionally necessary, Augustine did not doubt. That it could ever be a "good," he denied wholeheartedly. "Why are the words 'glory' and 'victory' used to veil the truth [about war]?" Augustine asked. "Take away the screens of a morbid fashion and let the naked deeds be examined; let them be weighed naked, judged naked."[72] The state of war frees and tends to encourage, even to legitimize, the obvious evils of lust and greed. The state of war results in the even more intense suffering of the human beings involved. "Let every man, then, reflect with sorrow upon all these great evils so horrible and so cruel and admit that this is misery."[73] Peace is a good, then, in that it spares men, albeit only for brief periods, from the horrors of war.[74]

---

[69]*DCD* 19.12, 19.11. See also ibid., 19.14; and Oliver O'Donovan, *The Problem of Self-Love in St. Augustine* (New Haven: Yale University Press, 1980) 20.

[70]*DCD,* 19.10, 19.11. See also Barrow, 218-19, 228.

[71]Saying this was not to imply that war was to be avoided at all costs, as we shall see, although Augustine's pronouncements upon the evil of war have often been "mined" by pacifists. See Windass, 27.

[72]*DCD* 3.14; *Con. Faus.* 22.74; *DCD* 3.18, 3.26, 19.7. See also Bainton, 99; Deane, 154, 161; Windass, 26-27; Eppstein, 67; Russell, 16; and Hartigan, 198.

[73]*DCD* 19.7. I have retranslated *"miseriam fateatur"* here. See also Francis Firth, O.S.B. "The Importance of Saint Augustine," *Canadian Catholic Review* 4 (September 1986): 291.

[74]"As to wars, when has the earth not been scourged by them at different periods and places?" *Ep.* 199.10.35. See also Lavere, 144: "This earthly peace forever eludes those who place their trust in it." As to Roman imperial expansion, often justified as a means of "keeping the peace," Deane, 169, notes with Augustine: "But even if we suppose that there were no peoples left outside the Empire, it would not follow that peace would reign throughout the world." According to

A second reason for the high value of peace has to do with the purpose of the *saeculum* as a preview of the life to come. As potential citizens of the city of God, human beings need a certain amount of quiet time, an atmosphere of tranquillity within which to contemplate life's majesties and mysteries, not to mention their own future holy estate. "Human peace is so sweet for procuring the temporal salvation of men."[75] A time for contemplation of the Scriptures should be very high on a person's list of priorities, according to Augustine. It had been the peace provided by the Roman Empire, after all, that had allowed God's Word to spread by way of the expanding church.[76]

Two points must be emphasized with regard to this reason for the value of peace. First, needless to say, earthly peace is not the "final" peace of the city of God. It does not even approximate that final peace. It is both temporary and tentative. It is "a solace for our wretchedness" rather than "a positive enjoyment of blessedness." As Deane says rightly, "it is primarily a negative peace—the absence of overt conflict and hostilities—maintained by restraint, coercion, and discipline." The final peace, on the other hand, would have no need for restraint and coercion, said Augustine, "since nothing either in ourselves or in another will be at war with any one of us."[77]

Second, earthly peace carries with it an obligation to use it well. If one uses it to feed one's desires for earthly power and wealth, it has little ultimate value. If on the other hand one uses it to contemplate God and God's mysteries and to help one's fellow human beings, then it is very much a good.[78]

Augustine (*DCD* 19.7), "The very extent of the empire has begotten wars of a worse kind; I mean social and civil wars, by which the human race is more wretchedly shaken, whether while they are actually being waged for the sake of calm at last or while they are a source of fear lest a new storm arise." See also *DCD* 4.3; and Butterfield, 183.

[75]*Ep.* 189.6. See also *Ep.* 220.3; *DCD* 19.4, 19.13, 19.17; Brown, *Augustine*, 324; and Barrow, 226.

[76]See, for example, *Conf.* 11.3; Versfeld, 80.

[77]See *DCD* 19.27. See also ibid., 15.4, 22.24; *Ep.* 189.6; Barrow, 259; Fortin, "Consciousness," 339-40; Brown, *Religion*, 40-41; and Deane, 64, 102.

[78]*DCD* 15.4, 19.13. See also Barrow, 226, 229; and Fortin, "Consciousness," 342: "Augustine was at once more hopeful for the destiny of the individual and less hopeful for that of society at large."

THE NECESSITY OF WAR

War is a plague. It is either a constant fact or a constant threat in the *saeculum*. "Wars are inevitable as long as men and their societies are moved by avarice, greed, and lust for power, the paramount drives of sinful men. It is, therefore, self-delusion and folly to expect that a time will ever come in this world when wars will cease and 'men will beat their swords into ploughshares.' "[79] Most wars are "internecine quarrels within the earthly city," as Deane puts it. They are exercises in lust and greed and nothing more. However, on occasion war is necessary and appropriate; in this way it is "just," not as a positive advancing of "justice" but as a negative restraining of "rank injustice."[80]

What are these occasions? When *is* war appropriate? For what reasons should one go to war? Paradoxically, Augustine said that the only proper reason for going to war is to preserve, or to recapture, the peace; that is, one wars for peace.

Such a proposition is less incongruous than it may appear to be. For Augustine, it was in fact a truism. Leaving aside evaluation of specific wars, wars are generally fought in order to obtain peace, whether in the sense of "profitable settlement," or in the sense of "harmonious ordering." When human beings choose warfare, for example, they "desire nothing but victory;" they seek profitable settlement. "What else is victory but the conquest of the other party to the fight? And when this is achieved, there will be peace [a profitable settlement]. . . . Even those who prefer that a particular settlement [*pax in qua sunt*] should be upset do so not because they hate peace but because they desire a different settlement that will meet their wishes." Moreover, in every inclination to war, there is the "natural" motivation for a "harmonious ordering." Such a desire "does not follow from the nature of war, but because war is waged by and within persons who have some natural being." By nature human beings seek harmony and agreement with their fellows. Although seriously tainted by sin, they remain in some important ways "natural beings." At any rate peace of some sort is always the goal of war.[81]

---

[79]Deane, 155. See *DCD* 18.13 and n. 77 above.

[80]Deane, 157. "Rank injustice" is Deane's phrase (161).

[81]*DCD* 19.12-13 See also ibid., 15.4; *Con. Faus.* 22.75, where he spoke of "the

Some settlements are better than others, however. The "just" war seeks a "just" settlement. A just settlement, of course, is not one that manifests complete justice, but rather one that is as relatively in line with natural harmony as one can expect peace to be in the *saeculum*. A relatively good settlement, then, is one that results in what R. S. Hartigan calls, "a harmonious ordering of rights and duties among men, and between men and God."[82] It is not a settlement based solely on coercion, imposed from without on unwilling subjects, although it might originate in coercion. Rather, it is a harmonious order based on "agreement" (*concordia* and *consensio*), broad in its scope and reflecting a respect for human beings as God's special creatures, a "fellowship with all [one's] fellow men."[83] Only wars waged with such settlements in view can themselves be termed "just."[84]

Saying this is not to suggest that there was in Augustine any kind of crusading zeal. Wars are not to be taken lightly. One does not upset an existing and relatively stable peace because it is "relatively unjust." War is the last resort. Yves LaBriere eloquently stated Augustine's point here: "Recourse to armed force necessarily produces evils so great, so horrible, so cruel . . . that one is under the most serious obligation never to resort to a procedure so risky and so tragic when there exists even a slim possibility of procuring by any reasonable means the result sought."[85] Before going to war, all

---

natural order which seeks the peace of mankind"; and Russell, 16; as well as note 73 above. One could certainly argue with Augustine on this point. Yet it would be difficult given his expansive use of "peace." See his description of the mythical Cacus as one who seeks peace (*DCD* 19.12.) See also John Langan, S. J., "The Elements of St. Augustine's Just War Theory" (Paper presented to American Society of Church History meeting, Union Theological Seminary, Richmond VA, 23 April 1982), p. 17. (I am grateful to Professor James F. Childress for calling this paper to my attention.) For an eloquent presentation of a contrary idea, see J. Glenn Gray, *The Warriors: Reflections on Men in Battle* (New York: Harcourt, Brace and Co., 1959) 215-16.

[82]Hartigan, 199. See also *DCD* 19.13.

[83]*DCD* 19.12. See also ibid., 5.17, 19.13; Deane, 171; Ramsey, *War and Conscience*, 30; and Martin, 212.

[84]*Ep.* 189.6; Hartigan, 199; Bainton, 95. See also Windass, 29-30: "As the worldly kingdom is to be scorned, it is hard to see how St. Augustine could justify killing for it . . . The nearest he ever gets to resolving this tension is when he suggests, on a number of occasions, that the worldly kingdom, for all its transitoriness, has *some* value, that worldly peace is at least *some* kind of peace."

[85]Yves de La Briere, "La conception de la paix et de la guerre chez Saint Augustine," *Revue de Philosophie*, n.s., 1 (1930): 565 (my translation). See also Deane, 159.

diplomatic remedies should be exhausted. Augustine wrote in praise of the young Count Darius, "my deservedly illustrious and most distinguished lord and son warmly cherished in Christ," for his attempts to settle through diplomatic means the conflict with the Goths in North Africa: "It is a greater glory to slay war with a word than men with the sword and to gain and maintain peace by means of peace, not by means of war."[86]

When war is necessary it is always to be regretted. In castigation of Roman "just wars," Augustine did not dispute the propriety of these wars generally, made "just" by the "aggression" and "wrongdoing" of Rome's neighbors; rather, he lamented the existence of such awful necessities, and denounced Roman complacency: "He prays badly who prays for someone to hate or fear, in order to have someone to conquer." Perhaps the Romans should have added a new goddess to the pantheon, that of "External Aggression"; "for we see that she contributed greatly to the growth of the empire." While in the eyes of many Romans the expansion of empire had been "a gift of fortune," it should rather have been seen as "a necessary evil." For "without a doubt it is better fortune to live in peace with a good neighbor than to subdue a bad neighbor in war." In sum, Augustine lamented in a later book, "the wise man, they say, will wage just wars. As if he would not all the more, if he remembers his humanity, deplore his being compelled to engage in just wars; for if they were not just, he would not have to wage them, and so a wise man would have no wars."[87]

What, more specifically, are the occasions appropriate for waging war, then? In an oft-quoted sentence, Augustine said, "Just wars are usually defined as those which avenge injuries."[88] Yet Augustine did not readily accept the "usual" definition. Although human beings might sometimes be conscious instruments of God's wrath, they are more likely to be prideful slaves to their own lust for power.

---

[86]*Ep.* 229.2.

[87]*DCD* 4.15, 19.7. See also Deane, 156; and Bainton, 99: "What Augustine said of the judge he would also have said of the general."

[88]*QH* 6.10. This sentence is incorrectly cited by Russell, 18, as "Just wars avenge injuries," omitting the significant phrase "are usually defined." This is no doubt a small point, but the possibility exists that Augustine sought to distance himself somewhat from the "usual" definition and for this reason purposefully included the *"definiri solent."* Russell does cite the full Latin quotation in a footnote (#8).

For this reason, I would argue, Augustine purposefully omitted any detailed tenets of "just cause." He mentioned some particular historical examples of appropriate warfare. The "defensive" wars resulting in Rome's imperial expansion, made necessary by attacks on Rome from without, passed muster, as did armed resistance to the barbarian invasions of North Africa.[89] Yet even defensive wars are not automatically appropriate. In an interesting exception, Augustine seems to have admired the example of the Saguntines, who had chosen to keep faith with the Romans and commit national suicide rather than resist obvious Roman aggression.[90]

In some cases aggressive war may be appropriate. The Israelites' war against the Amorites over the Amorites' refusal to grant innocent passage had been a "just war." Moses' wars against the Egyptians likewise had been "just wars," as had been Joshua's war against the people of Ai.[91] Indeed, any war waged by God's explicit and conscious messenger as a punishment to the wicked is a "just war."[92] God, in his ultimate wisdom, may very well send war as a punishment and a scourge.[93] The wars of Moses and Joshua had been "just" only because those men had been the direct representatives of God, however.

To say these things is therefore not to attribute to Augustine a self-righteous, crusading spirit. Because God's plan is known to God alone and because pride is the primary sin, the appropriate attitude for human beings is always one of humility and forbearance. One can never be *sure* that God is using one for good; one will always be uncertain. While one may know that God's will should be followed, one can never know for sure what that will requires in a specific situation. Augustine's defense of Moses was thus predi-

---

[89]*DCD* 4.15; *Ep.* 220.3 and 7. See also *Ep.* 99.2, 189, and 228.10-12; as well as Figgis, 65. For discussion of the propriety of defensive wars, see *De Lib. Arb.* 1.5; Bainton, 96; Deane, 160; La Briere, 564.

[90]*DCD* 22.6; Bainton, 96. Deane, 160, says that for Augustine a defensive war is "obviously" a just war.

[91]*QH* 4.44, referring to *Numb.* 21: 22-25; *Con. Faus.* 22.74-78; and *QH* 6.10.

[92]*Con. Faus.* 22.71-72. See also Hartigan, 198; and Russell, 20.

[93]Indeed, from the perspective of God's all-knowing Providence, all wars are ultimately good, for God uses even human sin to accomplish the divine purpose. See Hartigan, 199; and Russell, 19. Compare *Ep.* 220.8: "Nevertheless, I do not want you to be of the number of those evil and unrighteous men whom God uses to scourge with temporal punishments those whom he chooses."

cated on the realization that Moses' role as God's messenger became clear only after his deeds had been recorded in Scripture.[94]

Augustine was therefore no advocate of the "holy war" idea that was prominent in the High Middle Ages. In that view war, as Frederick Russell has defined it, was "fought for the goals or ideals of the faith and . . . waged by divine authority or the authority of some religious leader."[95] Augustine never spoke of war as an instrument of Christian expansion. Indeed, with one notable exception, any kind of "religious coercion" was unacceptable to him.[96] Although God may use war to punish sinners, neither political nor ecclesiastical officials should assume the role of God's direct representative without clear and explicit command.

Frederick Russell makes a very sound case for seeing Augustine as a major contributor to trends in Christian political thought that later resulted in the holy war idea. Yet I do not read Russell to mean that Augustine himself undertook to justify holy war. In expanding the Ciceronian idea of "just cause," according to Russell, Augustine "made of the just war a much more comprehensive doctrine." "Injuries" came to mean both "crimes" and "sins." Thus, Augustine's just war doctrine was a defense of "the whole moral order." "Divinely ordained" wars were automatically "just." Given this expansion, Russell concludes, it was a small step to link the "divinely-inspired just war . . . to the Pauline derivation of ruling authority from God with the result that wars to defend righteousness could be waged by rulers even without an express divine command."[97]

It is difficult to deny that the later medieval thinkers drew on Augustine's Old Testament interpretations to formulate their own doctrines of holy war. However, it is also important to point out that Augustine's writings on war do not lead automatically to the medieval conclusion. As John Langan has so perceptively put it, "the elements

---

[94]*Con. Faus.* 22.79. See also, for example, Langan, 8.

[95]See Russell, 2. See also Walters, "Five Classic Just War Theories," 417; and LeRoy Walters, "The Just War and the Crusade: Antitheses or Analogies?" *Monist* 57 (1973): 594. For other definitions of "crusade," see Edward LeRoy Long, Jr., *War and Conscience in America* (Philadelphia: Westminster Press, 1968) 37; and Walzer, 113-14.

[96]The exception is, of course, the Donatist schism.

[97]Russell, 23, 19, 25, 20. See also Michael Walzer, "Exodus 32 and the Theory of Holy War: The History of a Citation," *Harvard Theological Review* 61 (January 1968): 4-8; Hartigan, 203-204; Windass, 34.

[in the Augustinian writings about war] could be put together in support of a just war position or a holy war position or a pacifist position."[98] A particular principle does not follow inevitably from Augustine's very unsystematic remarks on the subject of war.

Although Augustine sanctioned Old Testament wars in *Quaestionum in Heptateuchum* and *Contra Faustum,* he also, in numerous later writings, specifically denied the possibility of translating the transcendent justice of God into any particular course of action within the *saeculum.* The Christianization of Rome, to the mature Augustine, was more historical coincidence than divine ordination. Indeed, Augustine sought to *deprive* the state of its "aura of divinity."[99]

Moreover, he repeatedly condemned the sin of self-righteousness, of facile confidence that one is in the right in a specific situation.

> Because Thy truth, O Lord, does not belong to me, to this man or that man, but to us all, Thou hast called us to it with a terrible warning not to claim it exclusively for ourselves; for if we do we shall lose it. Anyone who chooses to regard it as his sole possession, will be expelled from the common possession to his own, that is, from truth to lie.[100]

Intercivic war within the *saeculum,* he said, is as much the war of an individual with oneself as it is a war of essentially good people with essentially bad people. No one can ever be sure what they would do on the morrow. Any righteous action is inevitably tainted by sin.[101]

Finally, Augustine seems to have allowed for the possibility that *both* sides to a conflict may be right. There has been some disagreement among scholars about this aspect of Augustine's thought, as might be expected. Bainton, for one, interprets Augustine to say that "a just war can be just on one side only." Others interpret Augustine as clearly recognizing the fundamental difficulty in such facile categorization. According to Edward Leroy Long, Augustine "understood how the use of arms was brought about by a contest between relative forms of justice. No completely righteous cause is likely to be found in human relationships. The Christian cannot

---

[98]Langan, 27-28.

[99]Dawson, 77. See also Rist, "Exercise of Power," 372-74.

[100]*Conf.* 12.25. See also, for example, *Conf.* 10.36, 10.37; and Ramsey, *War and Conscience,* 32.

[101]See *Ep.* 130.2 4; *Conf.* 10.5; *Ep.* 188.

expect his cause to be universally regarded as completely right, that of his opponent as totally wrong." In addition, Paul Ramsey notes that Augustine's understanding of a "people" as a multitude united by a common love calls into serious question any interpretation that has Augustine seeing clearly "the presence of justice on one side, its absence on the other." Even Frederick Russell, who ties Augustine indirectly to the later holy war tradition, intrepets him as allowing for the possibility that both sides may be right.[102] Unfortunately, not one of these scholars can point to a specific passage in Augustine's writings supporting his interpretation. Yet the interpretation of Augustine's writings allowing for the possibility that both sides may be right seems to follow clearly from his various premises. Every temporal institution and every individual human being is inevitably a mixture of good and evil. Hence, any conflict between two temporal institutions would be, almost by definition, a conflict between two sides each "partially right."

Many aspects of Augustine's thought work against an interpretation of him as "holy warrior," then.[103] As Eppstein says, "the true emphasis in the saint's writings as a whole is far less upon righteous battles than upon peace and mercy, forbearance and long suffering."[104]

In attempting to determine the specific situations when war was appropriate for Augustine, therefore, it is important to remember that Augustine did not intend to detail a doctrine; rather, he sought to resolve a tension. As bishop of a firmly established church he found himself confronted both by the essential otherworldliness of his religion and by the necessity of maintaining the church's position *in the world*.[105] In order to reconcile these two, in a sense opposing, necessities, Augustine conceived of "just war." However, one fights not for "justice" but for "peace." More important, one fights not with confidence and enthusiasm but with resignation and humility. One listens for God's will in the particular circumstances and attempts to follow God's lead humbly, remembering all the

---

[102]Bainton, 99; Long, 26; Ramsey, *War and Conscience*, 28, 31; and Russell, 21. See also Jaspers, 77.

[103]See Markus, *Saeculum*, 69, 178, where he labels Augustine's *res publica* as inherently "pluralistic." See also Windass, 34; and Dawson, 76-77.

[104]Eppstein, 67.

[105]Windass, 31-32. See also Russell, 16-17.

while that one is ultimately blind both to one's own true motivation and to the historical consequences of one's action. One tries always to remember the underlying paradox of "just cause."

For responsible statespersons in the nuclear era, the recognition of such paradox adds an inescapable complicating factor to foreign policy decision making. For Augustine's paradox, that we must war for peace, that, in our day, we may be required to prepare for a war of total devastation *in order to prevent it,* strikes us as on its face absurd. Yet our circumstances may demand a recognition and a confrontation of just such a paradox.

CHAPTER TWO

Human Sin and Political Authority: Who May Wage War?

> *"For there is no power but of God."*
>
> Romans 13:1

THE REQUIREMENT of authority, like Augustine's other requirements for just war, was acutely paradoxical. Although it may lend itself to systematic analysis, it does not lend itself to systematic application. On the one hand, authority is simply a matter of power; whoever has the power has the authority. On the other hand, authority is scarcely related to power; indeed, power represents a perversion of the natural order.

The central truth underlying this paradox is that for Augustine the human being is a curious and complex mixture of both nature and perversion. One is neither wholly natural nor wholly perverted; yet one is both simultaneously. A human being is both God's special creature, possessed of absolute worth and dignity, and a depraved and perverted being, possessed by sin. In order to understand the meaning and place of authority in Augustine's just war thinking, therefore, it is necessary first to grapple with Augustine's understanding of human nature, human perversion, and the relationship between the two.

HUMAN NATURE, HUMAN PERVERSION

By nature, by original creation, human beings are equal, free sociable, cooperative, and pointed toward God. "By nature," Augustine said, "in which God first created man, no man is the slave

. . . of another man." God ordained an "equality with one's fellows" (*aequalitas cum sociis*).[1] Futhermore, humankind has by nature "free will"; one is "able to be without evil."[2] Humankind is naturally sociable and cooperative. The creation of the entire human race from one man is clear evidence of this characteristic, for Augustine.

> That God created man one and alone did not . . . mean that he was to be left in his solitary state without human fellowship. The purpose was rather to ensure that unity of fellowship itself, and ties of harmony might be more strongly impressed on him, if men were bound to one another not only by their similar nature but also by their feeling of kinship. For not even woman herself, who was to be joined to man, did He choose to create as He did that very man, but He created her out of that man in order that the human race might derive entirely from one man."[3]

This purpose is borne out by empirical observation: "Whoever reviews at all, with me, the pattern of human affairs and our common nature observes that . . . there is no man who does not wish peace."[4] Finally, a person's natural inner direction is toward God; one's natural home and resting place is one's Creator. "Man," said Augustine, "being a part of Your creation, desires to praise You; . . . You created us for Yourself and our hearts are restless until they rest in You."[5]

In the natural society of human beings, then, there is no need for force and coercion. All coercion and the power behind it are immediately suspect; they are unnatural. Because they tend toward hierarchy within the human race, they subvert natural human equality; by nature human beings are to rule only over the irrational creatures, not over other human beings.[6]

---

[1]*DCD* 19.15, 19.12. See also *De Doctr. Christ.* 1.23.23.

[2]*DCD* 12.22; *De Perf.* 6.14. See also *DCD* 22.30; Niebuhr, *Christian Realism*, 6, 183; Deane, 25-27; and Vernon Bourke, introduction to Portalie, xxxiii.

[3]*DCD* 12.22. See also ibid., 12.28, 14.1, 15.16-17; *De Bono Coniug.* 1; Deane, 78-79, 85; Baynes, 292; Figgis, 38; and Brown, *Augustine,* 224.

[4]*DCD* 19.12. See also *Ep.* 138.2.11.

[5]*Conf.* 1.1. See also ibid. 6.16, 10.23, 12.10; *DCD* 8.4, 14.6, 14.17-18, 19.12, 19.13; *De Doctr. Christ.* 1.4.4; *In Epist. Ioann.* 2.14; Deane, 41; Versfeld, 35; Portalie, 40; Niebuhr, *Christian Realism*, 130; Brown, *Augustine*, 431; Markus, *Saeculum*, 87-88; and Chroust, 198, 200.

[6]*DCD* 19.15.

Yet by nature human beings are also free. This natural freedom is the source of their troubles. Human beings use their freedom to turn away from God, to rebel against God as their natural home and resting place, and instead attempt to build a home in the created world, a home of perverse self-love. Rather than accept God as the center and source of things, they use their freedom to establish themselves as their own center and source, shunning not only God but also the natural harmony and equality of God's human creation. This misuse of freedom is what Augustine called sin.

Sin is thus not a particular transgression of a particular biblical standard, such as an act of theft or adultery. Sin is not an "act," it is a fundamental, if perverse, orientation of the will. Sin is the self-directing of the will toward the created world and away from the Creator. It is "misdirected love, which causes the will to fall away from an unchangeable to a changeable good"; it is the "love of so many vain and hurtful things." As Lee McDonald says, sin for Augustine is not "love lost but love misplaced—which means misdirected, warped, corrupted."[7] It is the condition of the will "having gone wrong" (*peccatum*).

Significantly, Augustine stressed that the created world itself is not the problem. As Deane says, he did not "advocate a completely negative, ascetic attitude toward the world; nor does he encourage the view that possessions and other earthly goods are *per se* evil." "The lapse is not to what is bad," Augustine said, "but to lapse is bad." To lapse means to make some part of the essentially good created world the ultimate object of one's affection, and thus to live in full conformity with it. For example, "The flesh is good, but to leave the Creator and live according to this good is the mischief."[8]

Sin is thus not a matter of an inherently good person being perversely drawn to an inherently bad material world. The things of the created world, including both the bodies and souls of persons, are good.[9] Sin is rather a kind of spiritual defect, a spiritual denial of the supremacy of God. "Just so does the soul defile itself (*fornicatur*) when it turns away from You and seeks outside of You the

---

[7]*De Perf.* 2.4; *DCD* 12.8, 22.22; Lee C. McDonald, *Western Political Theory* (New York: Harcourt Brace Jovanovich, 1968) vol. 1, *Ancient and Medieval*, 112. See also Deane, 16.

[8]Deane, 43; *DCD* 12.8, 14.5 See also *De Lib. Arb.* 1.4; and Niebuhr, *Nature and Destiny*, 1:231.

[9]Augustine refers frequently to Gen. 1.

things clear and pure which it cannot find until it returns to You." Whether one elevates spirit or flesh, soul or body, to ultimacy, the result is the same: one still lives "according to humankind." "For he that makes the soul's nature the greatest good and the body's the greatest evil, does both carnally desire the soul, and carnally avoid the flesh."[10]

The goods of the world should not be avoided; they should be used and enjoyed. However, they should only be enjoyed as evidence of God's creative power and mercy, and not as ends in themselves. "Use the world: let not the world hold you captive." As Deane puts it, sin is "the *desire* for money and goods, *not* their *possession;* . . . poor men can be just as guilty of [sin] as rich men."[11]

The heart of sin, in a sense the source of sin, is pride. And "what is pride but a craving for perverse elevation? For it is perverse elevation to forsake the Ground in which the mind ought to be rooted, and to become and be, in a sense, grounded in oneself."[12] Pride is thus self-centeredness; it is the centering of one's attention and one's affection on oneself.[13] But pride is also self-exaggeration (*superbia*); it is a refusal to accept one's status as a creature in a created world, and an attempt to set oneself up as creator of one's world. "So pride is a perverse imitation of God."[14]

In attempting to create one's own world, the proud person seeks to dominate others, who are by nature one's equals, and to use them as extensions of one's own will. Hence pride "abhors a society of peers under God," and "seeks to impose its own rule, instead of His, on society." Pride is possessed by a lust for mastery, a *libido dominandi*. This *libido dominandi* "brings many evils upon the human race and grinds it down."[15]

---

[10]*Conf.* 2.6; *DCD* 14.2, 14.5. See also, for example, *Conf.*, 1.13, 2.3, 5.12; *Con. Faus.* 22.78; *DCD*, 14.3, 14.4, 14.15; *De Perf.* 8.19; Versfeld, 50; and Brown, *Augustine*, 374-75, 389.

[11]*In Ioann. Evang.* 40.10; Deane, 110. See Deane's discussion generally, 107-112, and the references therein. See also ibid., 41-44; and Butterfield, 184.

[12]*DCD* 14.3, 14.13, See also *In Ioann. Evang.* 25.16; Deane, 16-17; Niebuhr, *Nature and Destiny*, 1:186n1; Jaspers, 84-85; and Niebuhr, *Christian Realism*, 122.

[13]*Conf.* 10.36.

[14]*DCD* 19.12. See also *DCD* 14.13; *Conf.* 5.3, 10.39; Deane, 16; and Rist, "Exercise of Power," 374.

[15]*DCD* 19.12, 3.14. See also *DCD* 1. Pref.; *De Doctr. Christ.* 1.23.23; *Conf.* 3.8; Deane, 17, 48-49, 230-31; Brown, *Religion*, 36-37; Martin, 213. For an eloquent description of the effects of *libido dominandi* in wartime combat, see Gray, 52-55.

Human pride and consequent sin are only possible, of course, because of natural human freedom. Because a person is free, because one in this way rises above the natural order, one is tempted to *reside* above the natural order. As Cochrane describes the connection, "The presumption of mankind may, indeed, lead him to suppose that, in his consciousness of existence and of activity, there is evidence that he embodies a scintilla of the divine essence, the mere possession of which constitutes a prima-facie claim to divinity, lifting him above the natural order of which he forms a part."[16]

Several points need to be emphasized here regarding Augustinian sin. First, sin is universal; all human beings are sinners. Second, sin is ingrained; human nature is radically and chronically altered by sin. Third, the source of sin is in human beings themselves; it is a self-directing of naturally free human will away from the goodness of God. Fourth, God knew that human beings would sin even before they did so. Last, the paradox that humankind is both naturally free and universally enslaved by sin, though insoluble, is not inherently contradictory.

For Augustine all human beings are sinners. "All men are a mass of sin [*massa peccati*]," he wrote. "No man . . . can be without sin, even if he wish it." More than once he quoted 1 John 1:8: "If we say that we are without sin, we deceive ourselves and the truth is not in us." To Sixtus, later bishop of Rome, Augustine wrote, "Yet whatever progress you make in the love of God and of your neighbor and in genuine godliness, do not imagine that you are without sin, as long as you are in this life."[17] Augustine was quite willing to admit and to discuss his own sins. Book 10 of his *Confessions* details the many instances of his deviation from the path of God, continuing even as he wrote. "The amazing Book Ten of the *Confessions*," says Brown, "is not the affirmation of a cured man; it is the self portrait of a convalescent." As van der Meer notes in his justly renowned *Augustine the Bishop,*

> In the pulpit he stood, as it were, in the company of his own people under the light of the Word,; he did not address them as "you," but

---

[16]Cochrane, 406. See also Niebuhr, *Nature and Destiny,* 1: viii, 17, 150; and Rist, "Exercise of Power," 374.

[17]*De Div. Quaest. ad Simplic.* 1.2.16; *De Perf.* 7.16; *Ep.* 189.8. See also *DCD* 19.10; and Figgis, 43-44. For Augustine's citations of 1 John 1:8, see, for example, *In Epist. Ioann.* 1.6; *De Perf.* 12.30; *Serm.* 56.11; and *Ep.* 153.

invariably used the word "we." He would publicly recall his own faults, and if, as he sometimes did, he administered a quite sharp rebuke, he was ready to take this as applying, if necessary, to himself.[18]

Sin is universal primarily because it is so deeply ingrained in human beings from their origin; it is *original* sin. As all human beings are brothers through Adam, so all are sinners through Adam. "We were all in that one man," he said. How so? Clearly, "We did not yet have individually created and apportioned shapes in which to live as individuals." However, what did exist with Adam, *in* Adam, was "the seminal substance from which we were to be generated." Obviously, then, "when this substance was debased through sin, no man could be born in any other condition." We are all, "as it were from a diseased root." For "man's genesis from man is not like man's genesis from dust."[19]

Evidence, for Augustine, of the deep-seatedness of sin abounds in the world. Consider even the infant, he suggested. Fresh from the womb, infants are clearly a "mass of sin," regarding themselves as the absolute center of things. They scream and cry for the things they want, until they get them. Actions such as these are easily, quickly, and rightly forgiven by adults, yet they point directly to the degree to which perverse self-love is ingrained in the fiber of human beings. They show that "it is the weakness of the limbs of infants that is innocent, not their wills."[20]

As an adolescent, Augustine engaged in a childish prank that later appeared to him as further evidence of the self-corruption of the human will: the renowned "pear-tree episode." He and his companions raided a neighbor's pear tree and threw their booty to some pigs. The crime itself was a minor one, of course, but upon reflection the middle-aged Augustine came to see in this episode a deeper significance. Why had he stolen the pears? What gain was there in the act? He came to see that his enjoyment had not been in the product of the theft, but rather in the act of theft itself. "It was foul, and I loved it; I loved my

---

[18]*Conf.* 10. 30-40; Brown, *Augustine,* 177; van der Meer, 420. See also *De Doctr. Christ.* 4.31.64; *Ep*. 111.4; Malcolm Spicer, "The Conversion of Saint Augustine," *Canadian Catholic Review* 4 (October 1986): 330-31.

[19]*DCD* 13.14, 13.3. See also ibid., 15.1; *Retr.* 1.9.3; Niebuhr, *Nature and Destiny,* 1:261; Bonner, 370-75; Deane, 17; Brown, *Religion,* 35; and Firth, 292.

[20]*Conf.* 1.7. See also ibid., 1.6; *De Peccat. Meritis* 1.35.66; and Deane, 56-57; as well as Giovanni Papini, *St. Augustine,* trans. Mary Prichard Agnetti (New York: Harcourt, Brace and Co., 1930) 33, noting Augustine's anticipation of Freud.

undoing, I loved my misdeed, not that for which I misdid, but the misdeed itself." "If any of those pears entered my mouth, it was the crime itself that gave it flavor."[21]

In his later years, Augustine could appreciate not only the corruption manifest in children and adolescents, where it is perhaps more evident as well as more forgivable, but also the perversity woven into the fabric of adult souls. Even mature and praiseworthy deeds can be mere masks concealing distorted and blameworthy motives."Pride lurks even in good deeds," he wrote to the nuns of Hippo. "What avails it to lavish money on the poor, and become poor oneself, if the unhappy soul is rendered more proud by despising riches than it had been by possessing them?"[22] To make the point even more forcefully, Augustine proposed a litmus test for individual human sanctity.

> Whoever does not want to fear, let him probe his inmost self. Do not just touch the surface; go down into yourself; reach into the farthest corner of your heart. Examine it then with care: see there, whether a poisoned vein of the wasting love of the world still does not pulse, whether you are not moved by some physical desires, and are not caught in some law of the senses; whether you are never elated with empty boasting, never depressed by some vain anxiety: then only can you dare to announce that you are pure and crystal clear, when you have sifted everything in the deepest recesses of your inner being.

The rhetorical point was plain: the rare human being who presumed to have passed the test would in fact be the one who failed most miserably. For the essence of pride and thus of sin is the attribution of goodness to oneself.[23]

What Augustine was getting at in these later musings was that the human will is *not* completely free; it is enslaved by a sinful self. Through Adam, natural freedom, "to be able not to sin," was lost. What was retained was freedom of a sort, but a "drugged" sort of freedom, a "truant's freedom" (*fugitiva libertas*), a freedom to choose only between particular sins; human beings were no longer able to

---

[21]*Conf.* 2.4, 2.6. See also ibid., 4.4-5, 6.8.

[22]*Ep.* 211.6. See also *De Perf.* 8.17; and Deane, 81.

[23]*Serm.* 348.2. See also *Conf.* 10.38, 7.7; *DCD* 14.13; *De Correp.* 40; Jaspers, 90-91; Deane, 239; and McDonald, 114.

choose not to sin at all.[24] To say that sin ingrained itself in the human will is not to say that the human will is blameless. The fault lies clearly with the human will; sin is always "voluntary."

Such responsibility must be laid at the feet of human will, Augustine reasoned, because God is pure goodness; by definition God can not be responsible for evil.[25] Evil is thus a falling away from good, a "lack" (*privatio boni*), an "absence" of good. "Evil has in itself no substance; rather the loss of what is good has received the name evil."[26] Augustine was not denying the existence of evil, of course, only God's authorship of evil. Marthinus Versfeld explains the Augustinian position clearly.

> No one is further than Augustine from denying what we should call the reality of evil, but it remains true that its striking force is rooted in the good. If a man tortures me he is committing, and I am suffering, an evil. But the man can torture me effectively only insofar as he is good and uses means which in themselves are good. Steel is good, fire is good and so is the intelligence and ingenuity with which they are applied to me. Ontologically considered, and as far as his act is an act, it is good. His action is evil because of something lacking in the man and in the act, namely good will. Likewise the evil produced in me by torture is a deprivation of bodily integrity. It renders me less than I should be. I suffer as good, that is, as having consciousness, a sensitive body, and so on. It is the absence of what is no longer in me that is evil. To do evil is always a failure to do something or to be something.[27]

---

[24]*Conf.* 3.3 (for *fugitiva libertas*) 8.5, 8.8, 8.9, 8.10, 10.5, 10.37-40; *DCD* 22.22, 22.30; *Ep.* 27.1; *Serm.* 162.6. See also McDonald, 114-16; Deane, 25-27; Brown, *Augustine*, 205-206, 374, 389; Jaspers, 88; Figgis, 41; Niebuhr, *Nature and Destiny*, 1: 150. As Brown notes, Augustine grew into this awareness. Soon after his conversion. His Christianity was strongly infected with the facile confidence of the Platonists. By the time he sat down to write his *Confessions*, however, this confidence in reaching the goal of human maturity was lost. Ironically, it was a work of Augustine's early years, *De Libero Arbitrio*, a defense of full human freedom, that was used with such enthusiasm by his opponents, the Pelagians, to support their own position. See Brown, *Augustine*, 146-57. On this point see also Markus, *Saeculum*, 82; and David E. Roberts, "The Earliest Writings," in Battenhouse, ed., 123.

[25]*DCD* 11.10, 12.2. See also *De Lib. Arb.* 1.2; *Conf.* 7.5, 7.12.

[26]*DCD* 11.9. See also ibid., 12.3, 19.4; *Conf.* 3.7, 7.16. On the adequacy of Augustine's understanding, see Stanley Hooper, "The Anti-Manichean Writings," in Battenhouse, ed., 168.

[27]Versfeld, 40.

The responsibility for such failure belongs fully to humankind. From the beginning, humankind chose to disobey, to come up short of full obedience. Human beings themselves continue to make the choice; it is not forced upon them. As Figgis put it, "It is the will, not the nature, that goes wrong."[28]

Further complicating the matter is God's foreknowledge of human sin. God created humankind knowing all the while that humankind would sin. Yet this foreknowledge was not the cause of sin. Humankind sinned inevitably but not necessarily; human sin was pre-known but not pre-determined.[29]

Mention of Augustine's understanding of God's foreknowledge carries one into the heart of the paradox underlying Augustine's understanding of human political authority. How can human beings be both free to sin, thus responsible for their sin, and destined to sin at the same time? Many scholars have asserted that they could not, and thus that Augustine was simply playing rhetorical tricks. These scholars have argued that, all of Augustine's protestations to the contrary notwithstanding, he was a determinist; he could not have an omnipotent and omniscient God and a free human will in the same formula. Even John Hick, who appears to make every effort to follow Augustine, finds that the Augustinian formula "cannot be saved from the charge of self-contradiction and absurdity. And even if [Augustine's] strange hypothesis be allowed," Hick goes on, "it would still be hard to clear God from ultimate responsibility for the existence of sin, in view of the fact that He chose to create a being whom He foresaw would, if He created him, freely sin."[30]

---

[28]Figgis, 41. On this point see *De Nat. et Grat.* 3.3; *De Perf.* 6.13; *Conf.* 3.8, 5.10; *Con. Faus.* 22.78. See also Deane, 18-19; and Niebuhr, *Nature and Destiny,* 1: 241-42.

[29]*DCD* 5.9. See also *De Lib. Arb.* 3.2-5; *In Ioann. Evang.* 53.4-10; Vernon J. Bourke, *Augustine's Quest for Wisdom: Life and Philosophy of the Bishop of Hippo* (Milwaukee: Bruce Publishing, 1945) 256; Versfeld, 41; Figgis, 45-46; Niebuhr, *Nature and Destiny,* 1:150, 242; and Bourke, introduction to Portalie, xxxiii.

[30]John Hick, *Evil and the God of Love,* rev. ed. (New York: Harper and Row, 1977) 69; see also George W. Osmun, *Augustine: The Thinker* (Cincinnati: Jennings and Graham, 1906) 246; Dino Bigongiari, "The Political Ideas of St. Augustine," in *The Political Writings of St. Augustine,* ed. Henry Paolucci (South Bend IN: Gateway, 1962) 343; James W. Woelfel, *Augustinian Humanism: Studies in Human Bondage and Earthly Grace* (Washington: University Press of America, 1979) 41.

These objections are both pointed and relevant, and must not be taken lightly. Nevertheless, it is also important to examine carefully Augustine's claim that the simultaneous existence of divine foreknowledge and human free will is readily apparent. Augustine claimed that at base the two are, if not logically consistent, at least empirically evident; if they are strange bedfellows, they are bedfellows nonetheless.

Perhaps Augustine's most forceful defense of his claim was his attack on the Ciceronian understanding of fate in chapters 9 and 10 of book 5 of *The City of God*. In order to evaluate this attack fully, it may help to quote Augustine at some length. Augustine described the Ciceronian position this way:

> If all future events are foreknown, they will take place in the order in which their occurrence was foreknown, and if they are to take place in this order, then the order is determined for a foreknowing God. If the order of events is determined, the order of causes is determined, for nothing can happen that is not preceded by some efficient cause. But if there is a determined order of causes by which everything that happens happens, then all things that happen happen by fate. If this is the case, there is nothing really in our power, and the will really has no free choice.

Yet Augustine wanted to reconcile foreknowledge and free will. His attempt was as follows:

> Even if there is in God's mind a definite pattern of causation, it does not follow that nothing is left to the free choice of our will. For in fact, our wills also are included in the pattern of causation certainly known to God and embraced in His foreknowledge. For the wills are among the causes of deeds of men, and so He Who foresaw the causes of all things cannot have been ignorant of our wills among those causes, since he foresaw that these wills are the causes of our deeds. . . . How, then, can the order of causes that is fixed in God's foreknowledge deprive us of all use of our will, when our wills play an important part in the order of causes itself? . . . For we do many things that we certainly should not do if were unwilling. To this class of things belongs first of all the will itself. If we will, the will exists; if not, it does not. For we should not will if we were unwilling. . . . It is not true, then, that there is no reality in our will just because God foresaw what would be in our will. For when He foresaw this, He foresaw something. Further, He foresaw something real, not a

mere nothing. Hence assuredly there is something in our will even though God has foreknowledge of it.[31]

It is easy to see how one could interpret these passages as deterministic in substance. If one conceives of God including human will in the casual chain, foreseeing the content of that will and the behavior to which it led, is one not saying that the behavior, being pre-known, is pre-determined? Clearly Augustine thought not. Inclusion of human will in the causal chain is a dramatic departure from mere determinism, because one's will is *one's own*. A person's will is the innermost part of one's being. As Augustine said in another place, "My weight is my love; by it I am borne, wherever I am borne" (*pondus meum amor meus; eo feror, quocumque feror*).[32] A person's will, one's ultimate love, carries one's whole self wherever it goes. One's will may be influenced by many factors outside oneself, but in the end one's will is one's own.

Augustine's defense of free will appeared even more problematic, however, when he considered the pervasiveness of human sin. Through Adam all sin inevitably. No one is free to refrain from sin. How then can one be called free? Or, more significantly, how can one be held responsible for one's sins? That one is held responsible for one's sins is obvious, and that, for Augustine, is clear evidence that one ought to be.[33]

But *why* ought one be? According to Augustine, one must start with the proposition that God is all-powerful, all good, and the creator of all things. One accepts this proposition on faith through the authority of the Scriptures.[34] If God is all-powerful, then there can not exist any independent evil force or substance fighting against God for the possession of human souls. For if such a force existed then God would not be all-powerful. If God is all good, then God

---

[31]*DCD* 5.9-10. See also Brown, *Augustine*, 404-407; and William L. Rowe, "Augustine on Foreknowledge and Free Will," *Review of Metaphysics* 18 (December 1964): 356-63.

[32]*Conf.* 13.9. See also Gilson, *Christian Philosophy*, 157. On this point John Hicks has produced an impressive analysis and argument, both of which deserve careful attention. However, it is not my intent to try to determine the "adequacy" of Augustine's "theodicy"; rather, my intent is only to demonstrate the sincerity, the breadth and the depth of his "theodicy."

[33]See, for example, *DCD* 5.10; *De Grat. et Lib Arb.* 2.4. See also Fortin, "Consciousness," 327.

[34]*DCD* 11.21-23, 12.5.

simply can not be responsible for evil. Goodness itself would not commit evil acts, either directly or indirectly through, say, human beings. Finally, if all-powerful and all-good God is the creator of all things, then God would not (indeed could not) create anything either independently powerful or independently evil.[35]

For these reasons, evil must be a negative thing, a spiritual "privation," a "lack." Moreover, the source of evil must be external to God; it must arise out of the created world in some way. And the only place from which it could arise, because the only thing created "free," was humankind itself. Thus, through process of elimination, Augustine came to conclude that the human self is the source of evil.[36] So God must, and does, hold it responsible for that evil.[37] Although human beings now find themselves entrapped by a corrupt will, they themselves are the source and cause of the corruption. As Augustine said, "It is man's fault that he is not without sin on this account, because it has by man's sole will come to pass that he has come into such a necessity as cannot be overcome by man's sole will." Human beings find themselves locked in a cage that they themselves have constructed.[38]

This, then, is the central paradox: human beings are enslaved by their own free selves. To put it another way, they are simultaneously a part of nature and a perversion of nature; each is a divided, a discontinuous being. As Jaspers so pithily expressed humankind's "fundamental experience," "I will but I cannot will my willing."[39]

At the base of Augustine's understanding of political authority, then, is divided and discontinuous humankind. As natural beings—and they remain natural beings ("For no creature's vice is so completely at odds with nature that it destroys the very last traces of nature")—they ought not to be coerced; they possess absolute dignity and worth. Yet as sinful, corrupted beings they have to be coerced:

---

[35]See, for example, *Conf.* 1.6, 5.10, 7.2; *DCD* 12.3 and 12.5.

[36]*DCD* 12.3; *Conf.* 7.3, 7.5-17. See also Deane, 15; Niebuhr, *Christian Realism*, 183; and Jaspers, 91.

[37]*De Lib. Arb.* 3.19.53. See also Brown, *Augustine,* 152; Niebuhr, *Nature and Destiny,* 1:247. For a general discussion of these points, see *DCD* 14.10-15.

[38]*De Perf.* 6.13. See also ibid., 4.9; *Conf.* 6.12; and Jaspers, 90.

[39]Jaspers, 90. See also *Conf.* 8.11; Versfeld, 35; and Niebuhr, *Nature and Destiny,* 1:243.

"For there is nothing so social by nature, so unsocial by its corruption, as this race." Or as Niebuhr expressed the discontinuity: "The self is free to defy God. The self does defy God. The Christian conception of the dignity of man and of the misery [one could say "depravity"] of man is all of one piece."[40]

PARADOX AND AUTHORITY

What was the place of political authority in this formula? For Augustine, political authority has a twofold purpose designed to aid both precepts of the paradox: It is both a remedy and a punishment for sin, its purposes are both rehabilitative and retributive. As keeper of the civic peace, political authority helps human beings to recover their true nature; it gives them the opportunity to contemplate both their own perversion and God's saving grace.[41] As punisher of criminal acts, it prevents human beings from falling into even deeper depravity; it restrains them from mortal sin. Augustine thus followed closely Paul's conclusion in his *Letter to the Romans* (13:1): "The powers that be are ordained of God." Having foreseen human sin, God allowed for the institutionalization of political power.

According to Augustine, the immediate consequences of human sin are purely negative and destructive. Human sin is the original cause of both human mortality and human estrangement.[42] Sin's destructive effects are everywhere manifest.

> This very life, if life it may be called, pregnant with so many dire evils, bears witness that from its very beginning all the progeny of mankind was damned. For what else . . . is the love of so many vain and hurtful things, from which come gnawing cares, passions, griefs, fears, mad joys, discords, strifes, wars, plots, wraths, enmities, deceits, flattery, fraud, theft, robbery, perfidy, pride, ambition, murder, parricide, cruelty, ferocity, vileness, . . . oppressions of the innocent, calumnies, deceptions, duplicities, . . . brigandage and all the other evils which come not to mind, but still do not pass from the life of men? Yes, these are misdeeds of bad men, for they

---

[40]*DCD* 19.12, 12.28; Niebuhr, *Christian Realism,* 183. See also *DCD* 19.13.

[41]See, for example, *Ep.* 153.

[42]Human mortality is represented by the story of the Fall; see *DCD* 13.14, 12.22; Deane, 18. Human estrangement is represented by the story of the Tower of Babel; see *DCD* 16.4, 19.5, 19.7; Deane 62-63, 168; and Brown, *Religion,* 28.

spring from that root of error and perverse love with which every son of Adam is born.

Because of human sin, life on earth is continual misery.[43]

To assuage the misery, to minimize the destruction, and to punish the sinners, Augustine wrote, God permitted political authority; God ordained herarchical arrangements of human beings and a home for the legitimate use of force. "Because God does not wholly desert those whom He condemns," Augustine said, "the human race is restrained by law and education [*prohibitio et eruditio*], which, though themselves full of labor and sorrow, nevertheless guard against the ignorance that besets us and oppose our violent impulses." Political authority, manifest as "law and education," entails force and dominion, of course, since it arose out of human sin: it is essentially a human creation and thus is infected with human perversion.[44]

Augustine therefore departed from the classical understanding of political authority. The polity was no longer the highest and most noble form of human association, whose purpose was to form and educate its citizens so that they could become fully developed or fully "human" (Aristotelian *spoudaioi*). It was no longer an unadulteratedly positive good, but rather a necessary evil; its purpose was no longer to achieve justice in the world, but rather to minimize injustice. Ramsey accurately sums up the transition when he says, "Augustine demoralize[d] *res publica.*" The polity's "moral" purpose, while very real, was now only indirect: to keep the peace.[45]

In sharp contrast to the classical thinkers, then, Augustine asserted that political organization is not natural to humankind but is the result of the sinful condition of humankind. Political orga-

---

[43]*DCD* 22.22. See also ibid., 13.14, 15.4, 15.6, 19.5, 19.7, 19.15, 21.14; *Conf.* 4.6, 6.6, 11.31; Brown, *Augustine,* 293; Deane, 62-63; and Baynes, 292.

[44]*DCD* 22.22. See also Markus, *Saeculum,* 205-206; and Deane, 143.

[45]Ramsey, *War and Conscience,* 25; *Ep.* 153.6.16. See also Markus, *Saeculum,* 83-84, 99; Martin, 215-16; Deane, 11, 222; Lavere, 140-41, 144; Fortin, "Patristic," 196; Chroust, 202; and R. A. Markus, "Two Conceptions of Political Authority: Augustine, *De civitate Dei,* XIX, 14-15, and Some Thirteenth-Century Interpretations," *Journal of Theological Studies* 16 (April 1965): 98. As Markus, *Saeculum,* 75-76, noted, Augustine grew into this rejection. In his early writings, Augustine retained an affection for the classical model. As evidence Markus points to Augustine's use of *ordo* instead of *potestas* when he quotes Romans 13:1 from memory. (Augustine himself noted the slip in *Retr.* 1.12.8.)

nization is not natural primarily because it entails inequality: some rule; others are ruled. Yet God "did not wish a rational creature, made in His own image, to have dominion save over irrational creatures: not man over man, but man over the beasts."[46] Any hierarchical arrangement of human beings is a perversion of the natural order, a perversion that arises out of the *libido dominandi,* or "lust for rule."[47] Political organization is therefore unnatural not only because it perverts natural human equality, but also because it does so by force, by *"dominium."* Any human relationship based on force is fundamentally unnatural, for Augustine, because it treats one of the partners as an object, and not as a creature possessed of reason and created in God's image.[48]

Augustine's understanding of political authority has not been unanimously interpreted as being "unnatural." Thomas Aquinas, perhaps Augustine's most influential interpreter, forcefully denied such an interpretation. According to St. Thomas, Augustine saw political authority as a natural extension of the family. The good ruler was thus one who rules for the common good. The subjection of free people to a ruler would have existed even in the state of innocence and would have implied no diminution of their freedom. "Mastership [*dominium*]," said Aquinas, "has a twofold meaning." While "a master means one to whom another is subject as a slave," "a man is the master of a free subject by directing him either towards his proper welfare, or to the common good." Aquinas continued,

> Such a mastership [*dominium*] of man over man would have existed in the state of innocence for two reasons. First, because man is naturally a social being, and so in the state of innocence he would have led a social life. Now a social life cannot exist among a number of people unless someone should govern [*praesideret*], who directs them toward [*intenderet;*] the common good; for many, as such, are directed toward many things, whereas one is directed only toward one.

---

[46]*DCD* 19.15. See also ibid., 11.16; *Conf.* 6.1; *In Epist. Ioann.* 8.6; Markus, *Saeculum,* 84, 92-93, 204-205; Deane, 78, 96, 117; O'Donovan, 16; and Bourke, introduction to Portalie, xxxii.

[47]*DCD* 1. pref., 3.14, 14.15; *De Doctr. Christ.* 23.23; *In Epist. Ioann.* 8.8; *En. is Ps.* 1.1. See also Markus, *Saeculum,* 93-94, 207; Deane, 48-51; Markus, "Two Conceptions," 81; and Windass, 26.

[48]*De Serm. Dom.* 1.19.59. See also *In Epist. Ioann.* 8.6 and 8; and *Conf.* 1.9.

Thomas quotes as an objection Augustine's insistence on the absence of *any* dominion of human being over human being in the state of innocence (because of the absence of any *need* for it, the individual's direction and end—God—being naturally identical with any *communal* direction and end). *All* the objections, Thomas replies tersely, are valid only against mastership over slaves. Clearly, though, Thomas's interpretation marks a radical change of attitude toward political authority. For Augustine, political authority is inherently suspect, as it implies not a familial relation but a servile relation.[49]

In spite of the perversion intrinsic to political authority, however, Augustine insisted that such authority works to accomplish God's purposes and thus exists by divine fiat. Political organization is by no means a creation of God; it is very much a human creation. Yet in its very perversion, it works to cancel out the effects of human sin. By means of its coercive capability, governmental machinery can harness human ferocity itself for the important job of providing some minimal social order and cohesion in situations inherently tending toward disorder and disintegration. As a result, it was clear to Augustine that political authority is "ordained of God." God did not create human lusts, but once foreseen, God "used" them, in the *form* of political authority, both to control the chaos engendered by sin and to punish sinners.[50]

Augustine's writings were thus filled with references to Romans 13:1-2.[51] Even though political authority is unnatural, he reasoned, one owes it one's full cooperation and obedience. For in the act of obedience itself resides both one's deserved punishment and a potential means to one's salvation. Because political authority

---

[49]Aquinas, *Summa Theologica*, Quaest. 96, Art. 4. See also the article by Markus, "Two Conceptions," 82, 95, 100; as well as note 45, above. The Thomist interpretation is carried on by Chroust, 202, who describes Augustine as one who "follows Cicero" and for whom "the secular state is not the result of the sins of man, nor the product of an agreement among men. For it has its ultimate roots in divinely ordained laws and in the natural instinct of man and human nature." See his entire discussion, 201-202. See also Barker, xxvi, who says that for Augustine "all *dominium* is a form of *ordo*." Barker softened this stance a bit in subsequent discussion. See xxvi-xxviii. See also Figgis, 65.

[50]*DCD* 19.15; *Ep.* 153.6.16. See also Carlyle, 1:120; Chroust, 202; Deane, 143; and Markus, *Saeculum*, 95, 205.

[51]See, for example, *En. in Ps.* 118.31.1; *Serm.* 62.13; *In Ioann Evang.* 116.5; *Con. Faus.* 22.75; *Ep.* 87.7, 100.1, 153.6, 220.4.

arose out of human sin, out of the *libido dominandi,* much of it, indeed most of it, is unjust. Yet one should still obey, for unjust regimes may very well be God's way of punishing one's sins. This is not to say, of course, that God *sends* unjust regimes, but rather that God uses unjust regimes that already exist. Nevertheless, whatever the content of a specific regime, it can not gain or maintain power without God's acquiescence, for "there is no power but of God." God grants the power of both the just and the unjust, both Augustus and Nero, both Constantine and Julian the Apostate. Therefore, even if one should find oneself under the power of a Nero, one should obey. "The power to rule is not granted to such men unless by the providence of the supreme God, when He deems the human situation [*res humanas*] worthy of such masters." Although "by nature . . . no man is the slave . . . of another man," yet the slavery imposed upon their subjects by such men is "a punishment . . . also ordained by that law which bids us to preserve the natural order and forbids us to disturb it."[52]

The act of obedience comprises more than one's deserved punishment, however; it constitutes a potential means to one's salvation. As the absence of disrupting rebellion, obedience creates an atmosphere of peace. And as a potential member of the City of God, one can use this peace to attend to more important matters: one can contemplate one's distance from God and the miracle of God's saving grace.[53]

Moreover, the act of obedience reflects the only true obedience: obedience to God, which is "the mother and guardian of all virtues in a rational creature." Hence, one obeys political authority for the same reasons that one obeys any aspect of God's ordering of the world: obedience signifies a kind of humility, a recognition of one's partiality and finitude. Paradoxically, then, it is humility, as genuine obedience, that uplifts, elevates, and frees its possessor, whereas it is the self-exaltation of pride and the lust for rule that abases and enslaves. Such reasoning was at the base of Augustine's oft-quoted passage, "And surely it is a happier lot to be slave to a man than to a lust; for the most cruel overlord that desolates men's hearts, to mention no other, is this very lust for overlordship [*libido domi-*

[52]*DCD* 5.21, 5.19, 19.15. See also ibid., 4.33, 19.16; *QH* 1.153; Conf. 2.6; and Deane, 143, 224.

[53]*DCD* 19.17. See also Langan, 18.

nandi]." The humble and obedient servant, one who submits "not in crafty fear but in faithful affection," has his eternal reward as much as the prideful master had his eternal punishment. Augustine thus advised his flock, when confronted by obdurate political authority, "Let us bend easily, lest we be broken" [*Flectamur facile ne frangamur*].[54]

Not all rulers are proud and libidinous, of course, any more than all subjects are humble and obedient. Yet it is clear that Augustine encouraged a kind of "passive obedience" to political authority. It is also clear that, as Brown describes it, "an acute sense of the spiritual dangers of excessive claims to self-determination lies at the root of Augustine's doctrine of passive obedience."[55] Prideful disobedience inevitably does more damage to the rebel by ruination of one's soul, Augustine believed, than passive obedience could ever do by ruination of one's body. For these reasons rulers should be accorded virtually absolute obedience and respect, no matter how corrupt or wicked or cruel they may be.[56]

Augustine's understanding of political authority seems to imply a simple answer to the question, "Who may wage war?": the ruler has unbridled discretion, and since the ruler holds the power of rule, then, effectively, whoever has the *power* to wage war has the *authority* to wage war. This answer has not been an uncommon one. Deane, for example, concludes, "On one point Augustine is perfectly clear: it is the monarch, the chief of state, who has both the right and the duty to decide that a just war is to be undertaken."[57]

Yet the simple answer deceives in its very simplicity.[58] Within history, it is true, power equals authority. But human destiny lies beyond history, in eternal communion with God and the saints. In eternity power in the form of coercion does not exist, only authority, in the sole possession of the one true God. Attempting a comprehensive answer to the question, "Who may wage war?" then,

---

[54]*DCD* 19.15; *De Cat Rud.* 14.20. See also *DCD* 4.3, 14.12, 14.13, 19.15; Brown, *Religion*, 30, 35; Markus, *Saeculum*, 86; and Deane, 114, 143-44, 306n91.

[55]Brown, *Religion*, 31. See also Markus, *Saeculum*, 85-86; Deane, 149; Langan, 8, 19.

[56]*DCD* 4.3. See also Brown, *Religion*, 30; Deane, 143, 145, 224.

[57]Deane, 162. See also Russell, 22; Hartigan, 200.

[58]See Deane, 145-49, 295n153; Russell, 22; Langan, 8.

requires delving a bit more deeply into Augustine's understanding of providence, God's "seeing forward."

PROVIDENCE AND WAR

As humankind has two "pulls," the pull of nature and the pull of perversion, God, for Augustine, has two perspectives on human beings: the perspective of nature, the "natural" order, the order of God's original creation, and the perspective of history, the historical and political order, the order that God ordained as ruler of the *saeculum*. Augustine called these two perspectives the *ordo naturalis* and the *lex aeterna*. They are intimately related because "the eternal law . . . ordains the preservation of the natural order and prohibits its transgression."[59] Yet they are clearly distinct because they reflect two kinds of providence: the *providentia naturalis* (the inherent workings of nature) and the *providentia voluntaria* (God's will as active in the world).[60] Any attempt to explain Augustine's requirement of authority in warfare demands coming to terms not only with the dualism in humankind but also with this dualism of God.

An oft-quoted passage from Augustine's *Contra Faustum* provides an appropriate starting point. According to the standard translation, Augustine said, "the natural order which seeks the peace of mankind ordains that the monarch should have the power of undertaking war if he thinks it advisable."[61] But if the "natural order" "ordains" ruler discretion, thus leaving it unbridled, there is a serious contradiction in Augustine's thought. How could Augustine have reconciled such ordination with his repeated assertions that human authority is unnatural? There are, of course, contradictions in the thought of any writer, and Augustine was surely no exception. Yet this one appears too blatant.

In fact, though, the difficulty rests not with Augustine's thinking, but with the translation. In Latin the passage is, "*ordo tamen ille*

---

[59]*Con. Faus.* 22.73. See also ibid., 22.27, 28, 30, 43, 61, 78; *DCD* 19.15; and Markus, *Saeculum*, 90-91. Compare Martin, 213: "We have then, in Augustine's theory, two basic kinds of political values in the organization of states: the community principle, defined by basic social agreement, and the regime principle, defined by an imposed order."

[60]*De Gen. ad Lit.* 8.9.17 (*PL* 34:379). See Markus, *Saeculum*, 87.

[61]*Con. Faus.* 22.75 (*NPNFC*, 4:301). See also the translation by Eppstein, 69-70: "The natural order of mortal things, ordained for peace, demands that the authority for making war and inflicting punishments should rest with the ruler."

naturalis mortalium paci accommodatus hoc poscit, ut suscipiendi belli auctoritas atque consilium penes Principem sit. " The translator apparently failed to notice that the monks who provided the edition from which he worked capitalized *Principem.* Given its place in the sentence, and the place of the sentence in the context of the whole paragraph and of Augustine's thought in general, it is clear that by *Principem* Augustine meant *The Princeps,* that is, Godself.[62] Rendering "authority" and not "power" for *auctoritas,* and "judgment" for *consilium,* the passage would be, "the natural order, which seeks the peace of mankind, requires that the authority and judgment to undertake war rest with Godself." Augustine did not lodge unbridled discretion in the ruler, but rather in the only place such discretion could be lodged: with Godself. God designed and created a natural order, foresaw its perversion, and reserved to Godself full discretion to deal with the perversion.[63]

The fact of God's dualism is thus extremely important in identifying an "authoritative" waging of war. By nature there is no power, only authority, and all authority rests with God. Within history, of course, power does exist, and it exists with God's implicit acquiescence. What, then, are the practical consequences of this dualism? For rulers, the dualism means, on the one hand, unbridled discretion within history, and on the other, a requirement of full and direct obedience to God. For subjects it means essentially automatic obedience to rulers on the one hand, and thoughtful, *prayerful,* disobedience to them on the other.

To elaborate, the *providentia voluntaria* is a foreknowledge actively willing in the *saeculum.* From the human perspective, historical events appear as radically contingent. Bad people seem to prosper and good people to suffer. In politics, both good and evil people rise to rule without apparent pattern. Whole civilizations rise and fall without rational explanation. The city symbolic of the greatest civilization of the age, the "Eternal City" of Rome, was sacked by barbarians. And yet, Augustine insisted, there is a divine plan at work.[64]

---

[62]Actually, by *Princeps* Augustine probably meant more specifically Christ, the "Prince of Peace" (*Princeps pacis,* from Isa. 9:6) or Christ, the "Prince of the Kings of the Earth" (*Princeps regum terrae,* from Rev. 1:5).

[63]See Matt. 28:18 (the "Great Commission"); and Markus, *Saeculum,* 87.

[64]*DCD* 20.2, 4.7, 4.33, 5.19. See also ibid., 5.11, 5.22; Augustine, *Enchiridion*

It is not a plan known to, or even knowable by, human beings. As Dawson so appropriately put it, "God ordains all events in His Providence in a universal harmony which the created mind cannot grasp."[65] Regarding the fall of Rome, Augustine asked rhetorically, "Who knows the will of God in this matter?" Indeed, what God does God does "in accordance with an order of things and of times which is hidden from us but very well known to Him." "Who can tell what harms or benefits a man [in any particular circumstances]; in peace whether it be to rule or to serve, to be at ease or to die; in war whether it be to command or to fight, to conquer or to be killed?"[66] For human beings, one might say then, the future direction and course of human history remains radically unpredictable.

Augustine therefore denounced all millenarian speculation. "It is a waste of effort for us to attempt counting the precise number of years which this world has yet to go, since we know from the mouth of Truth that it is none of our business."[67] He departed forcefully from the Eusebian school of thought assigning obvious and ultimate significance to the Christianization of Rome.[68] If there are "six stages" in human history, they are not obvious as stages in God's gradual education and development of the whole human race. Rather, they serve only as helpful chronological dividing lines.[69]

Above all, Augustine stressed that God uses sinful human will and deeds to the ultimate advantage of Godself and God's saints.

24.95 (in Vernon J. Bourke, "Voluntarism in Augustine's Ethico-Legal Thought," *Augustinian Studies* 1 [1970]: 13); *De Grat. et Lib. Arb.* 21.42; Deane, 71; Markus, *Saeculum*, 15, 91; Cochrane, 388; Dawson, 65-66, 69; Butterfield, 184; Jaspers, 101; Niebuhr, *Nature and Destiny*, 1: viii; Mommsen, 355, 369-70, 371-72; Chroust, 195-97; and Fortin, "Consciousness," 326-27.

[65]Dawson, 66. See also Deane, 68; Fortin, "Consciousness," 328.

[66]*DCD* 4.7, 4.33; *Con. Faus.* 22.78. See also Fortin, "Consciousness," 328; and Markus, *Saeculum*, 25.

[67]*DCD* 18.53. See also *DCD* 20.7 and 9; *Serm.* 47; *Ep.* 199.1.1; Deane, 72; Markus, *Saeculum*, 20-21; and Mommsen, 349-50.

[68]See Butterfield, 179. See also Markus, *Saeculum*, 40; Fortin, "Consciousness," 330-38; Mommsen, 35-38; as well as n. 25 in chapter one above.

[69]*De Trin.* 4.4.7. The six are (1) Adam to Noah, (2) Noah to Abraham, (3) Abraham to David, (4) David to Babylonian Captivity, (5) Captivity to John the Baptist and the birth of Christ, and (6) Christ's birth to the "hidden end of time." See also William A. Green, introduction to *DCD* 5: ix-x); Mommsen, 373n43; and F. Edward Cranz, "The Development of Augustine's Ideas on Society Before the Donatist Controversy," *Harvard Theological Review* 47 (October 1954): 279.

The *providentia voluntaria* is an active incorporation of evil will into God's historical plan. "Just as God is superlatively good as creator of good natures," Augustine said, "so He is superlatively just as regulator of evil wills. The result is that when evil wills make ill use of good natures, He Himself makes a good use even of evil wills." Through God's historical providence, then, God is like a painter who uses dark colors to enhance the beauty of her canvas: "For a beautiful picture is improved by dark colors if they are fitly placed, and just so the universe of real things . . . is beautiful, sinners and all."[70] As *providentia voluntaria* God regulates everything that happens in history. God does not *determine* what happens in history, but harnesses and incorporates everything that does happen into the divine plan.[71]

For the individual ruler or subject, the fact of the *providentia voluntaria* implies a certain kind of relationship to power and a certain kind of behavior in the face of power. For the ruler, the holder of political power, such providence effectively means that the ruler has sole and complete discretion in matters of policy. His authority, that is, resides in his power. For he would not have gained power in the first place had not God acquiesced in his lustful climb to power. Whether his motives are good or ill, God foresaw those motives and incorporated them into the divine plan for the whole of history. So whatever the ruler may do during his reign God has already foreseen and either rewarded or neutralized.[72] If he wages war, the war will serve a purpose ultimately good.[73]

---

[70]*DCD* 11.17 and 11.23. See also, for example, ibid., 18.51: "For all the enemies of the church, however blinded by error or depraved by wickedness are useful. If given the power of inflicting bodily harm, they exercise her patience. If they oppose her only by their wrong opinions, they exercise her wisdom. Moreover, to bring it about that even enemies shall be loved, they exercise her benevolence or even her beneficence." See also Butterfield, 183-84; Figgis, 40.

[71]See, for example, *DCD* 5.22, 11.17; *Conf.* 6.7, 9.8. See also Deane, 157; and Eppstein, 66.

[72]*DCD* 5.19; *Con. Faus.* 22.70. See also Butterfield, 183.

[73]*DCD* 5.21. See also Langan, 6-7; Deane, 145; Butterfield, 183; Fortin, "Conscience," 149-50; Russell, 22. Interestingly, as Deane, 145, points out, the "logical consequence" of God's omnipotent will as present in history is that if a rebellion were to succeed, "and the former ruler [were] killed or routed, the usurper [would become] the rightful ruler." Yet, as Brown, *Religion,* 31, says, "Occasions for disobedience do not worry Augustine: what concerns him is the correct way to express an overriding love of God. One incident shows this plainly. That thoroughly

For the subjects of rulers, the fact of the *providentia voluntaria* means that they should obey, essentially without question. Whatever the content of a particular regime, it serves a purpose ultimately good and consequently should not be hindered through disobedience. God bestows power on representatives of all degrees of human perversion; nonetheless, Augustine asked rhetorically, "although the causes be hidden, are they unjust?" Consequently, subjects ought to be both passive and obedient in the face of superior human power. For them, too, power equals authority.[74] If the subjects are soldiers, they are obliged to carry out the orders of their commanders even if those orders require fighting and killing. If they kill under military orders they are not guilty of murder; on the contrary, if they do not kill when ordered, they are guilty of treason. Soldiers ought therefore to obey even the possibly unrighteous commands of infidels, such as Julian the Apostate. Even in such a case, "the soldier is innocent, because his position makes obedience a duty."[75]

Within the framework of historical providence, then, the matter of authority is a simple one: the ruler, whoever he might be and whatever he might do, rules with God's sanction. He can do nothing without God's foreknowledge of the deed and, if the deed issues from a perverted will, without God's ultimate compensatory historical intervention. Rulers thus war at their discretion, and subjects fight in obedience to their rulers.

Yet God has an additional, and complicating, perspective on human existence: that of the *ordo naturalis*. God is also *providentia naturalis*. As providence of nature, God ordains a definite and specific order to human existence, an order that transcends history, that points beyond history to eternity. As beings created in the image and likeness of God, human beings are inextricable parts of God's

---

un-Augustinian body of men, Augustine's own congregation at Hippo, had lynched the commander of the local garrison. Augustine is profoundly shocked. He agrees entirely that the man was a very wicked man; that his flock had been victimized by him. But the true, humble Christian, St. Laurence, on whose martydom he had been preaching, had limited his disobedience to a courteous refusal to sacrifice. Such a Christian would have nothing to do with an act of arbitrary violence against a man set above him by God for good or ill." (The reference is to *Serm.* 302.10-17.)

[74]*DCD* 19.15, 4.3, 18.49, 18.51. See also Deane, 157, 162-63; Russell, 6, 20-21, 26; and Langan, 18.

[75]*Con. Faus.* 22.75; *En. in Ps.* 124.7; *DCD* 1.26. See also *DCD* 1.21; *De Lib. Arb.* 1.4.9; *Ep.* 47.5; Russell, 22; and Deane, 163.

natural order. The mere fact of one's existence, the fact that one "is" at all, sufficiently indicates, for Augustine, that one's true home and destination is in the One who eternally and supremely "is."[76] Consequently, historical existence, being fundamentally "unnatural," is of only secondary significance to human natures as they genuinely "are." Even then, its significance lies only in its role as testing ground for the saints.

Augustine's primary concern, then, was not "secular history," the rise and fall of regimes, but "sacred history" (*historia sacra*), the story of God's saving work. History as the teleological operation of God in time, history directed toward the one goal of salvation, was the history that concerned Augustine.[77] Which individual human beings would transcend their positions in history by responding to the pull of the *natural* order, so that they might reside in eternal communion with God and the saints? This question gave to Augustine's thought its characteristic impetus.

From the perspective of the *ordo naturalis*, no human power is in and of itself "authoritative." A ruler's authority derives only from his personal (individual) self-directing of will toward God. The truly authoritative rulers are those who, as individuals, "are not exalted with pride, but remember that they are men," who "fear and love and worship God," who "spread the worship of God far and wide," who "esteem it more important to rule over their base desires than to rule over any nations," who "practice all the more self-restraint as they gain the means for self-indulgence," who, generally, "make their power a servant to the divine Majesty," and who, "if they do all this, [do it] not because of a passion for empty glory, but because they yearn for eternal happiness." Particular rulers must realize, Augustine insisted, that the possession of political power is in and of itself irrevelant to the natural human quest for salvation. Its relevance lies only in the conscience and will of the possessor. "Who is so ignorant, who is so foolish," Augustine wrote to Boniface,

as not to see that the health of this mortal body and the strength of

---

[76]*DCD* 12.2

[77]Markus, *Saeculum*, 11. Markus, 9, notes that Augustine did not use the phrase "secular history" but that "the distinction is thoroughly Augustinian." See also Hannah Arendt, "The Concept of History," in *Between Past and Future* (New York: Viking Press, 1961) especially 65-66; and K. Lowith, *Meaning in History* (Chicago: University of Chicago Press, 1949) 166-73.

its corruptible members, and victory over men who are our foes, and honor and temporal power and all other earthly blessings, are bestowed upon both the good and the evil and are taken away from both the good and the evil? But the health of the soul, along with the immortality of the body, and the strength of righteousness and victory over the desires that are our foes, and glory and honor and peace for evermore, are bestowed upon the good alone.[78]

Consequently, for Augustine, Moses exemplified the truly authoritative political leader: "this Moses, who humbly put from him this high ministry, but obediently accepted it, and faithfully kept it, and diligently fulfilled it; who ruled the people with vengeance, reproved them with vehemence, loved them with fervor, and bore them in patience, standing for his subjects before God to receive His counsel, and to appease His wrath." Most important was not *what* Moses did but how and why: "In wars carried on by divine command, he showed not ferocity but obedience." "It is therefore mere groundless calumny to charge Moses with making war, for there would have been less harm in making war of his own accord than in not doing it when God commanded him.[79]

Augustine summarized as follows: "In the order of nature the act, the agent *and* the authority for the action are all of great importance." To use another example, "if Abraham should sacrifice his son of his own accord, what is he but gruesome and mad? Should he do so at the command of God, however, what is he but faithful and devoted?"[80] Rulers can gain genuine authority over subjects only by attuning themselves to God's natural order. "Think, then, of this point first of all, when you are arming yourself for battle," Augustine wrote to Boniface, "that your strength, even that of the body, is a gift from God; in this way you will not think of using God's gift against God."[81]

For the subject of a particular regime, membership in the natural order signifies a similar stance. As natural beings, subjects are pointed directly to God. Any human power that sets itself above them is immediately suspect, for God and God alone is the final au-

[78]*DCD* 5.24, 20.2; *Ep.* 220.11. See also *DCD* 1.8, 4.33, 5.15, 5.26, 19.19; *Ep.* 155; Brown, *Religion,* 34; Butterfield, 181-83; Mommsen, 360.

[79]*Con. Faus.* 22.69, 22.74, 22.78. See also ibid., 22.71 and 72.

[80]*Con. Faus.* 22.73. The last two sentences are my own translation.

[81]*Ep.* 189.6.

thority. In practical terms this stance means that true obedience can be to God alone. For it is God alone who provides for humankind's eternal destiny. Human rulers may have sway over one's body, but they can not have sway over the destination of one's soul. The general rule of subject obedience is thereby limited by a potentially large and critical area of exception. Although "the Apostle himself says, 'Let every soul be subject to the higher powers,' . . . what if [they] enjoin what you ought not to do?" Augustine was blunt: "In this case by all means disregard the power through fear of the Power." Although the earthly ruler may "threaten a prison," God "threatens hell."[82]

The natural order thus assigns to all human beings a moral responsibility for their actions. In their ultimate accountability to God, they should, as individuals, maintain a prayerful distance from all particular regimes.[83] Soldiers in wartime are no more exempt from this responsibility than are private citizens in times of peace.

There has been some controversy among scholars over the existence of this responsibility in Augustine's thought. Hartigan, for example, makes a strong case for an Augustinian vision of the soldier as "automaton."[84] And when one comes to Augustine's writ-

---

[82]*Serm.* 62.13. See also *DCD* 19.21; *Conf.* 3.8; Brown, *Religion*, 30; Deane, 89, 147-48, 295n153. Augustine emphasized the distance between human law and God's will more in his early works. See, for example, *De Lib. Arb.* 1.6.15; *De Vera Rel.* 31.58; *Ep.* 105.2.27; Markus, *Saeculum*, 88-89; Chroust, 201; Bourke, "Voluntarism," 3, 5-6; and Fortin, "Conscience," 141.

[83]See, for example, *DCD* 5.17. See also Dawson, 76.

[84]Hartigan, 200. Hartigan bases much of his argument on the following passage from *DCD* 1.21 (Dods trans., in Hartigan, 200): "However, there are some exceptions made by the divine authority to its own law, that men may not be put to death. These exceptions are of two kinds, being justified either by a general law, or by a special commission granted for a time to some individual. And in this latter case, he to whom authority is delegated, and who is but the sword in the hand of him who uses it, is not himself responsible for the death he deals. And, accordingly, they who have waged war in obedience to the divine command, or in conformity with His laws have represented in their persons the public justice or the wisdom of government, and in this capacity have put to death wicked men; such persons shall have by no means violated the commandment, 'Thou shalt not kill.' " Note, however, the more literal translation of George McCracken (Green, et al. 1:95): "This very same divine law, to be sure, made certain exceptions to the rule that it is not lawful to kill a human being. The exceptions include only such persons as God commands to be put to death, either by enacted law to by special decree applicable to a single person at the given time—but note that the man who is

ings on obedience from the direction of his understanding of historical providence, such a vision is evident. Yet, as Louis Swift has pointed out, such a vision cannot account for the abundant references in Augustine's writings to the higher loyalty of all human beings to God. Augustine did insist that soldiers respond swiftly and earnestly to those military commands that are clearly in line with God's will, as well as to those that do not clearly contravene such will.[85] There is, however, as Swift shows, a third possibility: a military command might *clearly contravene* God's will.[86] On that point, Augustine was, as we have seen, very explicit.

What, specifically, is an order that contravenes God's will? Augustine confined his examples to the biblical proscriptions concerning idol worship. Hence, he explained, Christian soldiers serving under Julian the Apostate had dutifully obeyed orders sending them into battle, but rightly refused to obey orders that they sacrifice to pagan deities.[87] Confining his examples of appropriate disobedience to questions of idol worship did not mean that Augustine ruled out all other possibilities, however. Rather, it seems that he limited his examples in order to avoid unnecessarily excluding other possibilities. His overriding concern was that all persons should obey God; what such obedience requires may change with a change in circumstances. "To say . . . that what has once been done rightly must in no respect whatever be changed," he emphasized, " is to affirm what is not true."

> If the service of the ministers of the Old Testament, who were also heralds of the New, consisted in putting sinners to death, and that of the ministers of the New Testament, who are also interpreters of the Old, in being put to death by sinners, the service in both cases is rendered to one God, Who [varies] the lesson to suit the times."[88]

---

bound to this service under orders, as a sword is bound to be the tool of him who employs it, is not himself the slayer, and consequently there is no breach of this commandment, . . . in the case of those who by God's authorization have waged war, or who, representing in their person the power of the state, have put criminals to death in accordance with God's law, being vested, that is, with the imperial prerogative of altogether righteous reason." This latter appropriately places more emphasis on the need for express divine command.

[85]*Con. Faus.* 22.75.

[86]Swift, 371-73. See also Russell, 22.

[87]*En. in Ps.* 124.7. See also, for example, *Serm.* 52.13; *Ep.* 105.2.27.

[88]*Ep.* 138.1.4; *Con. Faus.* 22.79.

To describe Augustine's understanding of appropriate occasions for disobedience to political rulers is not to say that these occasions are obvious, or many, or painless. Knowing God's will is not easy; prideful self-delusion is both humankind's greatest enemy and its greatest obstacle to a clear vision of *providentia naturalis*. As Swift suggests, "the subordinate's epistemological problems are such that instances of justifiable disobedience . . . would be rare or virtually non-existent."[89] Whatever the occasion, Augustine insisted, the subject "must be sure that his divine command is not made precarious by any doubt." Finally, Augustine emphasized that disobedient subjects called down upon themselves appropriate earthly punishment, punishment that must be endured joyfully, even to the point of bodily death, for God's sake.[90] There is no earthly reward for "conscientious objection."

In answer to the question "Who may wage war?" then, Augustine presented no concise formula. His answer was simultaneously "anyone" and "no one." "Anyone" may wage war, because God has already foreseen those who will and figured into the unknowable divine historic calculus the effect any particular warring will have on one's destiny. On the other hand, no one may wage war, because warring itself is "unnatural"; it perverts the natural order. In general, only those *already* in possession of political power are legitimate instigators and prosecutors of war. Augustine wished to avoid upsetting the status quo; there is something to be said for peace, even when it is "unjust." Subjects, in their sin, ought to respond obediently to existing earthly power. However, by extension of the idea of providential dualism, there may be occasions when God commands even a private party to wage war, and at that point the particular person ought to respond only to God. Moses' war against the Egyptians exemplified just such a situation.[91] No particular party, in other words, is forever and obviously "authoritative."

Inevitably, the deciding factor in the particular determination is the setting, the particular circumstances. Referring to the appar-

---

[89]Swift, 373. Augustine presented a profound analysis of "time" in *Conf.* 11.14-18, explaining in great depth the extent to which human beings are prisoners of "time," and thus, by implication, the difficulty of saying with any confidence what is the appropriate course of action for a given "time."

[90]*DCD* 1.26; *De Cat. Rud.* 21.37. See also *DCD* 19.17.

[91]See *Con. Faus.* 22.70-71.

ent contradiction of Christ's injunction to his disciples in Luke 22:36 ("But now, . . . he that hath no sword, let him sell his garment, and buy one"), Augustine pointed to God's unknowable consistency in the face of changing historical circumstances. "Does not this [passage] show how, without any inconsistency, precepts and counsels and permissions may be changed, as different times require different arrangements?"[92] Indeed, "the times . . . are not like one another; for they are times." In a sense human beings are "slaves" to the times. Human beings "whose life is short upon the earth, . . . cannot compare the causes of former ages, and of other nations, that they have not experienced with those they have experienced." Yet the times "may easily observe, in one and the same body, day, or family, what is fitting for such a member and at what seasons, what parts and what persons." Consequently, Augustine asserted sweepingly, "when God commands anything to be done, against either the customs or constitutions of any people whatsoever, it is to be done now; if it were prohibited before, it is to be permitted now; and if it were never made a law before, it is to be made one now."[93] Humankind's duty is thus to listen for God's will in the particular situation, and then to obey God.

Augustine recognized that such a duty is impossible for sinful human beings to fulfill. It is an obligation but by no means an expectation. Human beings can not fulfill their duty because at their innermost core they are in contradiction with themselves. They are simultaneously *both* natural and perverted. In close conjunction with humankind's duty, then, is humankind's faith and hope: faith in a merciful providence and hope for a trans-historical resolution of its own self-contradiction.

---

[92]*Con. Faus.* 22.77.

[93]*Conf.* 3.7-8.

CHAPTER THREE

The Grace of Right Love:
How May War Be Waged?

> *"Love, and do what you will."*
> Homilies on the First Letter of
> John 7.8

FOR AUGUSTINE, war was justifiable only as an action arising out of right love. War's methods, therefore, ought only to be love's methods. These two statements may appear to verge on absurdity; yet seen within the context of Augustine's thinking about love they are quite sensible and consistent. How can this be so? Does not the waging of war entail killing human beings? How can the taking of human life be a manifestation of right love? Or did Augustine in some way preclude the taking of human life in wartime?

Answering these questions takes us into the very heart of Augustine's understanding of human love, an understanding that both erected right love as the overriding principle of all human living and simultaneously recognized its inadequacy to translate that principle into laws covering the myriad details of living. It was an understanding, then, that relied heavily on God's grace and individual, contingency-based prudence.

HUMAN WILL AND RIGHT LOVE

What is love, for Augustine? In its broadest meaning, love is psychological "attachment" (*dilectio*).[1] As such, love is not merely

---

[1]Augustine also used *caritas, amor,* and *cupiditas,* among others, to designate the idea of love. Only *caritas* and *cupiditas* have specific connotations devoid of con-

emotive preference; it emanates from the deepest levels of human being. Love is intimately connected with will, and will is the central human characteristic. As Jaspers described the Augustinian understanding, "in everything that he is man is ultimately will, and the innermost core of will is love." Augustine summarized his understanding in a frequently quoted passage from his *Confessions:* "My weight is my love; by it I am borne, wherever I am borne." Love is therefore the essential dynamic and primary energizing force of the human soul. Just as weight impels bodies, Augustine asserted, so "every soul follows what it loves."[2]

Love is at the very center of human existence. Augustine found nothing in human experience that is not directly related to human love. As Deane rightly puts it, "The soul moves toward and becomes like what it loves." One's essential self, therefore, consists of one's love. "To ask whether a man is good," Augustine remarked, "is not to ask what he believes or hopes, but what he loves." "A good man," then, "is not one who knows what is good, but one who loves what is good."[3]

The centrality of love in the human psychic makeup for Augustine cannot be overemphasized. He fended off the Scipionic definition of *populus* and offered his own: "A people is a large gathering of rational beings united in fellowship by their agreement about the objects of their love."[4] Love, not law or justice, is the foundation of political institutions. Moreover, love is the basis of all human knowledge and action. "What is known," Robert Cushman accurately presents Augustine as saying, "cannot be divorced from what is loved. At the very minimum all cognition is directly dependent on interest, and nothing is fully known to which the consent of the will has not been given." Fundamentally, then, "the comple-

---

text. *Caritas* is always love of worthy objects, that is, God and God's image in one's neighbor. *Cupiditas* is always love of unworthy objects, that is, some created good without reference to God. *Dilectio* and *amor* are love of either worthy or unworthy objects, depending on the context. See *DCD* 14.7; *In Ioann. Evang.* 123.5, as well as the discussion in O'Donovan, 11. See also Jaspers, 98.

[2]Jaspers, 95; *Conf.* 13.9; *In Ioann. Evang.* 7.1. See also *Ep.* 155; *Conf.* 7.10, 11.9; Meagher, 6; Deane, 40; Dawson, 59; O'Donovan, 20; and Gilson, *Christian Philosophy,* 136-37.

[3]Deane, 40; *Ep.* 155.4.13. See also Chroust, 197; and Jaspers, 95.

[4]*DCD* 19:24. See also Deane, 122; and Markus, *Saeculum,* 65-66.

tion of cognition lies with affection." As Augustine himself put it, "Who can welcome into his mind what gives him no delight."[5] The same principle applies to human action generally, "for a person lives in those things that he loves." Everything a person does, Augustine emphasized, even evil, is ultimately the result of love.[6]

Human beings find many things to love, of course, and experience many forms of love. The goal and the challenge of human existence, for Augustine, is to love the right things in the right ways. Human virtue is "ordered love." Thus one sings with Christ's bride, the City of God, "Order love within me!"[7]

To stop loving is clearly no answer to the human predicament; to stop loving is to be "inert, dead, contemptible, wretched." Rather one must transform, redirect, one's love: "Guide toward the garden the water that is flowing into the sewer." In other words, "Love what is worthy of love."[8]

The only true and right object of love for human beings is God. As the source of all being and goodness, as, indeed, Being and Goodness themselves, God is the natural direction and home for human love.[9] Augustine insisted that that beyond which humankind can find nothing better is most worthy of love. That, of course, is God. All true love is love of God. "Happy is the one who loves You, O God . . . for he alone loses nothing that is precious to him." In other words, "No one loses You, unless *he* lets *You* go." The joy that comes from loving God alone is therefore both ever fulfilling and indestructible.[10]

---

[5]Robert E. Cushman, "Faith and Reason," in Battenhouse, ed., 289; *De Div. Quaest. ad Simplic.* 1.2.21. See also Brown, 155 (" 'feeling' [*affectus*] . . . [is] the ally of the intellect"), and Jaspers, 95.

[6]*Ep.* 130.3.7; *DCD* 22.22 See also *Serm.* 46.1; *In Ioann. Evang.* 7.1; *De Div. Quaest. Ad Simplic.* 1.2.21; Brown, *Augustine*, 170; Brown, *Religion*, 32; and Jaspers, 95.

[7]*DCD* 15.22 (the reference is to *Song of Songs* 2: 4). See also Brown, *Religion*, 32; Deane, 83; and Penelope D. Johnson, "Virtus: Transition from Classical Latin to the *De Civitate Dei*," *Augustinian Studies* 6 (1975): 122.

[8]Quoted by Jaspers, 95. See also *Ep.* 155; and Brown, *Augustine*, 171.

[9]*Conf.* 1.1. See also, for example, *Conf.* 4.11, 7.3, 7.5, 10.23, 13.1; *DCD* 12.5, 12.26; *De Mor. Eccl. Cath.* 15.25; Jaspers, 73; Johnson, 122; and Gilson, *Christian Philosophy*, 137.

[10]*Conf.* 4.9. See also ibid., 1.4, 7.10, and 10.29; *In Epist. Ioann.* 9.9; *Serm.* 47.4; *De Doctr. Christ.* 1.8.8; *Ep.* 155; and Jaspers, 95.

There has been great controversy among scholars about whether Augustine's right love—the love of God as an end—is ultimately self-seeking or self-sacrificing or both. The attack launched upon the Augustinian position by Anders Nygren in his *Agape and Eros*, which characterized Augustine's right love as an attempted but unsuccessful synthesis of egocentric *eros* and theocentric *agape*, has resulted in what Oliver O'Donovan calls "a major interpretative battle on which the smoke still hangs heavy."[11] In brief, Nygren asserted that Augustine's right love is "acquisitive love," that it is "eudaimonist" in nature, in that it is above all else a desire for "happiness" by the lover, and thus that it is essentially selfish. Nygren admitted that this selfishness is "enlightened" selfishness, but he maintained that, in the presence of the Pauline agape, it is nonetheless ultimately selfish and egocentric; it is Platonic and Plotinian *eros*.[12] Critics of Nygren, such as John Burnaby and Oliver O'Donovan, generally have not denied that Augustine's right love is "acquisitive," "eudaimonist," and "egocentric," but they have insisted upon qualifying those terms. Moreover, they have insisted that, contrary to Nygren's assertion, *eros* and *agape* are not necessarily mutually exclusive terms, and thus that the synthesis of the two, which Nygren termed an impossibility, exists in fact in the Augustinian understanding.[13]

I have already argued that Augustine's right love is a love of God as object, as *summum bonum*. Such love is "natural" (in the sense described in chapter two) desire. "Man desires to praise You," he said, and "Our hearts are restless until they rest in You." Hence, right love is "acquisitive": it seeks to "acquire" its natural home in God, a home from which it has been cast by its own sin.[14] Moreover, in a

---

[11]O'Donovan, 10. See Anders Nygren, *Agape and Eros*, trans. Philip S. Watson (London: SPCK, 1953) 476-558. Among those attempting to refute Nygren are John Burnaby, John Rist, and Rudolph Johannesson.

[12]Nygren, 476, 502, 527, 530, 546, 557-58. See John Rist, "Some Interpretations of Agape and Eros," in Kegley, ed., 163-68; and Rudolph Johannesson, "Caritas in Augustine and Medieval Theology," in Kegley, ed., 188-89. Both argue that Platonic and Neoplatonic *eros* are *not* necessarily egocentric.

[13]See, for example, Burnaby, "Amor," 180-86; O'Donovan, 143-59; and Johannesson, 192-97.

[14]See *Conf.* 1.1. See also ibid., 2.10 and 11.31 ("O Lord my God, what bosom of Your deep secrets is that, and how far from it have the consequences of my trangressions cast me?"); as well as Jaspers, 70.

sense love is "eudaimonist," since what it seeks is "well-being" (*bea-titudo*), a well-being that it anticipates finding in God. Finally, Augustine's right love is "egocentric" in that the self is the seeker and the potential repository of well-being.[15]

Yet Augustine's understanding of right love is more complicated than these terms imply, as the following summary of Augustine's thoughts about love shows:

> In some inexplicable way, I know not what, everyone that loves himself, and not God, does not love himself; and whoever loves God, and not himself, he it is that loves himself. For he that cannot live by himself will certainly die by loving himself, he therefore does not love himself who loves himself to his own loss of life. But when He is loved by whom life is preserved, a man by not loving himself only loves the more, when it is for this reason that he loves not himself, that he may love Him by whom he lives.[16]

Augustine was undoubtedly right in suggesting that what he had in mind in composing this passage is "inexplicable," but one is obliged to try to make some sense of it anyway.

The key terms in the passage are "self-love" and "life," both of which are tremendously important in any consideration of love in warfare. O'Donovan's study of Augustine's understanding of self-love is helpful in deciphering this first term. As he says, Augustine's use of the term *self-love* carried three possible "evaluative tones:" "an unfavorable tone, with which [the phrase] represents the root of all sin and rebellion against God; a neutral tone, to represent the natural condition either of man's animal or of his rational nature; a favorable tone, to represent man's discovery of his true welfare in God."[17] In seeking the sources of these tones, one might say that Augustine recognized within himself what he interpreted as a general human trait: the simultaneous existence of a true self and a false or perverted "self." One's true self is God's image in oneself; it is God's free gift to each human being.[18] This self naturally tends toward God and reaches its perfection and its well-being in God alone, enjoying God for God's own sake. Love of true self is

---

[15]Burnaby, "Amor," 180. See also Meagher, 6-7; and *Conf.* 10.20, 10.22.

[16]*In Ioann. Evang.* 123.5.

[17]O'Donovan, 137. See also ibid., 162n3; and Deane, 87-88.

[18]*Conf.* 1.20. See also ibid., 7.1; Niebuhr, *Nature and Destiny*, 1:155.

thus a result of loving God as the giver of that self. In other words, since the true self issues from God, is based in God, and is naturally directed toward God, then loving God is effectively equivalent to loving one's true self.

On the other hand, all human beings also find themselves in possession of a perverted and sinful "self." This perverted self is the individual human being's own creation, one that seeks domicile in the created world. In so doing it invents its own notion of happiness, of well-being. It makes itself the center of its world and bases its love on the degree to which it believes created things add to that center. Its criterion for love is thus pleasure, whether bodily or spiritual. It lives "according to the flesh," that is, according to itself.[19] This perverted self turns against God in fabricating its own center and source; it "hates" God, perhaps not as a conscious action, but as the clear effect of a failure to recognize God's proper place. The gulf between Creator and creation becomes so vast as to suggest a "negation" of God in a love centered in and on the world. In hating God the perverted "self" hates, by extension, the true self that freely emanates from God. "He who loves wrongdoing," Augustine quoted the Psalmist, "hates his own soul."[20]

"Self-love," then, can mean either love of true self, which is equivalent to love of God, or love of perverted "self," which is equivalent to hatred of God, and hatred of true self. As O'Donovan mentions, there is also a "neutral" tone to the term *self-love* meaning the animal instinct for physical survival. This tone, however, had no normative connotation for Augustine.

The other critical term in the "inexplicable" passage quoted above is *life*. Life can mean either physical, bodily life—that is, "mortal life"—or spiritual, eternal life—that is, "immortal life." Augustine alternated these meanings with such swiftness that it is often difficult to keep up with him.[21] Perhaps the most intriguing, and the most illustrative, discussion in this regard occurs in book 13 of *The City of God*, beginning with chapter 6, entitled "On the evil of Death in general," and continuing through chapter 11, entitled

[19]*Conf.* 10.27; *DCD* 14.2.

[20]*Serm.* 34.8 and 336.2. See also *Ep.* 155.4.15.

[21]See, for example, *De Perf.* 8.17: "For it is plainly one thing to depart from the body, which all men are obliged to do in the present life, and another to be delivered from the body of this death." See also *Conf.* 1.5 ("Hide not Your face from me: Let me die lest I die, that I may see it."), 1.6, 4.12, 13.22.

"Whether anyone can at the same time be both living and dead."
In this discussion, Augustine made plain that (just as perverted self-
love can appropriately be called "self-hate") physical life in and of
itself can appropriately be called "death." "Indeed," he said, "from
the very moment that a person begins his existence in this body that
is destined to die, there is never a point when death is not coming
on." So,

> if a person begins to die, that is, to be in a state of death from the
> time that the process of death itself commences in him, then surely
> he is in a state of death from the time that he begins to exist in this
> body. For death is the diminution of life because, once life has been
> ended by diminishing, he will then be past the time of death, not
> in death. Indeed, what else takes place but death every single day,
> hour and minute until, when life is used up, death, which was going
> on, is complete and time, which comprised the period during death
> when life was being diminished, now enters upon the period after
> death?[22]

The point of Augustine's discussion here is that mortal life is a
kind of death, and that bodily death, if it is God's will, can issue in
eternal life. Thus the person who is physically alive may be spiritually dead, just as the person who is physically dead may be spiritually alive.[23] Most important, though, is that one of these "lives"
is true and one only a sad imitation of true life. As creatures of God,
human beings by nature seek true, eternal life in God. As perverted beings, they center themselves in physical life and its com-
forts; but what they find there is spiritual death. In Christ's words
(Matt. 10:39), "He that findeth his life shall lose it; and he that lo-
seth his life for my sake shall find it." In an important way, then,
loving life excessively is a kind of death, for by loving physical life
excessively one hates *true* life.

Returning now to Augustine's "inexplicable" passage armed
with an understanding of two kinds of self and two kinds of life results in a better understanding of its meaning: "Everyone that loves
[his perverted self], and not God, does not love [his true self]." And
"He that cannot live [truly] by himself [that is, on his own strength

---

[22]*DCD* 13.10.

[23]One can also, of course, be both physically and spiritually alive, if, during one's
physical life, one centers one's existence in God; just as one can also be both physically and spiritually dead if one chooses to deny God.

and merits] will certainly die [lose eternal life] by loving [his perverted self]." Augustine's other apparently contradictory passages about self-love now become more clear as well. For example, "Love God, and so learn to love yourselves!" Again, "Learn to love yourself by not loving yourself!" And again, "If we prefer any other object of love to God or regard any other object of love as God's equal, that shows that we do not know how to love ourselves." Finally, "It is no self-hate, this ruthlessness with yourself."[24]

In this light, it is not difficult to see that Nygren's categorization of Augustine's right love as "acquisitive," "eudaimonist," and "egocentric," oversimplifies considerably the Augustinian understanding. By nature, it is true, human beings seek to "acquire" God so that they may attain well-being, that is, completion and perfection of self. More imporantly, however, the self is *created* by God; the self exists only because God loved it first. When the self rightly loves itself it loves what God has freely given; it loves Love, which is God. It thus gives *back* the "love-currency" first given to it. So Augustine could say, "he who loves God makes no mistakes in the matter of loving himself."[25] As O'Donovan puts it, Augustine recognized the principle of right self-love "as entirely coincident and coextensive with the love of God." In other words, "there [is] no way in which God [can] be loved without the lover loving himself as well." Right self-love for Augustine is thus as much "theocentric" as it is "egocentric," and it is "acquisitive" and "eudaimonist" only indirectly. The primary motive for loving God resides in the creature's thankfulness to God for its very existence. Any well-being that is "acquired" is very much a by-product. As Jaspers put it, "to love God is to love Him gratuitously (gratis) and not to seek a reward apart from God."[26]

Augustine's right self-love is clearly not self-abandonment, although it can easily be seen as self-sacrifice. In addressing the two primary commandments, he asked, "What is there left of your heart for you to love yourself? What is there left of your soul? What is

---

[24]*Serm.* 40.6; 46.2; *Ep.* 155. 4.13; *En. in Ps.* 140.14. For other examples and further explanation, see *Serm.* 34.8; *De Trin.* 14.14.18; *In Ioann. Evang.* 51.10; and *Conf.* 5.2.

[25]*DCD* 19.14. See also *De Mor. Eccl. Cath.* 1.26.48; *Conf.* 1.20; *Serm.* 34; *In Epist. Ioann.* 7.6; *De Trin.* 6.5.7 and 8.8.12. For Augustine's intriguing comparison of love as currency with money as currency see *Ep.* 192.2.

[26]O'Donovan, 37; Jaspers, 96. See also Jaspers, 97-98.

there left of your mind? God says, 'With *all* . . .' He Who made you demands all of you." Yet, O'Donovan argues, "close as he comes to dissolving right self-love into the love of God, Augustine will not go that far. He continues to speak of the two loves even while he asserts that they are coextensive." Thus, Augustine continued in his discussion of the two great commandments,

> "But," you say, "if there is nothing left to me for love-of-self, because I am commanded to love Him 'with all my heart and all my soul and all my mind,' how am I to keep the second commandment and love my neighbor as myself?" . . . Shall I tell you how you are to love yourself? This is your self-love: to love God with the whole of yourself![27]

To love God with the whole of oneself is to love God as the source of oneself and thus to love oneself "in God."

Given this understanding of right self-love, what did Augustine say, more specifically, about right love of neighbor? How is one to "love [one's] neighbors as [oneself]?" It follows that right neighbor-love is also rooted in the love of God as primary object. "If you have not learned how to love yourself," Augustine said, "I am afraid you will cheat your neighbor as yourself." Loving God means loving God's creation, the evidence of God's love, the evidence that God is love. And loving the creation "in God," "for the sake of God," means loving each created person as a sign of God's love. "For he loves his friend in God who loves God's love in the friend."[28]

Hence, the *forms* of love differ as befitting the object, whether Creator or creature. Augustine used the preposition *propter*, the verb *referre*, and occasionally the verb pair *uti* and *frui* to highlight this distinction. As the final and highest Good, only God does one love as an end, for God's own sake. Thus only God does one "enjoy" (*frui*). One's fellows one loves "for the sake of" (*propter*) God; one "refers" (*referre*) them to God; thus one "uses" (*uti*) them for God.

> To pass through the pleasure one takes in an object of love, and to refer it to that end where one wishes to remain, this is "use," and can only loosely be called "enjoyment"; while to stay in it and remain with it, making it the end [*finem ponens*] of one's joy, that is

---

[27]*Serm.* 34.7-8; O'Donovan, 39. See also Gilson, *Christian Philosophy*, 137ff.

[28]*Serm.* 78.3.5; *Conf. Faus.* 22.78. See also *Ep.* 137. 5.17; *In Epist. Ioann.* 7.4-7; and *Conf.* 13.2.

what "enjoyment" properly means, and that we must never do except with that Trinity which is the highest and unchangeable good.[29]

Augustine later dispensed with *uti* as applying to love of neighbor, perhaps because of its tendency to "objectify" one's fellows, but he persisted in his understanding of the basic distinction. As he said in *Contra Faustum,* for example, "a man is just [righteous] when he seeks to use things only for the end for which God appointed them, and to enjoy God as the end of all, while he enjoys himself and his friend in God and for God."[30] One loves God wholly and without qualification; one loves one's fellows and oneself as signs pointing to God, as evidence of God's love for one.

Fellow human beings are worthy objects of love, then, but only as "means" to God, not as ends in themselves. As O'Donovan describes it,

> To love man "in himself" is to admit the false belief that he is a self-standing, independent being. It is to see him as though he were his own source of value and so set him in the place of the One Who is in fact his source of value. To love him "in God" is to recognize that his real nature can be grasped only by reference to his Creator, while love "in Christ" implies that he is what he is by virtue of membership in Christ's body. To love "Christ in him" or "God in him" is to make precisely the same assertion, identifying as the beloved's most valuable feature that which relates him to God.[31]

Augustine realized his own deficiency in this respect. As a young man he had grieved terribly over the death of an unnamed friend. Reflecting on the incident in his *Confessions,* he exclaimed, "O madness, which knows not how to love men!"[32]

What is lovable in one's fellows, as in oneself, is the *imago dei,* the "image of God." More than mere reason or intellect, this image comprises, as Niebuhr suggested, human beings' capacity for "self-

---

[29]*De Doctr. Christ.* 1.33.37.

[30]*Con. Faus.* 22.78. See also O'Donovan, 32; Markus, *Saeculum,* 66-67; and Jaspers, 96-97. For evidence of Augustine's sensitivity to the objectification of personhood, see O'Donovan, 29; as well as *De Trin.* 9.8.13; *DCD* 19.13; and *Conf.* 3.8. Compare, however, *DCD* 11.25; and Ramsey, *Basic Christian Ethics,* 122-23.

[31]O'Donovan, 32 (the reference to Augustine is to *In Ioann. Evang.* 6.1). See also Jaspers, 97.

[32]*Conf.* 4.7. See also ibid., 4.6.

transcendence," their "transcendent freedom over both the natural and historical processes in which [they are] involved." The capacity for self-transcendence is in human nature. Whatever use human beings might make of this capability, neither they nor their fellows can snuff it out. "His fundamental intention," Markus says of Augustine, "is clear and explicitly stated: man has never lost the image of God so entirely that there is nothing left in him to be reformed; the image is deformed [by sin] and in need of reformation, not lost."[33]

Significantly, Augustine emphasized that *all* human beings possess this image, this manifestation of God's goodness. One possesses it in the same way that one is captured by sin: one inherits it from the first man, Adam. "For we all came out of the same lump."[34] Moreover, through Christ, one is a candidate for redemption.[35] Thus all human beings are worthy of love and should be loved. As O'Donovan says, no matter how wicked and repulsive, "by virtue of his creation each man has a good 'nature' which is quite distinct from his empirical wickedness, and by virtue of God's redemptive work he has the possibility of being saved." Consequently, "what we love in our enemy is what he is essentially and what he may yet be."[36]

Whatever a person may do, one's fellow human being, as human being, deserves one's love. Yet to love one's fellows is not to condone their wrongdoing. Rather, it is to distinguish between the person and the wrongdoing. "We should hate our enemy for what is evil in him, that is, for his wickedness," Augustine asserted, "while we also love our enemy for what is good in him, that is, for his nature as a rational and social being." One should, that is, "love what God created, the man and not the error."[37]

---

[33]Reinhold Niebuhr, *The Children of Light and the Children of Darkness* (New York: Charles Scribner's Sons, 1944) 59; R. A. Markus, "*Imago* and *Similitudo* in Augustine," *Revue des Etudes Augustiniennes* 10 (1964): 142. Markus cites *Retr.* 1.26 (on *De Div. Quaest. LXXXIII* 67). See also *Conf.* 7.12, 10.8, and 12.22; *DCD* 12.3, 12.24; *De Doctr. Christ.* 1.22.20; and Niebuhr, *Nature and Destiny* 1:153-56, 267. Ramsey protests against this kind of ascription. See *Basic Christian Ethics,* 94.

[34]*Conf.* 12.26. See also *DCD* 12.22; O'Connell, *Odyssey,* 186-87; Deane, 15; and Jaspers, 98.

[35]See, for example, *DCD* 18.49; *Conf.* 5.2, 7.18, 10. 43. See also Jaspers, 98.

[36]O'Donovan, 30. See also *De Trin.* 8.6.9; *Serm.* 336. 2; *In Ioann. Evang.* 65.2; and Williams, 10-11.

[37]*Con. Faus.* 19.24; *In Epist. Ioann.* 7.11. See also *DCD* 14.6; *Conf.* 10. 4; and *Ep.*

Thus when one loves God in a person, one loves not only God's "image" but also God's "likeness" (*similitudo*), that is, the resemblance of the "image" to the original. Right neighbor-love and right self-love encompass not only what O'Donovan calls the "cosmic" love of God, but also the "benevolent" love of creature for creature. In this way they encompass "the will that something which has its existence from God should fulfill its existence for God."[38] It should, that is, become more "like" God. We love our neighbor when we "wish him good" ("*velimus bonum*"), when we are "concerned for [him] that he should love God," and when we, if necessary, "exhort him to love God."[39]

One might conclude from this description of Augustinian right love that Augustine offered such love as a simple possibility. If human beings ought to love, one might conclude, then they can. It is easy to see how one might reach this conclusion, for immediately behind Augustine the thinker was Augustine the preacher and the rhetorician. In presenting to his listeners the obligation to love rightly, he leaned toward simplistic slogans. Such language inevitably carries with it an undertone of possibility, in reference to the acts it describes. Because one ought, one can; obligation begets possibility. But behind Augustine's simplistic rhetoric of love was an acute awareness of love as the *impossible* possibility. Humankind's obligation and humankind's innate freedom make right love a possibility, but humankind's corruption and pride at the very core of one's being make it an impossible possibility. One might *know* that one is to love one's enemies—also God's special creatures—as reflections of God's creative power, but one can not *do* it.

Love does have definite implications for action, however, for love remains a kind of possibility. Although right love does not arise spontaneously out of intrinsically perverted selves, love does happen in the world and it modifies human action in a very fundamental way. What then is the *source* of right love? Where does it

---

153.3. Additionally, see Windass, 25: "We can even find in St. Augustine's sermons the rather odd view that we should love our enemies *more* than our friends, for the very logical reason that our friends may flatter and pamper us, and so bring us nearer to eternal damnation, whereas our enemies, by making us suffer, give us an invaluable opportunity to come nearer to the Kingdom of God"(*Serm.* 62).

[38]O'Donovan, 33. See also Markus, "*Imago*," 142.

[39]*Ep.* 192.1; *DCD* 19.14 and 10.3. See also *De Serm. Dom.* 2.12.43; *De Doctr. Christ.* 1.22.21; and *Ep.* 153.

come from? Augustine answered: the source of right love is the source of all good, God, who is love itself. Right love, a free gift of God, is a form of grace.

GRACE

Augustine's understanding of grace was an essential element in his understanding of right love, for his emphasis on the indispensability of God's grace showed clearly his vision of right love as both wholly directed to God and wholly dependent upon God. This emphasis separated him dramatically from both the Greek "erotic" tradition of Plato and Plotinus and from the Christian rationalist position of the monk Pelagius and his followers.

Albert Outler offers a good introduction to Augustine's concept of grace.

> Grace is God's unmerited love and favor, prevenient and occurrent. It touches man's inmost heart and will. It guides and impels the pilgrimage of those called to be faithful. It draws and raises the soul to repentance, faith, and praise. It transforms the human will so that it is capable of doing good. It relieves man's religious anxiety by forgiveness and the gift of hope. It establishes the ground of Christian humility by abolishing the ground of human pride.

Finally, says Outler, "God's grace became incarnate in Jesus Christ, and it remains immanent in the Holy Spirit in the Church."[40] Grace is God addressing individual human souls and calling them to God. Grace is thus an infusion of right love into individuals who are, of themselves, wholly incapable of such love. God announced for all time the reality and possibility of grace by means of the person of Christ, and left with the church the responsibility to continue making the announcement.

Grace was indispensable to right love. As Augustine said,

> In order . . . that this love may be possessed, even as far as it can possibly be possessed in the body of this death, the determination of the will avails but little, unless it be helped by God's grace through our Lord Jesus Christ. For as it must again and again be stated, it is "shed abroad in our hearts," not by our own selves, but "by the Holy Ghost which is given unto us." And for no other reason does

---

[40]Albert Outler, introduction to *Augustine: Confessions and Enchiridion*, ed. Albert Outler, The Library of Christian Classics, vol. 7 (Philadelphia: Westminster Press, 1955) 15. Compare Deane, 20-21.

Holy Scripture insist upon the truth that God's commandments are
not grievous, than this, that the soul which finds them grievous may
understand that it has not yet received those resources which make
the Lord's commandments to be such as they are commended to
us as being, even gentle and pleasant; and that it may pray with
groaning of the will to obtain the gift of facility.[41]

It should not be difficult to see how such an understanding of grace
marked a dramatic departure from the Platonic and Neoplatonic
positions on the one hand, and from the Pelagian position on the
other.

There has been some controversy about the extent to which
Augustine's understanding of love was Platonic, that is, "erotic." As
Nygren said, "Neoplatonism is a school he does not leave, even as
a Christian he never breaks with it. All his life he remains a Neoplatonic Christian." Nygren has not been alone.[42] But more recent
scholars appear to have reached a consensus somewhat in opposition to the position of Nygren and the others. While they acknowledge that Augustine was profoundly influenced by the
Neoplatonists, as Augustine himself admitted, and that the Platonic tradition continued to hold a special place in his heart, recent
scholars take more seriously Augustine's own description of his
conversion to Christianity and his subsequent frontal attack on
Greek "eudaimonism".[43]

---

[41]*De Perf.* 10.21. See also Firth, 292-93.

[42]Nygren, 458; others include Boissier, Harnack, and Alfaric. See P. Boyer,
Christianisme et Neo-Platonisme dans la Formation de S. Augustin (Paris, 1920), cited by
D. J. Leahy, *St. Augustine on Eternal Life* (New York: Benziger Brothers, 1939) 1n.
See also W. R. Inge, *The Philosophy of Plotinus,* cited by Cochrane, 376; and Por-
talie, 15-16.

[43]See, for example, *Conf.* 7.20; *DCD* 8.4 and 8.10. For Augustine's vision of his
break with the Neoplatonists, see *Conf.* 7.20 and 7.21. The actual conversion experience is described in *Conf.* 8.6-12. For Augustine's attack on Greek "eudaimonism," see *DCD* 19.1-9. For interpretive descriptions of Augustine's break with
Neoplatonism, see Jaspers, 94; Alfred Warren Matthews, *The Development of St.
Augustine, from Neoplatonism to Christianity,* 386-391 A.D. (Washington: University
Press of America, 1980) 3-4; Cochrane, 377, 387; Brown, *Augustine,* 146-81, esp.
155, 178, also 327; Niebuhr, *Nature and Destiny,* 1:154-58; Ernest L. Fortin, "Reflections on the Proper Way to Read Augustine the Theologian," *Augustinian Studies*
2 (1971): 263; Battenhouse, 19; John A. Mourant, "The Emergence of a Christian
Philosophy in the Dialogues of Augustine," *Augustinian Studies* 1 (1970): 69; and
Eugene TeSelle, "Porphyry and Augustine," *Augustinian Studies* 5 (1974): 123, 124-

Augustine identified the essence of this attack in book 7 of the *Confessions* when he posed the rhetorical question, "When would these books [of the Neoplatonists] teach me . . . the difference between presumption and confession!"[44] The basis of the distinction, summarized so elegantly by the two contrasting words *praesumptio* and *confessio,* lies in the mediation of grace. God's love for individual human beings, as symbolized by the Incarnation and Crucifixion, is the source of all right human love. Without the gift of grace all human love falls short of true love because it rests on a "presumption" by individual human beings that they are its source. Only in the humility of "confession," of the simultaneous "accusation of oneself" and "praise of God," can true love find a home.[45]

In similar fashion, Augustine battled the monk Pelagius. While seeking to retain the indispensable element of free will in his understanding of grace, he relentlessly opposed the efforts of the Pelagians to gain official sanction for the idea that one could through baptism choose a life of sinlessness, and thus that one could love rightly as a result solely of one's own effort.[46] The Pelagians sought only to battle the simple determinism that they saw as representative of the church, but in so doing, according to Augustine, they raised free will to a status of autonomy within the individual, and

---

25, 128. Earlier but similar interpretive descriptions are in Portalie, 15-17; and Sister Mary Patricia Garvey, R.S.M., *St. Augustine; Christian or Neo-Platonist?* (Milwaukee: Marquette University Press, 1939). An exception among recent interpreters is Robert J. O'Connell. See his *St. Augustine's Early Theory of Man* (Cambridge: Belknap Press, 1968) 4-5; as well as his *Odyssey,* 36, 188.

[44]*Conf.* 7.20.

[45]*Serm.* 17.2. See also TeSele, 123.

[46]See, for example, Brown, *Augustine,* 365-66; and Bonner's superb summary, 352-93. J. H. Baxter, xxiii, calls Pelagianism "an outbreak of paganism within the Church." Such characterization is perhaps a bit strong, but one can note some important common ground. See Brown, *Augustine,* 350. Whether Augustine succeeded in retaining free will in his understanding of grace has been a matter of some controversy. Some scholars (for example, J. B. Mozley, *A Treatise on the Augustinian Doctrine of Predestination,* cited by Bonner, 386) have argued that Augustine's understanding was equivalent to Calvinist predestination, while others (for example, Portalie, 214ff) have argued that it retained a large measure of free will. My inclination is to follow the latter, and to say with Williams, 8, "Divine grace upholds and fulfills a right use of freedom; it does not destroy freedom. This is Augustine's view." See also the excellent discussion in Bonner, 383-89; and Portalie, 213-23; as well as Papini, 301; Deane, 18; and Cranz, 282.

thus, by extension, made a mockery of the Incarnation and the Atonement.[47]

Augustine insisted on emphasizing the mysterious nature of human decision making. "There is something of man that even the spirit within him does not know."[48] He came to view "delight" (*delectatio*) as the motivation of human will; but delight was, as Brown says, "discontinuous" and "startlingly erratic." "Who can embrace wholeheartedly what gives him no delight?" Augustine asked. "But who can determine for himself that what will delight him should come his way, and, when it comes, that it should, in fact, delight him?" In sum, the way human beings make choices is more complex than common sense often suggests. An act of choice extends far beyond merely knowing what to choose. Loving and feeling are intimately connected to choosing. Yet in human beings, the capacity to know and to feel in full, coherent fashion has come to be radically deficient. Responding to the Psalmist's plaintive cry, "O that my ways were directed to keep Thy statutes," Augustine asks rhetorically, "And *who is there* who says that he chooses [*optare*] what he thus has in his own power of choice [*in arbitrii potestate*], in such a way that he needs no help to bring it [the choice] about?" To the extent that human beings do unite feeling and knowledge, they do so only by drawing from a source outside their own powers of self-determination.[49]

In contrast to the Pelagian understanding, therefore, Augustine saw that individuals are involved in the sin of perverse love on a level much deeper than any conscious choice. As Brown puts the contrast,

---

[47]See, for example, *De Perf.* 7.16. Ironically, Pelagius quotes from Augustine's piece "On Free Will" in support of his own views (Brown, *Augustine,* 148-49). It was in that work that Augustine sought to overcome Manichean determinism by writing in support of unfettered human will, saying, for example, good will "needs only to be willed in order to possess it" (*De Lib. Arb.* 1.12.26). Yet, as Robert J. O'-Connell, "De Libero Arbitrio I: Stoicism Revisited," *Augustinian Studies* 1 (1970): 67-68; points out, the *second* book "On Free Will," written three to five years *after* the first (Brown, *Augustine,* 74), is in effect Augustine's "retraction" of the unfettered human will of the first book. See *De Lib. Arb.* 2.18 and 2.20. For a decription of Augustine's youthful optimism soon after his conversion experience, see Brown, *Augustine,* 115-27, esp. 122. See also Cranz, "Donatist Controversy," 278.

[48]*Conf.* 10.5. See also Brown, *Augustine,* 170, 179.

[49]*De Div. Quaest. ad Simplic.* 1.2.21; *En. in Ps.* 118.4. The reference is to Ps. 118:5. See also Brown, *Augustine,* 155, 373; Jaspers, 90-91; and Cochrane, 395.

The Pelagian man was essentially a separate individual; the man of Augustine is always about to be engulfed in vast, mysterious solidarities. For Pelagius, men had simply decided to imitate Adam. . . . ; for Augustine, they received their basic weakness in the most intimate and irreversible manner possible; they were born into it by the mere fact of physical descent from this, the common father of the human race.[50]

Hence the perversity of the will can only be overcome with God's help. Although "we were able to deform the image of God in us, . . . we cannot reform it." Only "the Creator who fashioned it . . . can do this." "Our experience gives abundant evidence," Augustine went on, "that in punishment for this sin our body is corrupted, and weighs down the soul, and the clay tabernacle clogs the mind in its manifold activity; and we know that we can be freed from this punishment only by gracious interposition."[51]

Such interposition exists in the person of Christ. Through Christ, "God who is blessed and bliss-creating has become a participator in our humanity and so provided a short-cut [*compendium*] towards our participation in his divinity."[52] Christ showed the "depth of God's humility and of His love for sinful men," as Deane appropriately describes Augustine's account, not simply as Incarnation, "but by His willingness to undergo rebuffs, punishment, and, finally, the most ignominious of all deaths, death by crucifixion, in order to ransom the captives of sin and error."[53]

Two points must be emphasized regarding Augustine's understanding of grace. First, as represented by Christ, grace is wholly unmerited. Augustine pointed emphatically to Paul, who "obtained God's grace . . . without any merits of his own," but indeed, "with many evil merits." Individual human beings are thus totally dependent upon God for their salvation. One of Augustine's favorite metaphors for the human being's relation to God was the infant's relation to its mother's breast. "For what am I without You,

---

[50]Brown, *Augustine*, 365-66.

[51]*Serm.* 43.4; *Con. Faus.* 22.78. See also *De Trin.* 13.7.10; *Conf.* 4.12, 9.1, 10.4, 11.2, 13.8; *De Perf.* 8.17, 12.30; McDonald, 116; van der Meer, 124; Chroust, 197; and Cranz, "Development," 288.

[52]*DCD* 9.15. I have departed from Wiesen's translation of *compendium* as "short and easy path." The path is short but from the human perspective it is not "easy." See also *De Perf.* 2.1, and *Conf.* 7.18.

[53]Deane, 23. See also *Conf.* 7.18 and 10.43.

but a leader to my own downfall? Or what am I, even at my best, but an infant sucking your milk and feeding upon You, the incorruptible Food."[54]

The second point is that the infusion of grace in this life does not rule out subsequent sin. For Augustine grace is a continuing need throughout one's life as a Christian; baptized Christians do not cease to be sinful human beings.[55] This point is especially worthy of attention due to the forceful critique of the Augustinian understanding of grace launched by Reinhold Niebuhr in his *The Nature and Destiny of Man*.

According to Niebuhr, the Augustinian conception of grace saw sin as "essentially the loss of an original perfection, rather than the corruption of the image of God in man." Thus Augustinian grace was "the completion of an imperfect nature." It emphasized "what is good but incomplete in nature" rather than "the element of corruption which always places 'nature' and 'grace' in contradiction."[56] Although Augustine did not "affirm the sinlessness of Christians, . . . he is convinced that the sins which remain are 'venial' rather than 'mortal.'" In other words, "he regards expressions of self-love, after redemption, as incidental, and not as the expression of a basic attitude." However, Niebuhr stated, "The actual situation is that man may be redeemed from self-love in the sense that he acknowledges the evil of it and recognizes the love of God as the only adequate motive of conduct; and yet may be selfish in more than an incidental sense." As examples Niebuhr mentioned "the pride of a bishop, the pretensions of a theologian, the will-to-power of a pious businessman, and the spiritual pride of the Church itself," which are not "mere incidental defects," nor "merely 'venial' sins"; rather, "they represent the basic drive of self-love." This faulty

---

[54]*De Grat. et Lib.* 6.14; *Conf.* 4.1. See also, for example, *Conf.,* 12.18, 13.14-15; *De Nat. et Grat.* 21.23; Brown, *Augustine,* 351-52; van der Meer, 6; Cranz, "Development," 293; Mourant, *Introduction,* 313; and Firth, 292-93.

[55]It is just such reasoning that is at the base of Augustine's championing of infant baptism in his later writings. See, for example, *De Peccat. Meritis.,* especially 1.39.70 and 2.27.43.

[56]Niebuhr, *Nature and Destiny,* 2:139-40. In the last sentence, Niebuhr was alluding to Thomas Aquinas's statement, "Grace does not annul nature but perfects it." Part of the problem with Niebuhr's interpretation, then, is his apparently unconscious acceptance of the "modern" understanding of the term "nature," an understanding that such "classical" thinkers as Augustine and Aquinas obviously could not have had.

understanding of grace, according to Niebuhr, led Augustine to identify too closely the City of God and the visible church, and therefore kept him from fully apprehending the "tragic quality of the spiritual life."[57]

It is not difficult to see how Niebuhr arrived at his description of Augustinian grace. Augustine did say, in effect, that grace is a "perfecting" of "nature." Through God's grace one may regain one's natural freedom and thus may seek what one naturally desires. Yet Augustine also said that sin, the basic attitude of perverse self-love, is in the "seminal substance" of human beings. Not simply "venial" sins continue to trouble Christians, but the "mortal" sin of pride, of craving for perverse elevation in the sight of others, and of undue consciousness of one's own righteousness. Augustine emphasized to his flock that even baptized Christians remain invalids. Although, like the man found near death by the Good Samaritan, their life has been saved by baptism, they are still "in process of healing in the inn [that is, the church]." And the "inn" "shall be a home we shall never leave" in this life. "Meanwhile we gladly receive our treatment [and] we do not glory of sound health, lest through pride . . . our treatment fails to cure us." Human nature is acutely and chronically infected with sin; it can, and will, be fully cured only at the end of time.[58]

There existed in Augustine's thinking about grace a fundamental tension, therefore. Although God is *able to* remake human beings, human pride stands forever in God's way. Thus grace both is and is not a historical possibility. God is able and willing to forgive and to inspire, but humankind is simultaneously forever unwilling to *be* forgiven and to *be* inspired. This tension is both troublesome and puzzling. On the one hand, if humankind is forever and consciously rebellious, of what value is the organized church, staffed as it is by human beings? On the other hand, if grace is a real possibility in the world, perceptible and accessible to all by way of Jesus

---

[57]Niebuhr, *Nature and Destiny,* 2:137. See also Niebuhr, *Man's Nature and Communities,* 43-44.

[58]*Sermo* 81.6. See also *Conf.* 10.36; *Ep.* 111.4, 143; *Retr.* 2.27 (quoting 1 *Cor.* 4:7); Brown, *Augustine,* 365; Deane, 35. Indeed, Augustine pointed out, as long as they live human beings remain trapped in time and space. See *Conf.* 11.11-18. See also Cranz, "Donatist Controversy," 290. Interestingly, Niebuhr appeared fully convinced by the Augustinian understanding of sin. See *Nature and Destiny* 1:158, 2:137.

Christ, how can humankind fail to glorify and to revere the one historic institution whose express purpose is to make known the possibility of God's grace and consequent human salvation? Inevitably, as Niebuhr was quick to show, Augustine got caught in the throes of his own tension. As one fully aware of the centrality of sin in the makeup of human beings, he denounced human pretension and the various schemes of self-salvation; yet as one fully committed to the evangelizing mission of the church, he had to downplay the existence of sin *within the church*. Hence, to read Augustine on grace and the possibility of human perfection is to wonder if one is reading the same Augustine who wrote book 10 of the *Confessions* and book 19 of *The City of God*.

Unfortunately but understandably, then, Niebuhr's criticism of what he saw as Augustine's understanding of grace hinged on a quotation from *On Human Perfection in Righteousness,* which Niebuhr failed to examine in its full context. "He . . . is not unreasonably said to walk blamelessly," Augustine had said there, "not who has already reached the end of his journey, but who is pressing on towards the end in a blameless manner, free from damnable sins, and at the same time not neglecting to cleanse by almsgiving such sins as are venial." It is odd that Niebuhr would have based his criticism of Augustinian grace—as implying a kind of Pelagianism—on a passage from one of Augustine's explicitly anti-Pelagian works. Indeed, if one looks at the piece as a whole one can discern some difficulties with Niebuhr's interpretation.[59]

Augustine began his treatise by attacking the Pelagian position regarding humankind's ability to overcome sin. Although human nature is good, and is able "to be free from evil," it can not be free "so long as the soul is oppressed by the body which is hastening to corruption." "No man, therefore, can be without sin [the basic attitude], even if he wish it, unless he be assisted by the grace of God through our Lord Jesus Christ." Yet "this perfection" can not be reached until "the conflict with death is spent [that is, at the end of time]." Moreover, in the last judgment only those "will be found righteous who with sincerity [*faciliter*] pray: 'Forgive us our debts, as we forgive our debtors.'"[60]

---

[59]*De Perf.* 9.20. *De Perf.* was addressed specifically to a paper by the Pelagian Coelestius.

[60]*De Perf.* 6.14, 7.16, (One must keep in mind that by "body" Augustine meant the whole spectrum of earthly desires.) See also *De Perf.* 8.19; and *Ep.* 189.8. In this life, only Christ may be said to be without sin (*De Perf.* 11.24).

The basic theme of the entire piece on "human perfection in righteousness," then, was that the essence of grace is forgiveness: God's forgiveness of us and our forgiveness of each other. Without the practice of the latter and a continued desire for the former, there is no evidence that one has truly received God's grace. The sentence immediately following the one on which Niebuhr appears to have rested his interpretation (distinguishing "mortal" from "venial" sins) summarized Augustine's position in this treatise: "For the way in which we walk, that is, the road by which we reach perfection, is cleansed by clean prayer. That, however, is a clean prayer in which we say in truth, 'Forgive us, as we ourselves forgive.' "[61]

Saying, "in truth," "Forgive us as we forgive" is the road to perfection. But that articulation, said Augustine, is impossible without true faith, which is impossible without God's grace. Moreover, that articulation is the only possible basis for true love. And "full righteousness . . . will only then be reached, when fullness of health is attained; and this fullness of health shall be when there is fullness of love." Therefore, "whoever tries to persuade us that such a prayer is not proper for faithful members of Christ, does in fact acknowledge nothing else than that he is not himself a Christian."[62]

As long as they live, faithful Christians are acutely aware of both their own mortal disease and God's healing grace. Hence, although it is true, as Niebuhr pointed out, that Augustine allowed for the possibility that some would be "without blame," that is, "free from damnable sins," he insisted that such freedom can result only from "clean prayer," which includes both sincere request for forgiveness and actual forgiveness of one's fellows. These ingredients can only be found in the true humility that comes from grace. Hence those "without blame" are not *aware* that they are "without blame." Au-

---

[61]*De Perf.* 9.20. See also *DCD* 15.7; and *Ep.* 153.

[62]*De Perf.* 3.8, 7.16. "If, again it is through himself that a man is able to live without sin, then did Christ die in vain, But 'Christ is not dead in vain' " (ibid., quoting Gal. 2:21). See also ibid., 6.14, 8.18-19, 11.24; and *Ep.* 153. Evidence that Augustine took to his own heart these assertions about sin and "clean prayer" was offered by Possidius, his first biographer, and the only biographer who knew Augustine personally. According to Possidius, when Augustine was near death he asked that the seven penitential Psalms be copied on sheets and hung in his small room. He then asked to be left undisturbed except during the times when his physician visited and when food was brought. For the ten days before his death he prayed, says Possidius, tearfully and wholeheartedly. Possidius, *Vita*, 31.1-3. See also Bonner, 155; and van der Meer, 273-74.

gustine did not see "the pride of a bishop, the pretentions of a theologian, [and] the will-to-power of a pious businessman" as "mere incidental defects." On the contrary, he clearly condemned all forms of human pride as, effectively, "hatred" of God.[63]

Augustine was not unaware of the possibility of "spiritual arrogance" in the church.

> It is not so much when the Church is involved in so many evils, or amidst such offenses, or in so great a mixture of very evil men, and amidst the heavy reproaches of the ungodly, that we ought to say that it is glorious, *because kings serve it*—a fact which only produces a more perilous temptation—but then shall it rather be glorious, when that event shall come to pass of which the Apostle also speaks in the words, "When Christ, who is your life, shall appear, then shall ye also appear with Him in glory" [Col. 3:41].

Until then the church inevitably contains both "spot" and "wrinkle" (Eph. 5:27). Those "without blame" are few even among Christians, and they, almost by definition, do not know who they are; for to be *conscious* of one's own goodness is to lack the ground of "clean prayer."[64]

LOVE IN ACTION

With the content and the source of Augustinian right love as background, one can begin to understand the link between love and war in Augustine's thought. Augustine could connect love with war because he saw love as implying human action and assertion. Right love is both forgiveness of one's neighbor and an active concern for the neighbor's eternal welfare. Augustine drew a rather hazy line between active concern and spiritual coercion, finding the latter to be, in general, beyond the bounds of right love.[65] Yet right love may

---

[63]See especially *Ep.* 21.1: "First and foremost, I beg your wise Holiness to consider that there is nothing in this life, and especially in our own day, more easy and pleasant and acceptable to men than the office of a bishop or priest or deacon, if its duties be discharged in a mechanical and sycophantic way, but nothing more worthless and deplorable and meet for chastisement in the sight of God; and, on the other hand, that there is nothing in this life, and especially in our own day, more difficult, toilsome and hazardous than the office of a bishop or priest or deacon, but nothing more blessed in the sight of God, if our service be in accordance with our Captain's orders."

[64]*De Perf.* 15.35 (emphasis added).

[65]Although he himself stepped over the line in dealing with the Donatists.

include physical coercion; it may include war. Augustine's pithy summarization of his position was "love [*rightly*, it goes without saying], and do what you will" (*Dilige, et quod vis fac*).[66]

Love may include rebuke. If circumstances are appropriate, love *requires* rebuke. "For just as it is no kindness to help a man at the cost of his losing a greater good, so it is not blameless behavior to spare a man at the cost of his falling into a graver sin." Hence, "We ought not to refrain from reproving and correcting a brother lest he incline toward death in false security." "Nothing is more truly a misfortune than that good fortune of offenders, by which pernicious impunity is maintained, and the evil disposition, like an enemy within the man, is strengthened." "When, however, men are prevented, by being alarmed, from doing wrong, it may be said that a real service is done to themselves."[67] That rebuke may result in repentance was clear to Augustine.

> It is a usual experience and a common occurrence for one who is reproved to be mortified at the time and to wrangle and be recalcitrant, yet afterwards to reflect within himself in silence, alone with God, where he is not afraid of displeasing men by being reproved, but is afraid to displease God by refusing correction, and thence forward to refrain from doing the thing for which he was justly rebuked, and in proportion as he hates his sin, to love the brother whom he realizes to have been the enemy of his sin.[68]

Moreover, rebuke is clearly possible as love: "For just denunciation of a defect in some natural creature doubtless implies praise of the creature itself, since a defect is justly denounced precisely because a praiseworthy creature is degraded by that defect."[69]

---

[66]*In Epist. Ioann.* 7.8. One can read this sentence as merely a tautology, since by Augustine's definition "love," in a sense, *means* "will." Yet it is difficult to believe that Augustine did not mean this in its apparent sense: Any action motivated by right love is permissible. See Gilson, *Christian Philosophy*, 140.

[67]*DCD* 19.16; *Ep.* 210.2, 138.2.14, and 47.5. Rebuke may thus include anger, if such anger is in servitude to God. See *DCD* 9.5. In responding to concern in the early church about Christ's injunction to "turn the other cheek," for example, Augustine cited Christ's reaction to being struck by the high priest's officer in John 18.23. See *Ep.* 138.2.13. See also *De Correp.* 3.5; Deane, 164-65; and van der Meer, 127.

[68]*Ep.* 210.2. See also *De Correp.* 5.7; *Conf.* 9.8.

[69]*DCD* 13.1. See also *De Serm. Dom.* 1.20.63. Although love may imply rebuke, the implication is neither inevitable nor automatic. See *DCD* 1.9.

Love may include physical coercion, as both prevention and punishment of sin. It "involves the obligation not only to do evil to no man but also to restrain a man from sinning or to punish him if he has sinned." Punishment is necessary "so that either the man himself who is chastised may be reformed by his experience or others may be deterred by his example." Although coercion is of itself a perversion of natural freedom, it is sometimes appropriate, "for the person from whom is taken away the freedom which he abuses in doing wrong is vanquished with benefit to himself."[70] Punishment should always reflect a fatherly kind of love. "For in the correction of a son, even with some sternness, there is assuredly no diminution of a father's love." Instead, fathers exercise a "benevolent severity" (*benigna asperitas*); their harshness is motivated by their love. A father may find himself "by love made fierce," just as one may find a man "by iniquity made winningly gentle." "A father beats a boy, and a boy-stealer caresses. If you name the two things, blows and caresses, who would not choose the caresses, and decline the blows? [But] if you mark the persons, it is love that beats, and iniquity that caresses."[71]

Loving punishment can even include the taking of human life. In such extreme cases, as exemplified by Moses' instructions that his own people be slain for worship of idols, there must be specific and unequivocal command of God, who is Love. Augustine was convinced that "Moses acted as he did, not in cruelty, but in great love." Such love "may be seen [by the way] in which he prayed for the sins of the people: 'If Thou wilt forgive their sin, forgive it; and if not, blot me out of Thy book.' "[72] Augustine could reconcile love and killing, using the example of Moses, because, first, God "knows the suitable command in every case"; and, second, the death of the body is not necessarily the death of the soul: only God can kill the

---

[70]*DCD* 19.16; *Ep.* 138.2.14. See also *Ep.* 173.2-3; Deane, 165.

[71]*Ep.* 138.2.14; *In Epist. Ioann.* 7.8 (I have changed the translator's "charity" to "love" in this last passage for the sake of consistency). Augustine was undoubtedly familiar with the phenomenon of child "abuse," but was speaking here of true parental love. See also Deane, 165; and Russell, 17.

[72]*Con. Faus.* 22.71 and 22.79 (the quotation is from Augustine's version of *Exodus* 32:32). See Bainton, 97. See also *DCD* 16.32 concerning Abraham's preparation to kill his own son.

soul.[73] Nevertheless, the crux of this entire matter is that only one who loves rightly is "fit to inflict punishment."[74]

Any discussion of Augustine's understanding of love in action must address his response to the Donatist schism. Arising out of a condemnation of those Christian clergymen who "handed over" copies of sacred scriptures during Diocletian's persecution (thus earning for themselves the appellation "*traditores*") and fueled by a strong African nationalist sentiment, the *pars Donati* was a power in its own right when Augustine assumed the episcopate at Hippo in 395.[75] For almost twenty years, until the Carthage Conference of 411, the phenomenon of Donatism occupied the great bulk of Augustine's time. It is the prime example of Augustine's justification of religious coercion as a manifestation of love.

There has been some controversy about the extent to which Augustine's support of imperial edicts against the Donatists represented a logical extension of his thoughts about love, or instead went against the grain of such thinking.[76] Frederick Russell, who apparently sees support of Donatist persecution as flowing logically from Augustine's thought as a whole, says, "Augustine viewed all forms of religious belief other than orthodoxy as a common threat to the faith." Thus, "since wickedness included the sin of improper belief, Augustine saw a divine purpose in [religious] persecution." Peter Brown, while emphasizing the "evolution" of Augustine's thought on this point, also appears to see such evolution as perfectly logical. "This evolution," he says, "took place less abruptly and with less hesitation than many commentators would admit."[77]

---

[73]*Con. Faus.* 22.72; *DCD* 1.11 and 1.12. See also Bainton, 92. Interestingly, in view of Augustine's allowance for "just" war, he consistently opposed the imposition of the death penalty in criminal cases, because it ruled out the possibility of repentance. See *Ep.* 153.18; and Brown, *Augustine,* 194-95, 241.

[74]*De Serm. Dom.* 1.20.63. See also Russell, 17.

[75]There are several good accounts of the Donatist schism and Augustine's part in attempting to resolve it. Among the best are Bonner, 237-311; Brown, *Augustine,* 212-43; Deane, 172-220; and Willis.

[76]The edicts, in effect, coerced the Donatists to join the Catholic church. See Brown, *Augustine,* 240-41, for the specifics.

[77]Russell, 23; Brown, *Religion,* 44. See also ibid., 263-64; and Brown, *Augustine,* 235. In a less sophisticated but similar vein see Joseph McCabe, *Saint Augustine and His Age* (London: Duckworth and Co., 1902) 410-11; Rebecca West, *St. Augustine* (New York: D. Appleton and Co., 1933) 138-42; and Osmun, 243-44.

Against this position is the view that Augustine consistently distinguished coercion of belief from coercion of action, and that he refused, throughout most of his life, to admit right love into the arena of religious coercion. According to this view, Augustine's response to the Donatist schism was a circumstantially prudential attempt both to stem the violence of the Donatist terrorists (called *circumcelliones,* because they would capriciously rage "around the farmhouses"), and to end the antagonism among fellow Christians from which the violence arose. The great advantage of this view is that it rests upon some rather explicit statements by Augustine as well as the generally agreed-upon fact that the circumcellion violence was both willful and senseless.

In several places Augustine said quite clearly that he abhorred the idea of religious coercion. Concerning one incident of Donatist violence he wrote,

> God knows (for to Him the secrets of the human heart are manifest) that, as I love Christian peace, so I am disturbed by the profane deeds of those who basely and impiously persist in dissenting from it; He knows too that my indignation springs from a desire for peace and that my object is not to drive anyone into the Catholic communion against his will, but to have the naked truth made known to all who are astray and revealed by God's help through my ministry, commending itself so well that they may embrace and follow it.

In another place, at the height of the controversy, he wrote that although his opinion had been "that no one should be coerced into the unity of Christ, that we must act only by words, fight only by arguments, and prevail by force of reason, . . . this opinion of mine was overcome not by the words of those who controverted it, but by the conclusive instances [of Donatist violence and Catholic suffering] to which they could point." As he wrote in 409, "the effort to make men abandon even a great evil and cleave to a great good produces more trouble than benefit, if they act merely under compulsion and not from conviction."[78] Throughout the controversy Augustine sought continued conversation, in the hope that the issue could be settled peacefully and amicably.[79]

---

[78]*Ep.* 34.1, 93.5.17, 100.2. See also *Ep.* 173.7 and Deane's excellent summary of such passages, 185-87.

[79]See, for example, *Ep.* 88.10. Willis mentions, in addition, *Ep.* 23, 33-34, and 44.

Augustine came to religious coercion, therefore, as the result of a prudential decision to attempt both a quelling of circumcellion terrorism and a rekindling of Christian love within the church in Africa. Writing to the Donatist Bishop Januarius, he said, "the clemency of the Catholic Church would have led us to desist from even enforcing these decrees of the emperors, had not your clergy and circumcellions, disturbing our peace and destroying us by their most monstrous crimes of violence, compelled us to have these decrees revived and put in force again."[80] As van der Meer put it, "Augustine desired persuasion; he did not wish for force. . . . It was only the excesses of the circumcellions and the palpably malicious intentions of the Donatist leaders that induced [him] . . . to approve the compulsory imposition of the faith as the lesser evil."[81] Against the rampages of the terrorists, which included the maiming, pillaging, and murder of Catholic priests, among others, and against the determined hostility of the Donatist clergy, Augustine set the dangers of religious coercion, and, in prudential attentiveness, chose the latter.[82]

Throughout the period of Donatist persecution, however, Augustine insisted that Christian love be held as a beacon to light the way back to the Catholic fold. In a letter to his close friend, the magistrate Marcellinus, Augustine asked for mercy for those circumcellions who had confessed to the murder of the priest Restitutus and the maiming of the priest Innocentius. "Christian judge, fulfill the duty of a devoted father; be angry at wickedness, yet forget not humane considerations, and do not give rein to the desire to seek revenge for the atrocity of their sinful deeds, but exert your

---

[80]*Ep.* 88.6.

[81]van der Meer, 95. See also Willis, 127-29; Baxter, xx-xxi; Burnaby, ed., 257; and Frederick Dillistone, "The Anti-Donatist Writings," in Battenhouse, ed., 191.

[82]See *Ep.* 185.3.12-4.16, as well as, for example, *Ep.* 43. Deane, 194-97, notes that a major ingredient in Augustine's calculus was the apparent early success of the Imperial edicts in moderating the conflict. See, for example, *Ep.* 97.4. Regarding circumcellion behavior, Willis, 16, states, "As bandits they were extraordinarily cruel. They attacked and robbed by night the homes of priests. They stabbed people or blinded them with vinegar. When they found that people recovered from this, they took to adding quicklime to the vinegar." See also, for example, Baxter, xvi-xvii; and Dillistone, 179. Augustine referred to some specific cases in *Ep.* 34 and 133, among others. According to Possidius, Augustine himself narrowly escaped being murdered by circumcellions. See *Vita,* recounted by Papini, 247.

will to the curing of the sores of sinners." Decrying capital punishment, Augustine begged Marcellinus to "set them to some useful work . . . that justice be satisfied in such a way as to turn the wicked . . . from their mad frenzy to the peaceableness of sane men." Moreover, when particular Donatists abandoned the schism and returned to Catholicism, Augustine was the first to welcome them in rejoicing and to credit God for their change of heart. Finally, during the long course of the controversy, Augustine consistently urged patience and forbearance upon Catholics, insisting that they not respond to circumcellion violence in kind.[83]

One could argue, as Brown appears to do, that Augustine's public courtesy concealed a private harshness, and that, moreover, Augustine merely sought an acceptable public image.[84] These things may very well be true; however, the point at issue here is whether Augustine sought to promulgate a doctrine of religious coercion as consistent with his thought as a whole, or whether he sought such coercion only as a temporary, prudential expedient appropriate for the particular circumstances of the Donatist schism. It is clear that the latter was true: for Augustine, the Donatist policy was prudential, not doctrinaire. Love in action was his overriding principle, but the application of that principle to a specific situation hinged as much on Christian attentiveness as on Christian love. Confronted with historical circumstances requiring response, Augustine, in acute awareness of the paradox of coerced belief, nevertheless chose to approve coercion.

LOVE AND WAR

Right love could include war, for Augustine. War is not a requirement of love, nor are most wars wars of love. Love makes stringent demands on war. Yet, "love does not exclude wars of mercy waged by the good," as John's clear injunction to the soldiers in Luke 3 made clear to Augustine.

> If the Christian religion condemned wars of every kind, the command given in the gospel to soldiers asking counsel as to salvation would rather be to cast away their arms and withdraw themselves wholly from military service; whereas the word spoken to such was,

---

[83]*Ep.* 133.1-2. See also *Ep.* 88.9, 97.4, 100.1, 138.2.11, 139.2, 144.1, 153, 173.3; van der Meer, 98, 128; Russell, 24; Dillistone, 180, 193.

[84]See Brown, *Augustine,* 299.

"Do violence to no man, neither accuse any falsely, and be content with your wages,"—the command to be content with their wages manifestly implying no prohibition to continue in service.

Augustine also pointed to Jesus' words in Matthew 22:21—"Render unto Caesar the things that are Caesar's . . ."—and to the conspicuous absence in Jesus' short dialogue with the Roman centurion in Matthew 8 of any injunction that the man leave military service as additional, conclusive evidence that war and preparation for war can be appropriate endeavors for Christ's followers.[85]

To Count Boniface, a Roman army commander in Africa who wished to retire from military service and become a monk, Augustine wrote both in sympathy to his wishes and in encouragement that military action against the invading barbarians need not preclude salvation. Quoting the Apostle Paul he wrote, " 'Everyone has his own gift from God'. . . . Some, then, in praying for you, fight against your invisible enemies [of lust and greed]; you, in fighting for them, contend against the barbarians, their visible enemies." War against the barbarians is thus necessary in order that "the citizens of the kingdom of heaven, [being] subjected to temptations among erring and impious men, . . . may be exercised and tried as gold in a furnace." Boniface ought therefore to persevere in his campaign, for "we ought not before the appointed time to desire to live with those alone who are holy and righteous, so that, by patience, we may deserve to receive this blessedness in its proper time."[86]

War and its consequent physical death and injury may result from right love, for Augustine, because love is primarily a matter of inward disposition, not one's outward action. Many actions do arise out of love, of course; Augustine could and did speak of "love in action." However, the true moral content of the specific action always resides in the inward disposition, the motivation, of the one who acts. Hence, objectively speaking, anything is permitted as long as it results from an attitude of right love.

---

[85]*Ep.* 138.2.14, 15; *Con. Faus.* 22.74. See also *Ep.* 189.4; and Langan, 8. Unfortunately, Augustine did not attempt to explain the advice to "Do violence to no man." I suspect, however, given his understanding of the importance of the inward disposition that "violence" meant for him "spiritual violence" and was equivalent to hate or lust, for example.

[86]*Ep.* 189.5.

Regarding the phenomenon of war, Augustine asked, "What is the evil in war? Is it the death of some who will soon die in any case, that others may live in subjection?" No, he answered, "the real evils in war are love of violence, revengeful cruelty, fierce and implacable enmity, wild resistance, and the lust for power, and such like." Hence the dominical injunctions to "resist not evil" and to turn the other cheek require "not a bodily action but an inward disposition." For "what is 'not rendering evil for evil' but refraining from the passion of revenge." What these precepts require us to do, then, is "in the inmost heart, to cherish patience along with benevolence, but in the outward action to do that which seems most likely to benefit those whose good we ought to seek." For example, "when the Apostle was struck, instead of turning his other side to the man, or telling him to repeat the blow, he prayed to God to pardon his assailant in the next world, but not to leave the injury unpunished at the time. Inwardly he preserved a kindly feeling, while outwardly he wished the man to be punished." The "true murderer" is "one who hates": "No, you have mixed no poisons, you have not sallied forth with a sword; you have made no bargains with accomplices; arranged no meeting place; you have not appointed a time; and, finally, you have not committed a crime. All you have done is to hate, and therefore, although you have not killed another you have brought about your own death." As Hartigan appropriately notes, "It is clear that the physical evil of death is insignificant compared with the moral lapses which may occur because of war."[87]

Indeed, "moral lapses" may require war as a response.

> It is generally to punish these things [that is, "love of violence, revengeful cruelty, fierce and implacable enmity, wild resistance and the lust for power"], when force is required to inflict the punishment, that, in obedience to God or some lawful authority, good men undertake wars, when they find themselves in such a position as

---

[87]*Con. Faus.* 22.74, 22.76; *Ep.* 138.2.9; *Con. Faus.* 22.79; *Serm.* 49.7; Hartigan, 198. See also *Conf.* 1.18; *Serm.* 56.14; *Ep.* 210.2; *In Epist. Ioann.* 7.7; Deane, 161, 313n34; Russell, 16; Langan, 8; Bainton, 92, 96; George E. McCracken, introduction to *DCD*, 1:lxv; Johnson, 121-22; and Luc M. J. Verheijen, O.S.A., "The Straw, the Beam, the Tusculan Disputations and the Rule of Saint Augustine," *Augustinian Studies* 2 (1971): 18-19. Augustine often looked to Christ's example, who, when before the high priest in John 18.23, conspicuously failed to turn the other cheek, but rather spoke forcefully to his assailant. *Ep.* 138.2.13. Note Augustine's intriguing interpretation of the "other cheek" precept in *Ep.* 138.2.12. See also *Ep.* 138.2.11.

regards the conduct of human affairs, that right order requires them to act, or to make others act, in this way.

Although, as Deane rightly expresses it, "Christ's teachings require us to maintain patience and good will toward other men in our hearts," such teachings may require also "correcting and punishing [others'] misdeeds," At any rate, "they do not enjoin upon us absolute pacifism and passivity in the face of evil."[88]

Such language points to a confusing element in Augustine's understanding of love and war which he apparently failed to clarify. On the one hand, Augustine said that from God's perspective love resides solely in one's inward disposition, that is, one's true motivation. Outward manifestations of the right inward disposition, then, are effectively irrelevant. So long as one truly loves, *what* one does does not really matter: any action based in and arising out of true love is by definition "right." Yet on the other hand he insisted that from the human perspective one's true motivation is indecipherable; it is simply impossible to ascertain the true reasons one acts as one does. Even more importantly, Augustine claimed that at times certain *actions* were made "necessary" by the implacability of certain heathen or sectarian foes.

It is difficult not to conclude from Augustine's discussion of love in war, then, that although love and war *may be* connected, such connection is, from the human perspective, both futile and fruitless. For the person involved in political decision making, any reference to inward disposition, whether one's own or one's adversary's, would be both naive and absurd. One can not know about "inward disposition," so why should one bother? Should one not rather rest one's decision on things that one *can* know, that is, concrete actions?

To confront Augustine on these terms is to find in him an implicit—though genuine—and surprising conclusion. Augustine's language of love and war harbor, for the student of politics, a very Niebuhrian paradox. Although from God's perspective one's love frees one to "do as you will," from the finitude and fallibility of human perspective, one has to judge on the basis of deeds naked of motivations. Regarding these "judgments pronounced by men on their fellow men, which are indispensable in cities however deep the

---

[88]*Con. Faus.* 22.74 (I have altered the standard translation slightly); Deane, 164. See also Langan, 10; and Russell, 17-18.

peace that reigns within them," Augustine asserted, "how sad, how lamentable we find them, since those who pronounce judgments cannot look into the consciences of those whom they judge."[89]

In the decision either to initiate or to wage war, the political leader faces an inescapable and tragic dilemma. If he truly and rightly loves his foes, then of course the significance of his acts of war will transcend outward appearance. The acts, or consequences, of his love will be both curative and constructive. Yet his love can be true only *after* he recognizes his own personal inadequacy both to love rightly himself and to uncover the motives of his enemies. Love is a gift of God's grace that comes only to those who in devotion affirm their need for it and in fervent prayer beg forgiveness for the sin of pride that blinds them to just that need. Any political leader who commits an act of war and ascribes it to love, in other words, at that very moment falls prey to the presumption and pride that rule out true love. If he *does* act, this means he commits almost by definition the sins of presumption and pride. Yet the situation might very well be such that if he does *not* act he will in like manner commit by definition the sins of cowardice and ill faith. In either case even the conscientious leader is destined to come up short of genuine love.

The statement "Love, and do as you will" exemplifies, then, not only an Augustinian dispositional ethics but also an Augustinian political realism. It is as much a statement of obligation to preserve the existing social order through whatever means are necessary as it is an injunction to maintain a particular, God-directed, inward disposition. For the Augustine who enjoined his flock, "Love, and do as you will," is the very same Augustine who enjoined Boniface, "Let it be your necessity, and not your will, that slays the enemy who fights against you."[90]*Because* one can never know for sure either one's own inward disposition or that of any other, one must confront love's dilemma and give to existing, socially acceptable codes of conduct the benefit of the doubt. The fact of the existence of these codes, that is, ought not to be taken as without significance.

Love remains an obligation, however, even if the obligation is impossible for sinful human beings to fulfill. What this means is that, for Augustine, one's attitude toward the rules of right conduct in

---

[89]*DCD* 19.6.

[90]*Ep.* 189.6.

warfare ought to parallel closely one's attitude toward the rule of obedience to political authority. That is, one should give the rules the benefit of the doubt but continue always to listen for God's will in the particular situation. Obey the rules, one might say, without worshiping them.

Augustine therefore spent little time articulating principles of *ius in bello*. Indeed, principles of *ius in bello* are, in a sense, unnecessary, because if a war truly arises out of the right love of one's enemy, then the love itself will mitigate the conflict.[91] At the same time, if war is waged in the spirit of love, no particular course of action is ruled out, for Augustine. Ruses and ambushes, for example, may be appropriate. The only "act" that Augustine appears to have denied altogether to loving war is one that is intimately connected with one's inward disposition: lying. "It is said unto God, 'Thy law is truth,'" Augustine recounted, "and consequently what is against truth cannot be just. Now who can doubt that every lie is against truth? Therefore there can be no just lie." "When faith is pledged," he stated in another place, "it is to be kept even with the enemy against whom you are waging war."[92]

---

[91]As an example of this potentiality Augustine pointed to Alaric's sack of Rome in 410. The attack was a devasting one: innocent people were killed and left unburied, women were raped, and property was destroyed, all in keeping with "the customary procedures of war." Yet an interesting and welcome aspect of the sack was that Alaric, an Arian Christian, had set aside "basilicas of the most generous capacity" as "asylums of mercy for the people, where no one should be smitten, whence no one should be ravished, wither many should be conducted by compassionate soldiers for release from bondage, and where none should be taken captive even by ruthless foes." See *DCD* 1.7, as well as 1.12, 13, 14, 16, and 28. Augustine was of course not claiming that Alaric acted wholly out of love, but only that Christian commitment *can* be a truly mitigating factor in warfare. See Figgis, 65-66; and Bainton, 97.

[92]*QH* 6.10; *Con. Mend.* 15.31; *Ep.* 189.6. See also Deane, 166. "Augustine readily admits," Fortin ("Conscience," 145) tells us, "that the issue is a difficult and intricate one. He is willing to grant that both the liar's intention and the matter of the lie have no small bearing on the case. The man who lies in order to save a friend's life is surely less guilty than the one who lies out of malice or for the sake of gain. Likewise, a lie in matters of religion is far more grievous than a lie pertaining to other, less vital matters. It is also the case that one may conceal the truth by refraining from speaking whenever there are good reasons to do so; for it is one thing to utter a falsehood and another to pass the truth over in silence. But this does not alter the fact that all lies are intrinsically evil and sinful, no matter how praiseworthy the intention or how trivial the matter." See also *DCD* 22.6: "But the salvation of the City of God is such that it can be kept, or rather gained, along with

The point is that, with Augustine's unique understanding of the paradox of right love, discussions about the presence or absence in his writings of rules of *ius in bello* tend to miss the mark. Although human beings ought to love, they are *not able*—at least on their own strength and merits. More importantly, although with God's grace they *are* able to love, because of the blindness of their own sin they *do not.* Either they refuse God's grace flat out or they take themselves as deserving of it. In either case they commit the fundamental and irrevokable sin of pride, which precludes right love.

The rather heated controversy over whether Augustine's understanding of right love encompasses the principle of noncombatant immunity, therefore, results from positions taken that are both underdeveloped. Paul Ramsey and Richard Hartigan are the most notable exponents of the two positions, and each interpreter ends up oversimplifying the Augustinian understanding. Ramsey argues, in brief, that since, for Augustine, justified war springs from the right-neighbor-love command to punish sin, the killing of those who are, in the particular instance, sinless can not be condoned.[93]

According to Hartigan, on the other hand, Augustine insisted that the primary concern in the waging of war should be military necessity. Yet Hartigan lifts such "necessity" to a level of doctrine when he says, in describing Augustine's position, "so long as the Christian kills without feelings of personal rancor or vengeance he not only does not violate God's law of charity but in reality obeys that law by participating in an act of retributive justice, which in Augustine's moral philosophy is an aspect of charity." Augustine did not exempt innocents from attacks, according to Hartigan, because "the extremely intimate relationship which exists between individual and social morality means that an unjust nation will not be characterized by the presence of a just citizenry." Moreover, should there happen to be innocents among those slain, "it is lamentable but not condemnable," for Augustine's "frequently expressed attitude [is] that death is merely a physical evil and to suffer this fate is far better than to be guilty of bad motivation or vice." Hartigan thus has Augustine saying that killing innocents who could some

---

good faith, and by means of good faith, while if faith is lost no one can reach that City." One can of course ask whether "ruses" and "ambushes" are not "lies," but as far as I know Augustine did not answer.

[93]Ramsey, *War and Conscience*, 34-38. See chapter four below for elaboration and critique of Ramsey's position.

day "be guilty of bad motivation or vice" might even be doing them a favor. At any rate, "Any objective determination as to who are innocent or guilty among the enemy is not only impossible but is also irrelevant." Thus, "no moral guilt is attached to the slaughter of any particular persons."[94]

Hartigan's analysis is rigorous and soundly based. Augustine did say, for example, that the relation between individual and societal morality is an intimate one, a *populus* being "a large gathering of rational beings united in fellowship by their agreement about the objects of their love." Moreover, Augustine appears at times to have been remarkably complacent about physical death. "Those who are necessarily bound to die," he said, "need not care greatly by what accident they die, but must care where they are forced to go when they die." Finally, Augustine appears to have elevated military necessity to a doctrine in its own right when he said to Boniface, "Let it be your necessity and not your choice that slays the enemy who is fighting against you."[95]

Yet the Augustinian position can not be so simply enclosed in a doctrine of "military necessity." In the first place, Augustine insisted repeatedly on demonstrations of mercy to the vanquished. "Just as violence is the portion [*redditur*] of him who rebels and resists," he wrote to Boniface, "so mercy is the due [*debetur*] of him who has been conquered or captured, especially when a disturbance of the peace is not to be feared."[96] Hartigan sees such insistence as an "incongruity" to the doctrine of military necessity, but it is in fact a consistent reaffirmation of the supreme obligation of prudential love. Although Augustine insisted on distinguishing physical, mortal life from spiritual, potentially immortal life, he did not do so to the denigration of physical life. Physical life, too, is God's gift. Indeed, only the physically alive may beg forgiveness for their sins.[97] Above all, the moral scourging that may result from war, that is, the punishing of the wicked and the testing of the good, is good

---

[94]Hartigan, 201-203. See Russell, 19-20, for a similar view of Augustine's position on love in war.

[95]*DCD* 19.24, 1.11; *Ep.* 189.6. On the first point see also *DCD* 4.3 and 19.21. On the second point see also the discussion of death in *DCD* 13.10; as well as *Serm.* 84.2; and Bainton, 92.

[96]See *Ep.* 189.6; and, for example, *DCD* 5.26.

[97]See, for example, *Ep.* 133.1, 153; *DCD* 1.8; Deane, 18; Brown, *Augustine*, 407; Hartigan, 201.

only from the perspective of historical providence, wherein God uses evil deeds for ultimately good ends; it does not transform the act of war into a positive good. War remains an evil. Moreover, those involved in war are clearly involved in an evil; they are not crusaders but are, Augustine hoped, people of deep humility who seek with God's help to derive from the many competing demands on their responsibilities a particular course of action.

The idea of military necessity inevitably implies a kind of self-righteous confidence in one's own cause which is out of place in any human endeavor, but especially in that most tragic of human endeavors, large-scale organized conflict. To bow to military necessity is to bow to the god of victory; yet, Augustine said, "As far as security [*bonos*] and morality are concerned, those true values of human life, I am quite unable to see what difference it makes that some men are victors and others vanquished, except for the utterly empty pride in human glory."[98] God in the divine wisdom regulates the outcomes of conflicts according to the divine plan. One's obligation as an individual, whether as ruler or as soldier, is to pray continually for both forgiveness and guidance, and in so doing to attempt to remember that all human beings, as such, are creatures of God and deserving of love.

The proper means of waging war, then, rests firmly on the conscience of the statesperson who initiates it and the soldier who fights it. All participants are required at some point to examine their own motivations and to discern the connection between motivation and act. All, in other words, are obliged to perform that delicate moral balancing of concern and coercion, of humility and self-assertion, being always on the lookout for the motives of greed and revenge and for the love-destroying pride of self-righteousness.

The weight of conscience bears more heavily on statespersons and military leaders, of course, because in general, God requires obedience to these authorities. Yet love's only true authority is God

---

[98]*DCD* 5.17. See also Deane, 155. Augustine condemned private acts of self-defense, a condemnation based primarily on the pride that such resistance inevitably implies. See *De Lib. Arb.* 1.4-5; and *Ep.* 47. For descriptions and elaborations, see Hartigan, 196-97; Bainton, 97-98; Russell, 18; and Windass, 24, among others.

through Christ, and all people are responsible to God.[99] God requires everyone to make moral decisions. Augustine was convinced that such weight on individual conscience is not detrimental to the *res publica;* far from it.

> Wherefore let those who say that the teaching of Christ is incompatible with the state's well-being, give us an army composed of soldiers such as the teaching of Christ requires them to be; let them give us such subjects, such husbands and wives, such parents and children, such masters and servants, such kings, such judges—in fine, even such taxpayers and tax gatherers, as the Christian religion has taught that men should be, and then let them dare to say that it is adverse to the well-being of the commonwealth; yea, rather, let them no longer hesitate to confess that this teaching, if it were obeyed, would be the salvation of the commonwealth.[100]

Yet Augustine also recognized that while such weight in and of itself is potentially creative in politics, the inherently sinful human beings who carry it will never fully actualize its creative potential. Indeed, for the most part they will abuse it; they will rationalize the requirements of conscience according to their own selfish desires.

In sum, Augustine's understanding of the connection between right love and just war assumed a human race obliged to love, and "naturally" desirous of love, but in the end, incapable of love. That incapacity does not remove the obligation, however. Love remains what Reinhold Niebuhr called an "impossible possibility." Both positions on the question of Augustinian support for a principle of noncombatant immunity, this means, oversimplify what Augustine himself said. Emphasizing military necessity, while not inappropriate, ignores his view of the universal and overwhelming *obligation* to love. Emphasizing the *rule* of noncombatant immunity, on the other hand, ignores among other things both love's transcendence over humanly contrived principle and Augustine's view of humankind's universal and overwhelming incapacity to love.

---

[99]Fortin, "Conscience," 149-50, argues that for Augustine conscience is *purely* a matter of authority such that only the "educated" and the "wise" understand the pangs of conscience and need deal with them. Yet conscience resides not in reason but in feeling, not in the head but in the heart.

[100]*Ep.* 138.2.15.

CHAPTER FOUR

Paul Ramsey and Reinhold Niebuhr: War, Love, and Prudence

> *"Nothing which is true or beautiful or good makes complete sense in any immediate context of history; therefore we must be saved by faith."*
> Reinhold Niebuhr
> *The Irony of American History*, 63

WHAT IS the Augustinian response to the milieu of twentieth-century international relations? Do Augustine's writings *have* any relevance for this setting? At least two observers of contemporary international relations—Paul Ramsey and Reinhold Niebuhr—believe strongly that serious study of the Augustinian corpus has yielded a welcome intellectual and spiritual harvest for our times. Interestingly, though, Ramsey finds a man quite different from the man Niebuhr found. Ramsey finds a man of hopeful moralism; Niebuhr, on the other hand, found, in general, a man of ominous political realism. Whose discovery is correct? Are both right? Or are both wrong?

PAUL RAMSEY'S AUGUSTINE

According to Paul Ramsey, Augustine's writings form the foundation for Western just war theory. Augustine was, he says, "the first great formulator" of the Western just war idea. For this reason

Ramsey thinks it is imperative to return to Augustine to capture both the essence and the germ of the idea. Upon doing so, Ramsey insists, one will come to realize that most later formulations of the idea have been "radically unAugustinian."[1]

The essence of the Augustinian just war idea, for Ramsey, is "love-transformed justice." In other words, the basis for justified warfare lay not in mere self-preservation, nor in natural justice alone, but in a meshing of Christian love and natural justice. Natural justice alone cannot account for the whole of the just war idea. Natural justice requires response in kind; it cannot account for the tenacity of the *ius in bello* principle of noncombatant immunity. That principle is rather "a deposit or creation of the Christian love ethic." The germ of the just war idea (an idea that we have inherited in the body of contemporary secular international law) is Christian love, not natural justice.[2]

In returning to the one who first encouraged love's germination into just war, St. Augustine, Ramsey finds a clear line of descent from the primacy of love to the idea of just war. He finds, first, an understanding of a City whose nature is divine charity, a City "in which men together attain their final end." As a result of the understanding of this City, "even earthly cities began to be elevated and their justice was infused and transformed by new perspectives, limits, and principles." From its inception, he says, Christianity has proposed "that the basic norm and distinctive character of the Christian life is Christian love."[3]

Early Christian pacifism was thus "in the main a consistent deduction from the new foundation laid by Christ . . . of love for every man for whom Christ died." Yet the "change-over to just-war doctrine and practice was not a 'fall' from the original purity of Christian ethics." It was "a change of tactics only." Thus, the "basic strategy remained the same: responsible love and service of one's neighbors in the texture of the common life." When Christians, after Constantine, found themselves with "responsibility for the political

---

[1]Ramsey, *War and Conscience*, 15.

[2]Ibid., xviii-xix, 10.

[3]Ibid., xxi; Ramsey, *Deeds and Rules*, 2. See also Paul Ramsey, *Christian Ethics and the Sit=in* (New York: Association Press, 1961) xiv; "The Case of the Curious Exception," in *Norm and Context in Christian Ethics,* ed. Paul Ramsey and Gene H. Outka (New York: Charles Scribner's Sons, 1968) 91; and *Basic Christian Ethics,* 57, 90.

community as a whole," henceforth "love for neighbors threatened by violence, by aggression, or tyranny, provided the grounds for admitting the legitimacy of the use of military force." In sum, "Christians simply came to see that the service of the real needs of all the men for whom Christ died required more than personal, witnessing action. It also required them to be involved in maintaining the organized social and political life in which all men live."[4]

To elaborate, Ramsey finds this love ethic to be the truly vital aspect of Augustine's thought. He notes, first, that for Augustine the four primary pagan virtues—prudence, justice, courage, and temperance—were rather "four forms of love," and that since these loves aimed at essentially earthly ends, "Augustine criticized [them] as not only vain but also selfish." Without the love that can "bring the soul to rest in the one good End that eternally endures, and convert, transform, and redirect the love wherewith a man loves every good, . . . 'there can be no true virtue.' " Hence, "The heart of the matter of virtue or of justice consists in a matter of the heart." Only the "right inner intention or direction of the will alone" can " 'rightwise' . . . virtue." This was true "regardless of the 'formal' identity there may be between one 'justice' and another," for "the use of the same word [may] point to patterns of behavior, character, or relationships which arise from and are in-formed by quite different sorts of love."[5]

Ramsey thus appropriately chastises Barker for interpreting Augustine's view of earthly kingdoms as having manifested, as though on a kind of sliding scale, various degrees of "relative righteousness [*iustitia*]." "Such an interpretation," Ramsey says, "does not take seriously into account Augustine's belief that there can be no justice, or rendering man his due, unless God is given His due." A more accurate interpretation of the Augustinian view of political regimes, for Ramsey, would recognize Augustine's assertion that human will, that is, human love, is the foundation of regimes. Earthly regimes are distinguished from one another not by relative degrees of *iustitia* but rather by various common loves.[6]

---

[4]Ramsey, *War and Conscience*, xvi-xvii; Paul Ramsey, *The Just War: Force and Political Responsibility* (New York: Charles Scribner's Sons, 1968) 144.

[5]Ramsey, *War and Conscience*, 16-18. References are to *De Mor. Eccl. Cath.* 15, and to *DCD* 19.25.

[6]Ramsey, *War and Conscience*, 18-19, 23, and 26.

Most important, then, is Augustine's understanding of the essential discontinuity in human will, his "doctrine of the divided will," his understanding that human loves tend to be "fratricidal" as much as they try to be "brotherly." "According to Augustine fratricidal love and brotherly love based on love of God are always commingled in human history. There is no heart, no people, and no public policy so redeemed or so clearly contrary to nature as to be without both."[7]

Given this discontinuity of human will, whether individual or corporate, there existed for Augustine a *radical* difference between true *iustitia* and what particular regimes tried to call by the name "justice." Humankind's existence was "fallen," Ramsey points out. Although confronted by "the light of Christ," humankind lives inevitably in the "shadows" cast by that light. Consequently, "An unrectified nisus toward the eternal disturbs every people's purpose." Whereas every people tends to see in its good "*the* Good," every regime is not so much relatively just as forever, albeit to differing degrees, *un*just.[8]

Because of Augustine's insistence upon this radical discontinuity between true *iustitia* and the makeup of human regimes, the idea of *iustum bellum* "cannot have meant for him the presence of justice . . . on one side, its absence on the other." Hence, says Ramsey, "At least at the outset, the just-war theory did not rest upon the supposition that men possess a general competence to discriminate with certainty between social orders at large by means of clear, universal principles of justice." That is, it did not rest upon the idea of natural law. Rather it rested upon the possibility of "right conduct" in war. Human beings are not so rational and perceptive as to discern degrees of justice within regimes, but they do have "a capacity to know more clearly and certainly the moral limits pertaining to the armed action a man or a nation is about to engage in." They can, that is, discern the content of Christian love in action.[9]

The primary emphasis of the just war theory as fathered by Augustine, then, is on the *means* of war, the way in which war is waged; in technical language, the *ius in bello*. Ramsey rests his conclusion here upon the distinction Augustine made between, as Ramsey says, "killing as unjust agressor and killing the innocent." The latter act,

---

[7]Ibid., 30-31.

[8]Ramsey, *Just War*, 497-98; *War and Conscience*, 31. See also ibid., 21, 23, 25.

[9]Ramsey, *War and Conscience*, 32-33. See also ibid., 11, 18, 28, 29.

said Augustine, "is evidently more wrong than the taking of the life of him who so does violence by the one against whom the violence is done." This distinction, as Ramsey acknowledges, "is quite insufficient to be made the basis for Christian action," for Augustine, in this passage, expressly labeled any act of private self-defense an unseemly love of the world. Yet once authoritative action is taken, that is, public action based on protection of the innocent and thus right love of neighbor, then Ramsey sees Augustine as having made, by extension, a critical distinction between lethal force directed toward an "unjust aggressor" and the same force directed toward an innocent bystander. Christian (Augustinian) love permitted, and may have required, the former but prohibited the latter. The "justified war" (Ramsey's translation of *iustum bellum*) is primarily meant to be a "limited war," therefore; it should be limited by Christian love to direct attack only upon actual combatants.[10]

The degree to which a particular act might be "authoritative" is open to some question, of course, and Ramsey does not mean to imply that it is at all easy to determine proper authority. He simply notes that for Augustine the burden of proof was always on those not sitting in the seat of power. "The [reigning] king, more than any individual or party, could be expected to be the voice of this alignment of wills [the *populus*]." When the king has spoken, and initiated hostilities, "the Christian citizen finds himself called into responsible action because of the alliance of his will with the will (and love) that constitutes him with the rest of the multitude a people." Ramsey insists that the authority question "be faced, and frankly and openly debated," but he does not appear to assign to it a paramount significance. He extracts from Augustine no calculus for determining right authority other than this burden-of-proof idea.[11]

---

[10]Ramsey, *War and Conscience*, 36, 45, 59, and 32. Should noncombatants be harmed "unintentionally," that is, as a secondary effect of an attack directed primarily at combatants, such harm is both regrettable and tragic, but it is not in and of itself "immoral." This is the "rule of double effect." See ibid., 50-51, 64. Augustine's words are from *De Lib. Arb.* 1.5. He believed strongly, of course, that one's own physical life was not to be valued unduly.

[11]Ibid., 39, 132. See also ibid., 114. On the lack of "authority" calculus see, for example, *Just War*, 91-139 on "Selective Conscientious Objection," esp. 92-93. See also *Sit=in*, 75-98, as well as *War and Conscience*, xxi. Childress, "Just-War Theories," 435, in discussing the authority question generally, without specific reference to Augustine, combats the tendency to relegate it to the status of "secondary criterion."

Likewise, in dealing with the question of just cause Ramsey discovers in Augustine no firm principle. War is justifiably undertaken as an act of Christian love on behalf of innocent fellow human beings who are suffering unduly.

> While Jesus taught that a disciple in his own case should turn the other cheek, he did not enjoin that his disciples should lift up the face of another oppressed man for *him* to be struck again on *his* other cheek. It is no part of the work of charity to allow this to continue to happen. Instead, it is the work of love and mercy to deliver as many as possible of God's children from tyranny, and to protect from oppression, if one can, as many of those for whom Christ died as it may be possible to save.

Beyond this inevitably vague admonition Ramsey finds no specific guidelines.[12]

Only in the area of just conduct of war does Ramsey find a clear guideline to Christian action: the principle of noncombatant immunity. While insisting that just cause of war and just conduct of war are the "twin-born" of Augustinian ("agape-ic") just war theory, he lavishes considerably more attention on one of these adopted "twins" than on the other. It thus seems clear that for Ramsey the Augustinian love ethic focused primarily on the "How?" of war over the "When?" or the "Who?" As he says, "Christian love shapes itself for enactment in terms of certain principles of right or proper conduct, before ever calculating the consequences to see whether one effect justifies another."[13]

The important point is that Ramsey traces to Augustine an insistence upon the relevance of Christian love for political action. The primary manifestation of that love in all political endeavor is right conduct in relation to our fellow human beings. In the waging of war, as well as in the preparing for war, those who operate within the Christian tradition are obliged to direct their attack, whether actual or potential, only against "the force which should

---

[12]Ramsey, *Just War,* 143. See also ibid., 19-41 ("The Ethics of Intervention"), 500-501; and *War and Conscience,* 9-10, 37, 229; as well as James T. Johnson, "Just War Theory: What's the Use?" *Worldview* 19 (July-August 1976): 46; and Childress, "Just-War Theories," 443. This is not to say that Ramsey thinks just cause guidelines unnecessary; see *Just War,* 423-24.

[13]Ramsey, *War and Conscience,* 158. See also *Just War,* 143-44, 260-61, 423-24. For the relative imbalance of attention for the "twins," see, for example, *War and Conscience,* 136, as well as Childress, "Just-War Theories," 443.

be resisted." Christian love can never mean that we "kill another man's children directly as a means of weakening *his* murderous intent"; it can never mean, that is, that we "do wrong that good may come of it."[14]

It is this love, this overriding emphasis on the *means* of war, that, according to Ramsey, has been lost to just war theory and must therefore be recovered. On the one hand, post-Augustinian formulations of just war theory in the Catholic tradition have shifted "from voluntarism to rationalism in understanding the nature of political community" and thus have increasingly emphasized "the natural-law concept of justice in analysis of the cause that justifies participation in war." Although "rules for the right conduct of war [have been] drawn up," such rules are "usually dismissed as the weakest part of the traditional theory of the just war." Yet for Ramsey the true beauty of the Augustinian formulation is its insistence, first, on the relative injustice of *every* political regime, and, second, its awareness that although "natural reason falters in attempting to make large comparison of the justice inherent in great regimes in conflict," it might be "quite competent to deliver verdict upon a specific action that is proposed in warfare."[15]

On the other hand, modern Protestant ethics, while claiming Augustinian realism as its ancestor, has given way to an ethic of political expediency. In concentrating its efforts on determinations of "the 'lesser evil' or perchance the 'greater good' among the supposed *consequences* of actions," it has "sought to find the path along which action should be directed in order to defend some sort of values at the end of the road toward which action reaches, yet never reaches." It has become "wholly teleological," in the sense of "wholly future-facing." Yet such an ethic "amounts to the suspension of a great part of morality." For if "no more can be said about the morality of *action* than can be derived backward from the future goal" then "ethics has already more than half-way vanished, i.e., it has become mere calculation of the means to projected ends." Such an ethic therefore "produces some version of the opinion that the end justifies the means."[16]

---

[14]Ramsey, *War and Conscience*, xx, 11; *Just War*, 250. See also *War and Conscience*, xviii-xx, 6-7, and 33.

[15]Ramsey, *War and Conscience*, 32, 33. See also ibid., 159.

[16]Ibid., 3, 4-5, 8. See also ibid., 9, 13; and *Just War*, 392. Ramsey refers primarily to Reinhold Niebuhr as illustrative of this trend in modern Protestant ethics. See *War and Conscience*, 3.

The great benefit of a return to the Augustinian just war position, Ramsey insists, is that such a position rightly focuses on the primacy of human will or love in politics and thus the ultimate significance of means in the problem of war. On the one hand, it accepts the reality of human sin, of "divided wills," and hence of the persistence of the power element in human political relations. According to this position, "The use of power is of the *esse* of politics. By this I mean it belongs to politics' very *act of being* politics. You never have politics without the use of power, possibly armed force." Consequently, this position acknowledges forthrightly that war can be "a just resort of policy."[17] On the other hand, the Augustinian just war position insists also, according to Ramsey, on the reality of a divine charity "in-forming" a fallen world. Hence it refuses to rest content with an "unelevated commonwealth," with "significant citizenship in only one city."[18] Beyond the *esse* of politics it recognizes "the *bene esse*" of politics. It therefore seeks to elevate the use of power by specifying limits to its use. Rather than settle for either the Catholic natural law theory of politics or the primarily Lutheran view of political "necessity," the Augustinian just war position can "hold these divergent emphases together in balanced perspective." It can take full account of the three realms of *ordo* ("the order of power"), *lex* ("the legal order"), and *iustitia* ("the regulative ideal of all political action"), aware of the lack of "entire congruency" among them but noting always their small "area of coincidence or overlap" and attempting, in love, to stay within the bounds of this small area.[19]

This understanding of just war has clear implications for the modern era, and Ramsey is quick to draw them out. Most significantly, Ramsey's Augustinian theory disturbs the extreme positions frequently taken regarding nuclear deterrent strategy. On the one hand, it hangs as an ominous moral cloud over any policy of mutual assured destruction, or, as Ramsey puts it in *War and the Christian Conscience*, "the unleashing of counter-nuclear retaliation by means of push buttons." A policy based on such MAD-ness is a policy based on the potential for an act that would be, quite simply, "the most unloving deed in the history of mankind." For Ramsey's

---

[17]Ramsey, *Just War*, 5, 79. See also ibid., xv, 71.

[18]Ramsey, *War and Conscience*, xxi, xxii, xxiii. See also *Sit = in*, 60.

[19]Ramsey, *Just War*, xiii; 12. See also ibid., 5, and *War and Conscience*, 13-14.

part, "I had rather be a pagan suckled in a creed outworn, terrified at the sight of hands made impure by any shedding of blood, than a skillful artisan of technical reason devising plans to carry out such a deed." The horror involved in such a deed has to do with the complete lack of discrimination between combatants and noncombatants that it implies. Thus Ramsey condemns most forcefully the only uses to date of nuclear weapons—those on Hiroshima and Nagasaki—as a "use of violent repression directly against civilians as a means of forcing a decision to surrender on the part of the Japanese military command." The Christian, even in retaliation—not the case in the attacks on Japan—"can only totally reject counter-people warfare." He "cannot have complicity in poisoning the wells just because his enemy may do this." Besides, counter-value retaliation in the nuclear era would, "in the whole history of warfare," be the "most immoral, because the most stupid and politically purposeless." The all-out destruction one envisions from the activation of a MAD policy would be irrational because the "winners" of such a "war" would find not only that their own state was in shambles but also that they had had "to destroy utterly where they thought to conquer and to bend." At base, then, "*neither* deterrence *nor* warfare with these immoral means is or can be feasible." Deterrence based on massive deployment of counter-value weapons fails miserably as a strategy because it is based on a "psychological facade." Rather than deterring the enemy, therefore, "the first result" of "making the deterrent seem more and more horrendous" is that "we ourselves and our allies are deterred."[20]

In another, equally important way, then, Ramsey's Augustinian theory clears the moral skies for "counter-force" nuclear strategy. To the extent that nuclear weapons remain counter-force in design, intention, and use, they fall decidedly within the bounds of just war theory. Love prohibits the direct killing of innocents, but it clearly permits war directed against the guilty. The advent and coming-of-age of nuclear weapons do not change the applicability of the "rule of double effect," nor the moral responsibility to fight wars on occasion. In the nuclear age, as in any previous age, "the question is not only the humaneness or inhumaneness of certain means of putting fighters out of the war, and those closely co-operating in the attacking force. The question is whether the 'target'

---

[20]Ramsey, *War and Conscience*, 169, 170, 150, 270, 168, 234, 237. See also ibid., 10, 167, 231; and *Just War.* 168, 273.

has been so far enlarged as to obliterate the distinction between peoples and their government, between peoples and forces."[21]

Ramsey goes on to insist that a nuclear strategy based on counter-force tactics is not only the most moral response to a nuclear world, but is also the most rational deterrent. "War must be made morally possible, not only because it is not improbable at some distant time but because, even now, a nation's purpose has no embodiment and no effect until a substitute has been found, not for war, but for the deterrent that deters no one so much as ourselves." In short, a " 'deter the war' capability depends on a 'fight the war' capability." "Without the ability to fight the war," Ramsey goes on, "we cannot stop the relentless advance of an enemy. What cannot be used, cannot deter." Or, again, "deterrence is credible only if the war is credible."[22]

Specifically, Ramsey suggests for the United States a gradual, even if unilateral, phasing out of all "multi-megaton" weapons, weapons "whose every use must be for the purpose of directly killing non-combatants as a means of attaining some supposed good and incidentally hitting some military targets." Not only would the use of such weapons be "wholly immoral," but "the manufacture and possession" of such weapons, and the "political employment of [them] for the sake of deterrence, is likewise immoral."[23] At the same time he encourages the development of "an arsenal of fractional kiloton weapons," weapons by design more limited in their use, deployed in such a way (for example, on submarines) as "to keep in perfect invulnerability [our] retaliatory power." In this way the likelihood increases that "the only war that will actually occur will be 'just war,' i.e., against the attacking or counter-attacking power itself." Ramsey argues persuasively that such emphasis on production and deployment of counter-force nuclear weapons in conjunction with a *declared* policy to use them, should war come, would be both our most moral and most rational foreign policy direction. It would recognize the realities of power in the nuclear age while

[21]Ramsey, *War and Conscience*, 227. See also ibid., 10, 138-39, 148-49, 228-29, 232-33, 276, 294, 306. For a contrary view see Walzer, 276-83. See also O'Brien, 87.

[22]Ramsey, *War and Conscience*, 153, 244, 239. See also ibid., 168, 259-60; and *Just War*, 41, 213-16.

[23]Ramsey, *War and Conscience*, 162. See also ibid., 227, 235, 296; and *Just War*, 154.

simultaneously recognizing the moral limits on the use of such power.[24]

In response to those who suggest that baring an intention to limit our attack to military targets may mean defeat, Ramsey quotes favorably George Kennan: "I am skeptical of the meaning of 'victory' and 'defeat' in their relation to modern [all-out] war between great countries. To my mind the defeat is [such unlimited] war itself." Military defeat, in other words, may also mean moral victory. Although one seeks victory in both moral and military terms, a moral loss can be ultimately more devastating than a military loss.[25] Yet, at base, Ramsey thinks his policy suggestions are both morally *and* rationally (that is, militarily) sound.

PROBLEMS WITH RAMSEY'S AUGUSTINE: LOVE, SIN, AND PARADOX

Paul Ramsey has done contemporary Christian ethics a great service by attempting to inject some life into what many twentieth-century thinkers and statespersons had come to believe was a sterile idea: the idea of the just war. Not only has he enlarged the area of debate on the nuclear issue, but he has simultaneously mapped out a broad common ground on which many Protestant and Catholic thinkers can rest comfortably.

There are, however, some rather serious problems with Ramsey's interpretation of Augustine, and thus, by implication, with the just war idea itself. Interestingly, though, these problems arise not as a result of Ramsey's misunderstanding the fundamental Augustinian premises, but rather as a result of the ways Ramsey draws out the implications of those premises.[26]

---

[24]Ramsey, *War and Conscience*, 228, 221. See also ibid., 220; *Just War*, 16-17, 214, as well as Ramsey's "Suggested Policy Decisions," 235-45. Although Ramsey's position on "first use" of theatre nuclear weapons is not clear from these writings, drawing out the implications of his argument would lead one to believe that first use of *counter-force* nuclear weapons would be acceptable to Ramsey under certain conditions.

[25]George Kennan, "Foreign Policy and Christian Conscience," *Atlantic Monthly* 203 (May 1959): 44-49 (quoted by Ramsey in *War and Conscience*, 161-62, who provided the bracketed insertions). See also ibid., 151-52; *Just War*, 17.

[26]I therefore disagree with the conclusion of Charles E. Curran, *Politics, Medicine, and Christian Ethics: A Dialogue with Paul Ramsey* (Philadelphia: Fortress Press, 1973) 72-73, who suggests that Ramsey fails in determining the basic Augustinian premises.

Ramsey accurately identifies the three foundation stones of the Augustinian understanding of war: he notes, first, that right war arises out of a sense of loving responsibility for one's fellow human beings; second, that human beings are divided and discontinuous creatures; and, third, that right love limits the conflict. When he constructs a theory of just war on this foundation, however, Ramsey tends to leave Augustine behind. Indeed, Ramsey's theory does not rest fully upon the foundation stones he himself has identified.

To elaborate, Ramsey correctly identifies right love as the primary ingredient in the development of a just cause. War can be the loving response to "rank injustice." In this sense justice is always "transformed" by love. Yet Ramsey then goes on to draw out of the Augustinian understanding a sense of war as a positive good. When war is undertaken as a loving response to the repression and victimization of the innocents, the "little ones" whom Christ died to save, Ramsey says, there need be regret, but no remorse.[27] Ramsey is of course not a crusader, although his "farewell" address to "Christian realism," written during the Vietnam conflict, might lead some to perceive him as one.[28] Rather, he is clearly a sensitive observer of international politics who appreciates many of the tragic elements inherent in our "fallen world." Nevertheless, he is also one who insists that, under some circumstances—that is, when it becomes necessary to rescue or protect the "innocent and helpless"— war is an act, if not of unadulterated virtue, then at least of positive virtue.

This sense is more implicit in Ramsey's writings than explicit, but it is there nonetheless.[29] He does say of Augustine, "It is a lively sense of man's common plight in wrong-doing and of the judgment of God that overarches the justified war, and not . . . a sense of or clarity about the universal ethical standards that are to be applied."[30] Yet by referring to war under conditions of just cause as a "positive obligation," as a "requirement of charity," as "proper Christian action," as "an application of the supreme standard for Christian living," as indeed "justified," Ramsey implicitly attributes

---

[27]See Ramsey, *Deeds and Rules*, 188.

[28]See Ramsey, *Just War*, 479-88.

[29]See Childress, "Just-War Theories," 432, who refers appropriately to *Deeds and Rules*, 187-88.

[30]Ramsey, *War and Conscience*, 28.

a self-confidence about war to Augustine, a positive evaluation that did not really exist.[31] Although Ramsey notes the medieval tradition requiring soldiers "to do forty days' penance for fighting in any war, however just," and even suggests a possible revival of that tradition when states suppress or ignore claims of conscientious objection, he does not appear to see in such a requirement the Augustinian understanding that war is always an evil, that indeed evil is of the essence of war. Rather, he sees the traditional requirement as "a precaution in case [the individual soldier] had been involved in doing an injustice which . . . he had not to determine." Moreover, Ramsey's suggested reinstatement of such a requirement is pointedly directed at those individual Christians who "as soldier[s] during wartime [are required] to participate in the use of immoral means."[32] The clear implication in both instances is that one could conceivably be involved in a war and *not* be involved in an evil.

For Augustine such untainted involvement is not possible. Evil is of the essence of war. War is a confrontation characterized by force. As such it demonstrates a gaping lack of proper respect for the dignity of human beings. War, that is, can only arise out of human sin; it can never be a positive exercise, from the human perspective, only a "lesser evil." For that reason any involvement in war should elicit a response of remorse. Any other response is inappropriate.

Ramsey seems anxious to disparage such a response. In evaluating Joseph Fletcher's *Situation Ethics,* for example, Ramsey finds "the mood . . . of Niebuhrian Christian realism" to be "going about responsibly doing the greatest good possible and gaining a general sense of guiltiness by calling it the lesser evil," thus "fashionably self-censuring oneself as sinful."[33] Comparing such language to that of Augustine is instructive.

> Let every man, then, reflect with sorrow upon all these great evils, so horrible and so cruel, and acknowledge that this is misery. And if anyone either endures or thinks of them without mental pain, this is a more miserable plight still, for he thinks himself happy because he has lost all human feeling.[34]

---

[31]Ibid., 191; *Just War,* 500-501; *War and Conscience,* 10, 190, 28.

[32]Ramsey, *War and Conscience,* 115, 132-33.

[33]Ramsey, *Deeds and Rules,* 187-88. See also *War and Conscience,* 5.

[34]*DCD* 19.7. I have incorporated the translation Ramsey uses in *War and Conscience,* 27. See also *Conf.* 10.28.

In sum, although Ramsey accurately sees war as, on occasion, an appropriate response to a fallen world, he does not appear to have incorporated into his evaluation of the act of war the full Augustinian recognition of the immense distance between the human (that is, sinful) world and the City of "divine charity." A major reason for this lacuna is that Ramsey fails to draw out the full implications of the second Augustinian foundation stone: the essential discontinuity in humankind.

Ramsey begins his discussions of Augustinian just war with an appropriate and accurate account of the primacy of will (or love) in human beings. He goes on rightly to elaborate Augustine's understanding that such will is "divided," that "fratricidal love" and "brotherly love" were "commingled" in every human heart. As a result of Augustine's recognition of this moral discontinuity, Ramsey insists, "the just-war theory cannot have meant for him the presence of justice on one side, its absence on the other."[35]

Yet Ramsey then proceeds to have Augustine find human beings fully capable of a rational determination about right conduct.[36] If the will is truly primary, as Augustine declared, then it always rules over reason. Further, if the will is truly divided, then lust rules reason as much as love does. Self-love, the love of the world, sin—these are the most intimate aspects of human being. One cannot escape sin in this life any more than one can escape one's body in this life. For Augustine, then, every human act, every human judgment, and every human motive are immediately suspect. One's *own* acts, judgments, and motives are the *most* suspect. The point at which these things stop being suspect to oneself is the very point at which they are, objectively speaking, the most sinful. For the essence of sin is pride. Even when in the service of apparent beneficence toward one's neighbor, rational self-assurance undermines and may destroy the benevolence of the act.

Ramsey asserts on the one hand that "the limitation placed upon conduct in the just-war theory arose not from autonomous reason asserting its sovereignty over determinations of right and wrong . . .

[35]Ramsey, *War and Conscience*, 31.

[36]Part of the difficulty is that Ramsey uses the writings of the mature Augustine (the *Confessions* and *The City of God*) as illustrations to make his points about the divided will and the relative injustice of regimes, and then uses the "Platonist" work *On Free Will* to illustrate his point about right conduct. See *War and Conscience*, 15-39.

but from a quite humble moral reason subjecting itself to the sovereignty of God and the lordship of Christ."[37] Yet throughout his discussion of right conduct in war is the implicit assumption made explicit in his later article, "The Case of the Curious Exception": "Man's competence to know the good is, of course, not to be denied. Our capacity to reason morally is the only means by which we can, from whatever ultimate norm, articulate ethical principles or order the moral life, or improve our practices." Although "we can . . . grasp the fact that there is another law in our members," we can "anticipate the consequences of this . . . in rule-strengthening rules of moral reasoning that allow this to be taken realistically into account." Thus he can say in *War and the Christian Conscience,* "For it may well be the case that natural reason falters in attempting to make large comparison of the justice inherent in great regimes in conflict but is quite competent to deliver verdict upon a specific action that is proposed in warfare."[38]

The primary way in which Ramsey draws out of Augustine's idea of tainted reason an un-Augustinian confidence in human reason is through his development of the idea of "principled prudence." In essence such prudence is "the principle of proportion."[39] Responding to critics who suggest that he oversimplifies the art of statesmanship, relying excessively on clear principles and rules of action, Ramsey insists that there is a true home for artful statesmanship within the bounds of his just war theory.

> For the rest, decisions in regard to the political use of violence are governed by political prudence. This is to say, whether a particular war should be fought, or whether it should be fought at a higher level of violence for hopefully a shorter time or be de-escalated and fought for a longer time, and many another questions one must ask in justifying a particular political option rather than another, depend on one's count of the costs and the benefits, upon weighing greater and lesser evils in the consequences.

---

[37]Ramsey, *War and Conscience,* 59.

[38]Ramsey, "The Case of the Curious Exception," 118; *War and Conscience,* 33. For other illustrations, see ibid., 11, 32, 135, 269; and Paul Ramsey, *Who Speaks for the Church?* (Nashville: Abingdon Press, 1967) the "dedication": "To my daughter['s] . . . daughter. . . . She will grow up to comprehend better things."

[39]Ramsey, *Just War,* 503-504. See also James F. Childress, *Civil Disobedience and Political Obligation: A Study in Christian Social Ethics* (New Haven: Yale University Press, 1971) 92.

Thus, "The statesman responsible for policy decisions lives in a realm where 'the science of the possible' is definitive for all actions." In other words, the delineation of the moral limits on warfare "is the *context* for policy decision" and not the policy decision itself. "There remains a gap between the just-war theory, even if this is a normative theory of and for practice, and the actual practice of statesmanship."[40]

Ramsey is unwilling to surrender principle to the prudence of circumstance, however. In response to Robert Tucker's "realist" critique of Vatican II, he asserts, "In any discussion of the claims of reason to direct statecraft . . . it is of first importance to distinguish the unchanging principles which govern the use of force from the practice which these principles . . . require from age to age because of the changing shape of warfare." In other words, " 'prudence' has rightly to be understood in the service of some prior principle."[41]

However compelling Ramsey's idea of prudence may be, at base it exhibits an unAugustinian confidence in human reason, whether theoretical or practical. Ramsey's references to Aristotle indicate such confidence, as does the general tone of his language. "For sound judgment to be made that a certain conduct is commanded," he says, "the Christian must . . . also consult the consequence to see as best he can that the good outweighs the evil or that evil is minimized by his proposed action." In this way, "the good or the best or the lesser evil among the goal of action is to be chosen." "Whether [certain] effects are acceptable, or not, must be assessed by prudential reason balancing good and evil . . . consequences." Ramsey is optimistic about the possibilities of human reason to a degree Augustine would not have recognized. Speaking of the "difficulty . . . posed by how hard it is to pay attention to *all* of [the] morally relevant features" of a particular act, Ramsey states,

> This difficulty . . . does not flow from myopia or simply from habitual inattentiveness or . . . unresponsiveness in the decisions we make. It flows, rather, from the fact that the agent's moral 'outlook,' his ultimate norm or operational 'system of ethics' *selects in* the features of acts and situations that will appear morally relevant

---

[40]Ramsey, *Just War*, 503; *War and Conscience*, 309, 230, 309. See also ibid., 5-6, 8-9, 137-38; and *Just War*, 189, 217-18, 423-424.

[41]Ramsey, *Just War*, 397; *War and Conscience*, 4. See also *Just War*, 124-27, 391-92.

to him while *selecting out* characteristics that may, on a larger view, be not only relevant but necessary in order to comprehend all the moral wisdom needed for the direction of conduct."[42]

At this point Ramsey has completely lost track of the "divided will"; he has lost sight of what sin truly is, for Augustine. Sin is not the fact of human finitude and fallibility; sin is what human beings do with their finitude and fallibility. As Augustine emphasized repeatedly, sin is the *cause* of human finitude and fallibility. "It is by sin that we die," he said, "and not by death that we sin."[43] Sin is not a limited perspective on the good; it is the conscious and deliberate *rebellion* against the good. "It's no use trying to toe the line," asserted Rupert Birkin, in the mostly unAugustinian novel by D. H. Lawrence, "when your one impulse is to smash up the line." Or, as Augustine described his adolescent theft of his neighbor's pears, "It was foul and I loved it. . . . If any of those pears entered my mouth it was the crime itself that gave it flavor." Thus the difficulty of which Ramsey speaks *did* "flow [both] from myopia [and] from habitual [consciously rebellious] inattentiveness."[44]

All of this is not to say that Augustine had no appreciation for the wonder of human reason. Clearly he did. Rather it is to say that he understood, in a way Ramsey apparently fails to recognize, that human reason is *ruled*—ultimately and even tyrannically—by human will. Since human will is discontinuous at best and seriously perverted at worst, one *ought* continually to be ready to beg God's forgiveness for the will that propels even the best uses of one's reason. Human beings, Augustine believed, must act, and they must judge, but they ought never to believe that either their actions or their judgments are free of perversion.

The third point at which Ramsey slips off the Augustinian foundation concerns the limiting function of Christian love in warfare. Ramsey targets Augustinian love accurately when he says that right love both permits and limits warfare. When Ramsey proceeds to draw from this general observation the specific principle of non-

[42]Ramsey, *War and Conscience*, 4; *Just War*, 154; "The Case of the Curious Exception," 81. See also *War and Conscience*, 178. For references to Aristotle see, for example, *Just War*, 217-18.

[43]*De Peccat. Meritis* 3.20. Augustine was here rephrasing Rom. 5:12, according to Niebuhr, *Nature and Destiny*, 1:173.

[44]D. H. Lawrence, *Women in Love* (New York: Viking, 1920) 192; *Conf.* 2.4, 2.6.

combatant immunity, however, he pulls the roots of Augustinian love out of the ground.

For Augustine, right love is spiritual attachment to God alone. Human beings are "ways" to God; they are "signs" of God's presence. Thus, what one loves in human beings, if one loves rightly (which of course one can not do), is God's reflection. God's image is the critical element in each human being, and that image is not affixed primarily to one's body but to one's soul; it is not affixed to one's "matter" but to one's "spirit." Regarding death, then, the important thing is not *when* one dies but the state of one's soul at the moment of death. Were it possible to confine right love to a fixed principle, therefore, it would not be a principle such as noncombatant immunity, which identifies right love with saving physical life. An adequately Augustinian principle of right love would be one that identified right loving more with saving *spiritual* life.[45] Of course Augustine did not denigrate physical life, for it is only *during* one's physical life that one is able to grow into true, spiritual life. Christ's *first* great commandment, in other words, is followed closely by the second, the two being inextricably linked.

Most important, though, right love for Augustine can only with difficulty be confined to any "principle" more specific than Christ's first great commandment. Beyond this, the supreme rule is "Love, and do as you will!"[46] Thus Moses had demonstrated right love when he had ordered that his people be slain at random. So also Abraham had loved rightly when he had prepared to slay his own son, a perfect "innocent," on Ramsey's terms. So, too, Augustine believed it right love to persecute his fellow Christians, the Donatists, most of whom were wholly innocent of terrorist activities, a persecution that went wholly against the grain of his profound respect for divergent perspectives. Augustine, the Donatist perse-

---

[45]Compare Ramsey, *War and Conscience,* 163: "Seriously threatening to kill an innocent man for some good end, say, in order to compel him to take a Salk vaccination . . . is, as means, the same as threatening to kill him for some evil end, say, to get him to hand over his pocketbook," with Augustine's "love that beats." See also *Conf.* 3.11. Other critiques of Ramsey's interpretation of Augustine on this point, aside from Hartigan, 201-204 (mentioned in chapter three above), are Langan, 20-22; and Curran, 74-75.

[46]*In Epist. Ioann.* 7.8. See Ramsey's references to this passage in *Deeds and Rules,* 23; and *Basic Christian Ethics,* 90. The first great commandment appears in Matt. 22:37-38; Mark 12:30; and Luke 10:27.

cutor, was the same Augustine who exclaimed, "Thy truth, O Lord, does not belong to me, to this man or that man but to us all."[47]

Right loving involves for Augustine a series of paradoxes that Ramsey does not fully account for. The first of these, that one ought to love but that one can not, is intimately connected to the second; that love is real but indecipherable within oneself or others. Both of these lead directly to the third: true love, *especially* when it claims to involve political action, can exist only in true "confession." Thus, the "love" content of any political action is determined not by adherence to "rules" or to "principles," but by adherence to God, an adherence plainly impossible without the grace of "self"—forgetfulness.

In sharp contrast to Ramsey's enunciation of the principle of noncombatant immunity as "faith effective through in-principled love," then, Augustine presented nothing less than "faith effective through unadulterated love." For any *human* specification or limiting of right love, the love first shown to humankind, and given freely to humankind, by God, is inevitably a human tainting of a divine gift. Interestingly, in Ramsey's early work, *Basic Christian Ethics*, he appears to recognize Augustine's understanding of love's freedom most adequately. "Strictly speaking," he says, "this is a new 'principle' for morality only in the sense that here all morality governed by principles, rules, customs, and laws goes to pieces and is given another sovereign test. For this reason Christianity is relevant, as relevant as a revolutionary threat, to every culture yet identical with none. It announces to every age: man is not made for your institutions."[48] Ramsey finds love limited to principle only later in his career.

The separation of Ramsey's just war theory from each of its Augustinian foundation stones points to a common, and faulty, joist (or girder) in the theory's structure. In constructing his theory, Ramsey succumbs to the classical perspective. In the process he loses track of the distinctive character of Augustine's Christian perspective. Ramsey falls prey to the "*praesumptio*" of the classical perspective without fully appreciating the "*confessio*" of the Augustinian perspective.

To say this is certainly not to identify Ramsey as a pagan. However, it is to say that he is perhaps more Pelagian than Augustinian.

---

[47]*Conf.* 12.25.

[48]Ramsey, *Basic Christian Ethics*, 57. See also ibid., 39, 46, 53, 58, 90.

Ramsey is emphatic in his vision of God in Christ comfortably transcending the "fallen world" of human beings. Yet God in Christ appears to be little more than a paradigm for Ramsey. In *Basic Christian Ethics* he states, "Not only in what he said, but in what he did and in what he was, Jesus placarded before men 'the righteousness of God,' he became the standard for measuring the reign of God among men. Through him, Christians become those who 'have been taught by God to love one another.' " Hence, Christ is the "true prototype of divine-Christian love." The "righteousness of God" is "a supernatural measure." The more recent "The Case of the Curious Exception" contains similar language. "Christian ethics makes ultimate appeal to a divine performance," he says. We make "prototypical use" of the parable of the Good Samaritan. Therefore, it is not "that God is good because He is a father," but rather "that from the measure of His steadfastness we know something of the meaning to assign to 'good' fatherhood."[49]

For Augustine, God in Christ is much more than a model, a "proto-type." Without God human beings are nothing; they are empty, vacant. God fills human beings and contains them. God is the only source and ground of all human beings. "I could not be at all, my God, unless You were in me," said Augustine. Everything good that human beings have, they have from God. Even more, God in Christ is the *salvation* of humankind, a salvation needed desperately, even if human beings do not always seek it desperately. Any knowledge one has, one has from God; any truth one has, one has from God; any justice one has, one has from God; and, most important, any love one has, one has from God.[50]

The appropriate attitude for the individual human being, then, is one of constant confession, of simultaneous "accusation of oneself" and "praise of God." Right conduct can only arise out of humility, which is itself a gift of God. More importantly, right conduct can be known only by opening oneself fully to God's will, that is, by attentiveness to God in prayer.[51]

Where Ramsey departs from the Augustinian understanding, then, is at the point where he fails to appreciate fully Augustine's

---

[49]*Basic Christian Ethics*, 45, 19, 12 (quoting 1 *Thess.* 4:9); "The Case of the Curious Exception," 123.

[50]*Conf.* 1.3, 1.2, 1.5.

[51]See, for example, *Conf.* 3.9, and 13.1. Augustine defines "confession" for his audience in *Serm.* 17.2.

sense of paradox. Had he recalled more fully Augustine's sense of the tragically, in Ramsey's words, "unrectified nisus toward the eternal" that "disturbs every people's purpose," he perhaps would have kept in clearer view the remorse essential to the discussion of any human act, but especially to that most tragic of acts, organized violence. He perhaps would have remembered that in politics, as in all human activities, for Augustine, fear *and* guilt are the beginning of wisdom.[52] Hence, he would have seen more clearly the degree to which, for Augustine, sin is ingrained in the very fiber of human being, so that it colors one's every thought and action; the human being's "divided will" is indeed truly "divided." Finally, Ramsey would have followed more consistently love's freedom from humanly articulated principle. For Augustine, a true love of God, a love directed to God that can only *come* from God, is forever at war with human-based principles and programs, because it is forever mired in the paradox of self-impotence. It is thus a love that attends only God, that both heeds God and waits for God, knowing full well that "rules" could change at any time.[53]

Rather than relying upon Ramsey's Aristotelian prudence of principle, the contemporary Augustinian observer of politics, whether statesperson or scholar, would be one who attends to historical contingency and attempts to discern and follow God's will in the particular circumstance; one who values human experiential wisdom but recognizes the uniqueness of each historical situation and the inherent contradictions of human social existence; one whose hope rests in God's ultimate mercy and not in rationally derived rules. Perhaps understandably, Ramsey disparages this kind of approach to statesmanship, labeling it "consequentialist," and therefore dangerous.

> Those theologians who most stress the fact that Christian ethics is wholly predicated upon redemption or upon the Divine indicative,

---

[52]*DCD* 5.24. Compare Job 28:28; and Proverbs 15:33. The "unrectified nisus" quote is from Ramsey, *Just War*, 497-98.

[53]In *Deeds and Rules*, 92, Ramsey notes that he does not understand "Paul Lehmann's view" that "war *both* contradicts what God is doing in the world to bring about a new humanity and is instrumental to this activity." "Are we called in such wise," Ramsey asks disparagingly (95), "to take in trust the risk of trust that our decisions and actions may still by God's grace be found potentially instrumental to His activity in the world?" A true Augustinian would likely answer, "Yes! Exactly!"

and who say that decisive action is made possible by virtue of *justification* in Christ and by God's *forgiveness,* are often precisely the thinkers who strip politics of norms and principles distinguishing between right and wrong. For them policy decisions are always wholly relative or "contextual," pragmatically relating available means to ends. On their view, a policy may be inept or erroneous, but it is difficult to see how a decision could be *wrong.* This makes it difficult to see what there is in need of forgiveness, except inner motives.[54]

It is true that this kind of approach requires a "leap of faith." It requires a will to believe that, in the end, God is in charge of human affairs and that whatever happens, happens ultimately for the good. This approach is not passive, of course; it recognizes the need for responsible social action. Yet, while it has high hopes it withholds positive expectations about humanly contrived solutions to political problems.

REINHOLD NIEBUHR AS MODERN AUGUSTINIAN

Reinhold Niebuhr exemplified this Augustinian approach. Interestingly, though, Niebuhr was Augustinian almost in spite of himself. He distanced himself from what he saw as the moral pretension inherent in Augustine's "doctrine of grace," but in the process became a true Augustinian.[55] Throughout the middle third of the twentieth century Niebuhr used his pen as a pin to prick the balloons of modern self-righteousness, and thereby to expose the emptiness of human self-love. He apparently perceived himself as a one-man demolition team, called upon to explode the myths of human self-redemption and social progress. In spite of his castigation of what he saw as Augustinian grace, then, Niebuhr followed the Augustinian vision most completely and most faithfully.

There are three key points of congruence between the Augustinian and the Niebuhrian visions. For both thinkers human beings were, throughout their being and throughout their life, in contradiction; for both politics was hence a realm of little more than awful

---

[54]Ramsey, *War and Conscience,* 12-13. One could note in response that for Augustine the human predicament is grounded precisely in the unseemliness of such "inner motives."

[55]Niebuhr did think of himself as generally Augustinian, of course. See, for example, *Christian Realism,* 2.

necessities; and last, for both humankind's ultimate hope and salvation arose only from God's providential mercy and power.

Niebuhr had difficulty accepting "Augustine's horrendous conception that sin was transmitted from generation to generation through lust in the act of procreation,"[56] but he had no difficulty accepting the essentially Augustinian notion that sin is universally ingrained in human beings. For Niebuhr one of the primary truths about humankind is that human beings are thoroughly sinners; they are infected with sin. The essence of sin is "pretension"; human beings "pretend" to be more than they are. "Man is mortal," said Niebuhr. "That is his fate. Man pretends not to be mortal. That is his sin." "The dialogue between the self and God results in the *conviction* of the self." This conviction (that is, condemnation) results not from finiteness itself. Rather, the human self is "convicted . . . of its pretension or 'sin'; of claiming too much for its finiteness."[57] Such pretension is ingrained in the very makeup of human beings because it arises out of their essential freedom. *Because* human beings are free, they are "tempted to exceed [their] bounds and claim for the achievements of [their] spirit a universality which they can never possess."[58] For human beings sin is inescapable, even if it is not "necessary." It colors all human acts, judgments, and motivations, with an "ideological taint," giving rise, in the end, to "an impulse to dominion." "Man is a frail little insect buffeted by forces vaster than he. . . . What is more natural than that . . . he should desire enough power to hold the enmity of nature at bay and to intimidate his human foes."[59]

---

[56]Niebuhr, *Man's Nature and Communities,* 24.

[57]Reinhold Niebuhr, *Beyond Tragedy* (New York: Charles Scribner's Sons, 1937) 28; Reinhold Niebuhr, *The Self and the Dramas of History* (New York: Charles Scribner's Sons, 1955) 65 (emphasis added). See also, for example, *Structure of Nations,* 219-20, 298; *Nature and Destiny* 1: 24, 150, 173; 2: 1; and Kenneth W. Thompson, *Christian Ethics and the Dilemmas of Foreign Policy* (Durham NC: Duke University Press, 1959) 19.

[58]Niebuhr, *Beyond Tragedy,* 43. See also Reinhold Niebuhr, *Faith and Politics,* ed. Ronald H. Stone (New York: George Braziller, 1968) 79-81, 253; *Nature and Destiny* 2: 8; *Structure of Nations,* 122, 135, 291; *Beyond Tragedy,* 11, 29, 43; *Children of Light and Darkness,* 59; and *Christian Realism,* 143.

[59]Niebuhr, *Nature and Destiny* 1: 150; *Beyond Tragedy,* 98; *Structure of Nations,* 14. See also *Children of Light and Darkness,* 20; and *Leaves From the Notebook of a Tamed Cynic* (1929; reprint ed., New York: Living Age Books, 1957) 110. For discussion

Such pretension is universal, said Niebuhr. The historic cruci-fixion of Christ was final evidence of this universality: "He dies not because he has sinned but because he has not sinned. He proves thereby that sin is so much a part of existence that sinlessness can-not maintain itself in it."[60] As notable as the destruction of sinless-ness in the symbol of the cross was the instigation of the destruction by historic religion, by, indeed, God's chosen people. Thus, the universality of human pretension could and did claim religious jus-tification or rationalization. Augustine's "City of God," for exam-ple, became in the medieval period a "historic institution" and an "instrument of dominion." "The developent of papal absolutism represents a clear evidence of the perennial nature of the impulse to dominion."[61]

To say that human beings are universally and pathologically sinners is not, for Niebuhr, to say that they are "totally depraved." Indeed, Niebuhr said, "Total depravity is an impossibility, since man can be a sinner only because he is a child of God. He can do evil only because he has freedom; and freedom is the mark of his divine sonship."[62]

Human beings are thus curiously divided and internally contra-dictory creatures. They are simultaneously children of God, possess-ing absolute worth and dignity, and rebellious ingrates, deserving only of brutal chastisement. When they truly acknowledge their own fi-nitude and dependence, and the full transcendence of their Creator, they are the most creative of creatures. Yet when they pretend to be their own creators, turning away from their true source and ground in prideful rebellion, they are the most destructive of creatures. Hence, their creativity and their destructiveness are curiously mixed, provid-ing the spectacle of a human creativity that is inevitably destructive and a human destructiveness that is inevitably, in part, creative. As Niebuhr said, "there is no simple possibility of making nice distinc-

of the "ideological taint," see *Christian Realism*, 2-3, 75, 77, 123-24, 182-83; *Moral Man and Immoral Society* (New York: Charles Scribner's Sons, 1932) xx, 5, 8, 27, 40; *Love and Justice*, ed. D. B. Robertson (Gloucester MA: Peter Smith, 1967) 26, 102; *Structure of Nations*, 50; and *Children of Light and Darkness*, 139.

[60]Niebuhr, *Beyond Tragedy*, 167. See also *An Interpretation of Christian Ethics* (New York: Harper and Brothers, 1935) 49.

[61]Niebuhr, *Structure of Nations*, 107, 14. See also ibid., 35, 89, 92, 290; *Moral Man*, 69; *Love and Justice*, 76; and *Tamed Cynic*, 121-23.

[62]Niebuhr, *Beyond Tragedy*, 190.

tions between human destructiveness and creativity. In the words of Pascal, the 'dignity of man and his misery' have the same source." Thus, "Man stands perpetually outside and beyond every social, natural, communal and rational cohesion. He is not bound by any of them, which makes for his creativity; he is tempted to make use of them for his own ends. That is the basis of his destructiveness."[63] The primary point here, though, is that Niebuhr, in true Augustinian fashion, recognized that the moral discontinuity inherent in human beings follows them wherever they go, whether into politics or family life, into religion or into atheism. "Human nature is, in short, a realm of infinite possibilities of good and evil because of the character of human freedom."[64]

When such morally discontinuous beings enter communal life, that is, politics, they bring along their entire baggage of pretensions and contradictions. The only way they can cooperate effectively is by generating a "collective egoism" to substitute for their individual egoisms. There is a sense in which political life exacerbates humanity's destructive impulses. "In every human group there is less reason to guide and to check impulse, less capacity for self-transcendence, less ability to comprehend the needs of others and therefore mere unrestrained egoism than the individuals who compose the groups reveal in their personal relationships." Hence, the forces that "prevent anarchy in intra-group relations encourage anarchy in intergroup relations."[65]

Both the intercommunal and intracommunal interactions of human beings have to be based on power. As does Ramsey and as did Augustine, Niebuhr recognized power to be the *esse* of politics. "All social co-operation on a larger scale than the most intimate social group requires a measure of coercion." Communal life inevitably gives vent to "the brutality of human nature," so an authoritative, communal power is needed physically to restrain such brutality. Of course, "no state can maintain its unity purely by coercion." The entrance of individuals into communal life is motivated as much by loving responsibility as by *libido dominandi*, as much by desire for justice as by desire for power. "All communities of man-

---

[63]Niebuhr, *Christian Realism*, 6. See also ibid., 178, 182-83; *Structure of Nations*, 290-91; and *Nature and Destiny* 1: 150.

[64]Niebuhr, *Love and Justice*, 54. See also *Christian Realism*, 2.

[65]Niebuhr, *Moral Man*, xi, 16. See also ibid., 48, 91, 93.

kind, from the most primordial, the family, to the larger communities of nation and empire," asserted Niebuhr, "are dependent on the one hand upon some internal force of cohesion and on the other hand upon the unifying power of a central authority."[66]

The central point for Niebuhr here was that the wielding of power is essential to the development of even a "proximate justice"; yet, it is always morally dubious. The power that is "a *sine qua non* [for] public order and peace" is "the same power that is the source of injustice." Hence, "The fact that there is no peace without power justifies a qualified religious reverence toward historic centers of power which maintain a tolerably just relationship to the community." However, "The fact there there is no justice with power requires an unrelenting critical attitude toward all government."[67]

A tolerable social order, then, as a tolerable international order, is one in which "the individual or the group recognizes the possibilities of creative relation to other life, guards against excessive asertions of interest . . . , and balances competing vitalities as much as possible so that no force or vitality will be able to express itself unduly"; it rests upon a kind of "balance of power." Such an order "cannot be established . . . by pure moral suasion," but only by "some kind of decent equilibrium of power." Yet such balance must have an "organizing center," a "concentration of preponderant power at [its] center," and, therefore, be inevitably a kind of "dominion."[68]

Entry into politics, then, involves human beings in innumerable paradoxes: individual self-sacrifice entails communal pride; the harmony of even "proximate" justice requires coercion; the power necessary to establish and protect proximate justice entails dominion. These paradoxes are insoluble, Niebuhr insisted, because of the essential discontinuity inherent in human being. Human beings' creative capacities are so intimately joined to their destructive im-

---

[66]Ibid., 3; *Love and Justice*, 249, 73; *Structure of Nations*, 33. See also, for example, Harry R. Davis and Robert C. Good, ed., *Reinhold Niebuhr on Politics: His Political Philosophy and Its Application to Our Age as Expressed in His Writings* (New York: Charles Scribner's Sons, 1960) 193; *Structure of Nations*, 61, 134; and Ronald Stone, introduction to *Faith and Politics*, xvii.

[67]Niebuhr, *Love and Justice*, 73; *Faith and Politics*, 90. See also ibid., 86.

[68]Niebuhr, *Structure of Nations*, 31; *Love and Justice*, 52, 210; "The United Nations and World Organization," *Christianity and Crisis* 2 (25 January 1943): 1; *Structure of Nations*, 33; *Love and Justice*, 210. See also *Moral Man*, 31; *Structure of Nations*, 61; and *Children of Light and Darkness*, 174.

pulses that nothing they do can be purely creative or destructive. Everything they do is inevitably both.[69] Hence, "The fight for justice will always be a fight." Hence also, "Politics will, to the end of history, be an area where conscience and power meet, where the ethical and coercive factors of human life will interpenetrate and work out their tentative and uneasy compromises."[70]

Two conclusions flowed from this picture of political life, for Niebuhr. First, any good that arises from political activity, any justice, any respect for human dignity, arises only from assertion of power against power. There can be no purely creative results following on the heels of purely moral intentions. Right love is the "impossible possibility"; it is possible only as obligation, not as historical action. "In the realm of politics . . . , self-interest and power must be harnessed and beguiled rather than elminated." That is, "forces which are morally dangerous must be used despite their peril."[71]

In politics essentially sinful human beings interact in their *public* capacities, an added dimension that exacerbates already inherent pretensions. Representatives of groups or nations will not, indeed should not, sacrifice group interests spontaneously. The striving for *public* goods therefore requires means "such as self-assertion, resistance, coercion and perhaps resentment, which cannot gain the moral sanction of the most sensitive moral spirit." "Whenever religious idealism brings forth its purest fruits and places the strongest check upon selfish desire it results in policies which, from the political perspective, are quite impossible."[72] There inevitably arises, then, a "frank dualism in morals " distinguishing

---

[69]See, for example, Niebuhr, *Structure of Nations*, 13, 24, 71, 134, 218; *Moral Man*, 232, 249; *Children of Light and Darkness*, 57; and "Toward Intra-Christian Endeavors," *Christian Century* 86 (31 December 1969): 1664-65.

[70]Niebuhr, *Love and Justice*, 38; *Moral Man*, 4. See also the illuminating dialogue between Reinhold and H. Richard Niebuhr, "The Grace of Doing Nothing"; "Must We Do Nothing?" and "The Only Way into the Kingdom of God," *Christian Century* 49 (23 March, 30 March, and 6 April 1932): 378-80; 415-17, 447.

[71]Davis and Good, 133-36, 193.

[72]Niebuhr, *Moral Man*, 257, 270. Niebuhr used the example here (269) of the effort by Tolstoi and his followers to keep the Russian peasant movement nonviolent. Such a strategy, said Niebuhr, only "helped to destroy a rising protest against political and economic oppression and to confirm the Russian in his pessimistic passivity." See also *Love and Justice*, 46, 300-301.

political life from private life. "Political morality," Niebuhr insisted, "is in the most uncompromising antithesis to religious morality."[73] Although "to look at human communities from the perspective of the Kingdom of God is to know that there is a sinful element in all the expedients which the political order uses to establish justice, . . . it must also be recognized that it is impossible to eliminate the sinful element in the political expedients. They are, in the words of St. Augustine, both the consequence of, and the remedy for, sin." Thus, "political morality contains an inevitable ambiguity because the factors of interest and power, which are regarded as an irrelevance in pure morality, must at least tentatively be admitted to the realm of social morality." Although, for example, "self-interest may be a source of discord ultimately, . . . it is tentatively necessary to prevent the harmony of the whole from destroying the vitality of the parts."[74]

In the atomic bombing of the two Japanese cities at the close of World War II, Niebuhr found a superb example of this predicament of politics. From the standpoint of personal morality, dropping the bombs was abhorrent. Yet Niebuhr recognized that the statesmen involved in this decision were captives of their public responsibilities. Confronted by a German desire and potential to develop the bomb, responsible statesmen could not refuse to encourage its development for our own side. Once developed, and holding out the prospect of a quicker end to the war, responsible statesmen could only with great difficulty refuse to use it. Niebuhr's primary criticism of the statesmanship of the decision was of the "lack of imagination in impressing the enemy with the power of the bomb without the wholesale loss of life that attended our demonstration." Yet he was thoroughly realistic (and therefore Augustinian) in his resignation to the fact that, inevitably, "technical society produces total war, because it enables men to harness the resources of a society for a certain end totally; and its instruments of destruction become more and more total." Statesmen

---

[73]Niebuhr, *Moral Man,* 271, 259. See also ibid., 233. Regarding Niebuhr's point here, compare George Kennan, "Morality and Foreign Policy," *Foreign Affairs* 64 (Winter 1985/86): 206, where he notes in Niebuhrian fashion, "Government is an agent, not a principal. Its primary obligation is to the *interests* of the national society it represents, not to the moral impulses that individual elements of that society may experience."

[74]Davis and Good, 157, 328.

could not and would not renounce the use of available means of coercion if they perceived that their constituency depended upon the use of those means for its survival. They were caught in a web of both human pretension and historical circumstance. "That there should be such desperate contests of will between whole civilizations," said Niebuhr, "is really more shocking than that all resources to which human wills have access, should be used in the contest."[75]

Niebuhr's second conclusion about political life followed closely on this first. Because of these "hard and cruel necessities" inherent in political interaction, "There is no escape from guilt in history." Exercise of power can only properly entail remorse, doubly so when such exercise involves the organized destruction that is war. In contrast to Ramsey's "deferred repentance," and in conjunction with Augustine's "constraint to torture and punish the innocent," then, is Niebuhr's "agonized participation." At the outbreak of World War II, Niebuhr wrote, "We cannot contemplate our political life decently without a proper and grateful understanding of the 'grace' of God." Such grace is both "the providential working in history by which God makes the wrath of man to praise him, and transmutes good out of evil," and "the element of forgiveness." "There can be no acceptance of grace," Niebuhr insisted, "without repentance." "If we do not understand how sinful even good men and nations are, we will have no gratitude toward a merciful providence that makes us do good against our will and gives us a chance to serve mankind, even though we want to serve ourselves." In sum, "The only true peace within and among human communities is the peace of forgiveness which grows out of contrition for sin."[76]

In answer to Ramsey's accusation that his social ethics were "consequentialist" to the point of a "suspension of a great part of morality," Niebuhr asserted the inextricability of pure motives from

---

[75]Niebuhr, *Love and Justice*, 233; "The Spirit and the Body in War," *Christianity and Crisis* 2 (10 August 1942): 1. This is not to suggest that Niebuhr approved the use of nuclear weapons even on a counterforce basis. See *Structure of Nations*, 279-80.

[76]Niebuhr, *Love and Justice*, 222-23; Davis and Good, 206-207. See also *War and Conscience*, 11-12, 309, 310; *DCD* 19.6; Long, 41ff; Niebuhr, *Beyond Tragedy*, 60; Niebuhr, *Faith and Politics*, 13; and Niebuhr, quoted in *Reinhold Niebuhr: A Prophetic Voice for Our Time*, ed. Harold R. Landon (Greenwich CT: Seabury Press, 1962) 116.

morally discontinuous human beings. Niebuhr admitted that "nothing is intrinsically immoral except ill-will and nothing intrinsically good except good will." Still, "since it is very difficult to judge human motives, it is natural that, from an external [political] perspective, the social consequences of an action or policy should be regarded as more adequate tests of its morality than the hidden motives." The world of politics requires one to admit to moral contradictions. Particular means might be ethically wrong but politically right. "The realm of politics," he said, "is a twilight zone where ethical and technical issues meet." Indeed, "A political policy cannot be intrinsically evil if it can be proved to be an efficacious instrument for the achievement of a morally approved end." Yet, "neither can it be said to be wholly good merely because it seems to make for ultimately good consequences." Political action requires both a determination to succeed and a simultaneous humility of contrition.[77]

The third important point of congruence between Niebuhr's vision of politics (and hence, of war) and Augustine's, therefore, concerns right relation to the good. For Niebuhr, as for Augustine, that good can only come from a genuine faith in, and hope for, God's healing mercy beyond history.[78] The way out of the morass of politics is not to ignore its ambiguities by asserting moral rules, but rather to place one's final hope in a merciful providence, confessing both the inherent ambiguity of politics and one's personal responsibility for such ambiguity.[79] One functions adequately in politics, then, not through Ramseyan prudence but through atten-

---

[77]Niebuhr, *Moral Man*, 170-71. I am inclined, then, to see Niebuhr's approach to politics as an "extension" of Ramsey, rather than to agree with Ramsey's claim that his approach is an "extension" of Niebuhr. See Ramsey, *Just War*, 260. See also Niebuhr, *Love and Justice*, 219-21, 258; and *Faith and Politics*, 117.

[78]Reinhold Niebuhr, "Prayer and Politics," *Christianity and Crisis* 12 (27 October 1952): 138-39. Niebuhr noted in this short piece that, clearly, prayer can be "the final vehicle of [human] pretension" as much as "the proper response of contrite recognition of the vanity of human pretensions," but genuine prayer is always the latter.

[79]Niebuhr, *Structure of Nations*, 290-99; "Faith as the Sense of Meaning in Human Existence," *Christianity and Crisis* 26 (13 June 1966) 129, 131; "A Christian Journal Confronts Mankind's Continuing Crisis," *Christianity and Crisis* 26 (21 February 1966): 13. See also the important recent collection of Niebuhr's writings edited by Robert McAfee Brown, *The Essential Reinhold Niebuhr* (New Haven: Yale University Press, 1986), especially Brown's introduction.

tiveness to historical contingency. Since there is no escape from the inherent contradictions of political existence, the person in politics has to act *in the midst of* contradiction, having attuned himself both to the exigencies and contingencies of history and to a hope pointing beyond history.

Discerning the outlines of the Suez crisis of 1956 caused Niebuhr to reflect on this point at some length.

> The crisis in Egypt in the fall of 1956—and the evident desire of good people to find a right or "moral" solution for the issues— raised the problem of the precarious relations between moral ideals and international politics, and all politics, for that matter. The reason right and wrong cannot be defined so easily is because two or three moral values and loyalties come into conflict in a political decision, so that our decision in a particular instance usually depends upon historical contingencies which are not anticipated in any statement of Christian or moral principles.

Hence, "The hope of Christian faith that the divine power which bears history can complete what even the highest human striving must leave incomplete, and purify the corruptions which appear in even the purest human aspirations is an indispensable prerequisite for diligent fulfillment of our historical tasks." In sum, "We must establish tentative harmonies and provisional equities in a world from which sin cannot be eliminated, and yet hold these provisional and tentative moral achievements under the perspective of the Kingdom of God."[80]

Niebuhr thus embarked on a journey of fundamental political inquiry in his public life, a journey to call into question the excessively rational and consistent visions of politics prevalent in twentieth-century thinking. That task was clearly more of an Augustinian

---

[80]Davis and Good, 322; Niebuhr, *Children of Light and Darkness,* 189; Davis and Good, 153. Niebuhr did use the word "prudence" on occasion (for example, in *Love and Justice,* 154), but he also said, "a genuine charity is the father of prudence." See also Reinhold Niebuhr, *Christianity and Power Politics* (1940; reprint ed., Hamden CT: Shoe String Press, Archon Books, 1969); Bob E. Patterson, *Reinhold Niebuhr* (Waco TX: Word Books, 1977) 154; Reinhold Niebuhr, "Intellectual Autobiography," in *Reinhold Niebuhr: His Religious, Social, and Political Thought,* ed. Charles W. Kegley and Robert W. Bretall (New York: Macmillan, 1956) 19; Reinhold Niebuhr, "Reply to Interpretation and Criticism," in Kegley and Bretall, 439; Reinhold Niebuhr, *Justice and Mercy,* ed. Ursula M. Niebuhr (New York: Harper and Row, 1974) 22; *Children of Light and Darkness,* 188; *Christian Realism,* 182; *Beyond Tragedy,* 113-14; and Reinhold Niebuhr in Landon, ed., 116.

response to twentieth-century international politics than the construction of theories of "justified" war. It recalled with poignant simplicity that "we are 'justified' not by our own goodness but by the goodness of God."[81]

The Augustinian/Niebuhrian response to human political interaction thus withholds prospective, if hypothetical, moral judgments. Only when confronted with concrete historical circumstances can this response come into play. At that point it recognizes in deep humility and contrition the inevitably tragic element in its proximate solutions, while accepting in genuine social responsibility the challenge and the necessity of prudent action. Niebuhr thus found himself convinced both of the propriety of violent resistance to Nazi Germany and of the impropriety of violent assertions of Western self-righteousness toward the Soviet Union. "The problem of indiscriminate pacifism in a community in which order and justice are attained not by pure love or pure reason but by an equilibrium of various forms of economic and political power," he wrote toward the end of his life, "has given way [in the nuclear era] to the problem of curbing pure force in the international realm."[82]

Consequently, the Augustinian/Niebuhrian response cannot rest content with "rules" or "principles," whether of right conduct or of right consequences. In spite of Ramsey's attempt to label Niebuhr's "law of love" a kind of *ius naturale,* the law of love Niebuhr envisioned transcended all human expressions of "transcendent" principle. It did so simply because the traditional expressions of ultimate principle, of "natural law," were rationally based; they arose out of a human reason that saw itself as fully competent.[83] Yet, as Niebuhr insisted, human reason is forever "tainted." "All statements and definitions of justice are corrupted by even the most rational men through the fact that the definition is colored by interest." In short, said Niebuhr,

> Human nature is . . . a realm of infinite possibilities of good and evil because of the character of human freedom. The love that is

---

[81]Davis and Good, 207.

[82]Niebuhr, "Christian Journal," 13. See also *Structure of Nations,* 267-86, especially 281-86.

[83]Niebuhr, *Love and Justice,* 48-49. See also *Christian Realism,* 183. Ramsey's labeling is in Paul Ramsey, "Love and Law," in Kegley and Bretall, eds., 99-100.

the law of its nature is a boundless self-giving. The sin that cor-
rupts its life is a boundless assertion of the self. Between these two
forces all kinds of *ad hoc* restraints may be elaborated and defined.
We may call this natural law. But we had better realize how very
tentative it is.

For "insofar as . . . principles of justice are given specific historical
meaning, they also become touched by historical contingency." Indeed, "life and history are full of contradictions which cannot be
resolved in terms of rational principles."[84]

Hence, instead of marriage to principle humankind must forever be open both to the contingencies of history and to God's way
of reconciling those contingencies to God's transcendent plan.[85] In
conjunction with his mission to question, then, was Niebuhr's mission to open political decision making to a sensitivity to the human
existential paradox. While encouraging the prudential policy maker
in his search for "proximate solutions," Niebuhr insisted that proper
policy making must incorporate "the basic paradox in all human
morality." Such paradox is best exemplified in the fundamental, but
only apparently simple, command "Thou shalt love." Although that
command states "a possibility as an obligation," it also incorporates
an understanding that "the obligatory feature destroys it as a possibility"; for "it is of the character of love that it desires the good
freely and without compulsion."[86]

By means of his primarily Augustinian vision of politics and of
human contradictions, Niebuhr demonstrated most clearly the relevance of the fifth-century bishop for our time. His demonstration
was not entirely intentional or conscious. Toward the end of his life
Niebuhr wrote that "Augustine's Pauline realism was . . . excessively consistent."[87] Yet Augustine's thought as a whole was shot
through with Niebuhrian paradox. Human participation in politics, for Augustine as for Niebuhr, is a bundle of "both/and's." Yet,
although the human problems of political interaction are peren-

---

[84]Niebuhr, *Christian Realism*, 48; *Love and Justice*, 54; *Faith and Politics*, 105; *Nature and Destiny* 1: 165. See also "Niebuhr's Response," in Landon, ed., 122-23; and
Christian Realism, 173.

[85]See, for example, *Nature and Destiny*, 1: viii; and "Niebuhr's Response," in
Landon, ed., 122-23.

[86]Davis and Good, 134. See also Robert McAfee Brown, "Reinhold Niebuhr:
A Study in Humanity," in *The Legacy of Reinhold Niebuhr*, ed. Nathan A. Scott, Jr.
(Chicago: University of Chicago Press, 1975) 4.

[87]Niebuhr, "Toward New Intra-Christian Endeavors," 1662.

nial and insoluble, they are never hopeless. Although "nothing that is worth doing can be achieved in our lifetime," we are "saved by hope"; although "nothing which is true or beautiful or good makes complete sense in any immediate context of history," we are "saved by faith"; although "nothing we do, however virtuous, can be accomplished alone," we are "saved by love"; although "no virtuous act is quite as virtuous from the standpoint of our friend or foe as it is from our standpoint," we are "saved by the final form of love which is forgiveness."[88]

---

[88]Reinhold Niebuhr, *The Irony of American History* (New York: Charles Scribner's Sons, 1952) 63.

CONCLUSION

The problem of war in our own time appears to differ radically from that in the latter stages of the Roman Empire. Augustine wrote long before gunpowder, longer before air war and "obliteration bombing," and even longer before thermonuclear weaponry. The problem of modern warfare weighs on contemporary minds as a great deal less controllable and a great deal more deadly than what Augustine faced. After all, weapons now exist that if detonated more or less simultaneously would put an end to all earthly life as we know it. To many, humankind appears to have manufactured effectively autonomous weaponry, an exercise both useless and absurd. We have imagined the unimaginable, thought the unthinkable, and constructed weapons of pure and total destruction. Hence the chasm separating the modern problem of war from the classical problem of war appears unbridgeable.

Yet at least two modern observers, Paul Ramsey and Reinhold Niebuhr, have stepped forward to deny, each in his own distinctive way, that the problem of war in our time differs dramatically from that in Augustine's time. For both observers, modern war poses the very same moral and political questions that classical war did. Both agree that the problem of war arises not from a particular historical era's technology or weaponry, but from the human beings in that era who invent, threaten, and ultimately use that weaponry. Both Ramsey and Niebuhr find modern war to be still under human control, and hence not primarily a technological or strategic problem, but always a moral and political problem. War remains a contest of human will. Technological developments may determine the way *many* observers approach the fundamental moral and political issues involved in warfare, but Ramsey and Niebuhr both insist that these fundamental issues *undergird* and *define* the various technological/strategic concerns, and ultimately remain the focal point for all sincere and constructive thinking about war.

In confronting the fundamental questions, Ramsey and Niebuhr both point to Augustine as having been primarily responsible for the development of a Christian, *intellectual* context for evaluating war. And, clearly, Augustine's writings can serve as essential reminders of the constancy and primacy of the *human* aspects of warfare. Yet when thought of as an intellectual "developer," Augustine's value to us diminishes. For, ironically enough, attempts to transform his writings into consistent doctrine or systematic theory end up illuminating those aspects of his writings that seem most bound to his own historical era. Both Ramsey and Niebuhr, then, while attempting to interpret and to reinforce Augustine's doctrine, end up seriously oversimplifying his *life*. In Niebuhr's case the final irony is that in reacting against what he perceives as the "doctrinaire" aspects of Augustine's writings, he reacts with a genuinely Augustinian sense of paradox.

Augustine's value to our modern era lies not in his "doctrine." Although he, more than any other figure in Western history, first linked war, love, and judging into what has appeared to many to be an integrated whole, the appearance of wholeness dissolves rapidly upon close examination. For Augustine's "theory" is filled with paradoxes: the "cause" for right war is "just peace," but there is in the world neither true justice nor lasting peace; one ought to evaluate war but one can not; one's power is a mark of one's authority, but the powerful are not finally authoritative; one ought to obey one's earthly superiors, except when one ought not; love includes war, but true love is the absence of war; one ought to love rightly but one can not.

Although we may be led to Augustine, then, it is far from obvious what we should do with him when we get there. What part or parts of him should we bring back to our own time and condition? Should we bring back his understanding of true justice or his understanding of earthly misery, his understanding of citizenship within history or his understanding of citizenship beyond history? Should we return with his notion of power or his notion of authority, his notion of civil obedience or his notion of civil disobedience? Should we fetch for our time his idea of right human love or his idea of the impossibility of right human love? While it is the perennial temptation to bring back *only* parts, such partitioning inevitably destroys Augustine's value as a thinker, one who, as Karl Jaspers put it, quite properly "lets his thinking run aground on the shoals of contradiction."[1] The whole of Augustine, in other words, is much more than the sum of his parts.

For example, the inseparability of Augustinian "theology" and Augustinian "political science" means that in a secular age the Augustinian approach may yield a despairing Hobbesian realism, a conviction that human beings are obnoxious and forever irredeemable. In a religious age, on the other hand, it means that this approach may yield a naive, and sometimes brutal, idealism, a conviction that human beings *will* be good and *will* cooperate whether they like it or not. In any age, the attempt to keep Augustinian "civics" an integrated whole is almost bound to be awkwardly out of place. The Augustinian aproach is a child of light among the children of darkness and a child of this world among the children of light.

In insisting on the possibility of a "proper" cause to initiate or wage war the Augustinian approach disturbs the realists. Yet in insisting that such propriety is impossible to determine with certainty it disturbs the idealists. In insisting on the need for strong central power in politics and on the need to obey that power it disturbs the idealists. Yet in insisting on the possibility of "authorized" war by private parties and thus on "authorized" disobedience to political authority it disturbs the realists. Finally, in insisting that love can mean coercion it disturbs the idealists; yet in insisting that true love is real and that it means the highest demonstration of respectful worth and dignity toward human beings it disturbs the realists.

One can fully appreciate Augustine's contribution to human thinking about war, then, only if one considers his sense of paradox, his acute awareness of the inherent contradictions involved in human social existence. Twentieth-century investigators of the phenomenon of war can profit markedly from Augustine's insights, but they must resist the temptation to categorize his thinking. Perhaps Anton Pegis summarized the inescapable dilemma best:

---

[1]Jaspers, 111. Compare the recent and most comprehensive biography of Niebuhr by Richard W. Fox, *Reinhold Niebuhr: A Biography* (New York: Pantheon Books, 1985), esp. ix and 294-95, where Fox says much the same thing about the dangers inherent in attempts to apply *Niebuhr's* writings to the evaluation of contemporary events.

To attempt to portray the unity of a heart and a mind which lives as deeply and as intensely as did Augustine is always a rash undertaking. . . . He is eminently the disciple of the love of God. But this love is not a doctrine but a life, not an abstract analysis but a journey, not a theory but an experience. Now precisely, how is an *experience* communicated? It can be possessed only by those who live it, and it is as uniquely *theirs* as their own being. The greatest work that Augustine produced is his own life: how shall we read *that*?[2]

---

[2]Pegis, "The Mind of St. Augustine," 8.

BIBLIOGRAPHY

AUGUSTINE—PRIMARY SOURCES

Augustine. *The City of God.* Edited by Vernon J. Bourke. Translated by Gerald Walsh, S.J., Demetrius B. Zema, S.J., Grace Monahan, O.S.U., and Daniel Honan. Garden City NY: Doubleday, Image Books, 1958.

_____. *The City of God against the Pagans.* Translated by William M. Green, William Chase Greene, Philip Levine, Eva M. Sanford, and David S. Wiesen. 7 vols. Cambridge: Harvard University Press, 1968.

_____. *Confessions.* Translated by W. Watts. 2 vols. Cambridge: Harvard University Press, 1912.

_____. *Confessions.* Translated by R. S. Pine-Coffin. Harmondsworth, Middlesex: Penguin Books, 1961.

_____. *The Free Choice of the Will.* Translated by Francis E. Tourscher. Philadelphia: Peter Reilly, 1937.

Baxter, J. H., ed. and trans. *Select Letters of St. Augustine.* London: William Heinemann, 1930.

Burleigh, John H. S., ed. and trans. *Augustine: Earlier Writings.* The Library of Christian Classics, vol. 6. Philadelphia: Westminster Press, 1953.

Burnaby, John, ed. and trans. *Augustine: Later Works.* The Library of Christian Classics, vol. 8. Philadelphia: Westminster Press, 1955.

Corpus Christianorum, Series Latina. Turnholti: Typographi Brepols editores Pontificii, 1961.

Corpus Scriptorum Ecclesiasticorum Latinorum. Vienna: Academy of Letters, 1866–.

Howe, Quincy, Jr., ed. and trans. *Selected Sermons of St. Augustine.* New York: Holt, Rinehart and Winston, 1966.

Migne, J.-P. *Patrologiae Cursus Completus . . . series Latina.* 221 vols. Paris, 1844-1865.

Paolucci, Henry, ed. *The Political Writings of St. Augustine*. South Bend IN: Gateway, 1962.

————. *The Fathers of the Church*. New York: Fathers of the Church, Inc., 1951–.

Schaff, Philip, ed. *A Select Library of the Nicene and Post-Nicene Fathers of the Christian Church*, vols. 1-8. New York: Charles Scribner's Sons, 1887.

AUGUSTINE—SECONDARY SOURCES: BOOKS

Baille, John. *St. Augustine: A Biographical Memoir*. New York: Robert Carter and Brothers, 1859.

Bainton, Roland H. *Christian Attitudes toward War and Peace: A Historical Survey and Critical Re-evaluation*. Nashville: Abingdon Press, 1960.

Barrow, R. H. *Introduction to St. Augustine's "The City of God."* London: Faber and Faber, 1950.

Battenhouse, Roy W., ed. *A Companion to the Study of St. Augustine*. New York: Oxford University Press, 1955.

Bonner, Gerald. *St. Augustine of Hippo: Life and Controversies*. Philadelphia: Westminster Press, 1963.

Bourke, Vernon J. *Augustine's Quest for Wisdom: Life and Philosophy of the Bishop of Hippo*. Milwaukee: Bruce Publishing, 1945.

Brown, Peter. *Augustine of Hippo: A Biography*. Berkeley: University of California Press, 1967.

————. *Religion and Society in the Age of St. Augustine*. New York: Harper & Row, 1972.

Burnaby, John. *Amor Dei: A Study of the Religion of St. Augustine*. London: Hodder and Stoughton, 1938.

Burns, Thomas F., comp. *A Monument to St. Augustine*. New York: Dial Press, 1930.

Copleston, Frederick C. *Medieval Philosophy*. New York: Harper & Row, Harper Torchbooks, 1961.

Deane, Herbert A. *The Political and Social Ideas of St. Augustine*. New York: Columbia University Press, 1963.

Ebenstein, William. *Great Political Thinkers: Plato to the Present*. 4th ed. Hinsdale IL: Dryden Press, 1969.

Figgis, John Neville. *The Political Aspects of S. Augustine's "City of God."* London: Longman's, Green, 1921.

Freemantle, Anne, ed. *The Age of Belief*. New York: New American Library, 1954.

Garvey, Sister Mary Patricia, R.S.M. *St. Augustine: Christian or Neo-Platonist?* Milwaukee: Marquette University Press, 1939.

Germino, Dante. *Political Philosophy and the Open Society*. Baton Rouge: Louisiana State University Press, 1982.

Gilson, Etienne. *God and Philosophy*. New Haven: Yale University Press, 1941.

_____. *History of Christian Philosophy in the Middle Ages*. New York: Random House, 1955.

_____. *The Christian Philosophy of St. Augustine*. Translated by L. E. M. Lynch. New York: Random House, 1960.

Jaspers, Karl. *Plato and Augustine*. Edited by Hannah Arendt. Translated by Ralph Manheim. New York: Harcourt Brace Jovanovich, 1962.

Leahy, D. J. *St. Augustine on Eternal Life*. New York: Benziger Brothers, 1939.

McCabe, Joseph. *Saint Augustine and His Age*. London: Duckworth, 1902.

McDonald, Lee Cameron. *Western Political Theory*. Vol. 1, *Ancient and Medieval*. New York: Harcourt Brace Jovanovich, 1968.

Markus, R. A. *Saeculum: History and Society in the Theology of St. Augustine*. Cambridge: Cambridge University Press, 1970.

Matthews, Alfred Warren. *The Development of St. Augustine, from Neoplatonism to Christianity, 386-391* A.D. Washington: University Press of America, 1980.

Meagher, Robert E. *An Introduction to Augustine*. New York: New York University Press, 1978.

Mourant, John A. *Introduction to the Philosophy of Saint Augustine: Selected Readings and Commentaries*. University Park PA: Pennsylvania State University Press, 1964.

Nygren, Anders. *Agape and Eros*. Translated by Philip S. Watson. London: SPCK, 1953.

O'Connell, Robert J. *St. Augustine's "Confessions": The Odyssey of the Soul*. Cambridge: Harvard University Press, Belknap Press, 1969.

_____. *St. Augustine's Early Theory of Man*. Cambridge: Harvard University Press, Belknap Press, 1968.

O'Donovan, Oliver. *The Problem of Self-Love in St. Augustine*. New Haven: Yale University Press, 1980.

O'Meara, John. *Charter of Christendom: The Significance of "The City of God."* New York: Macmillan, 1961.

O'Meara, John. *The Young Augustine*. London: Longmans, Green, 1954.

Osmun, George W. *Augustine: The Thinker*. Cincinnati: Jennings and Graham, 1906.

Papini, Giovanni. *Saint Augustine*. Translated by Mary Prichard Agnetti. New York: Harcourt, Brace, 1930.

Portalie, Eugene, S.J. *A Guide to the Thought of St. Augustine.* Translated by Ralph J. Bastian, S.J., with an introduction by Vernon J. Bourke. Chicago: Henry Regnery, 1960.

Potter, Ralph B. *War and Moral Discourse.* Richmond VA: John Knox Press, 1969.

Regout, Robert. *La doctrine de la guerre juste de saint Augustin a nos jours d'apres les theologiens et les juristes canoniques.* Paris: Pedone, 1935.

Russell, Frederick H. *The Just War in the Middle Ages.* Cambridge: Cambridge University Press, 1975.

Smith, Warren Thomas. *Augustine, His Life and Thought.* Atlanta: John Knox Press, 1980.

van der Meer, F. *Augustine the Bishop.* Translated by Brian Battershaw and G. R. Lamb. London: Sheed and Ward, 1961.

Versfeld, Marthinus. *A Guide to "The City of God."* New York: Sheed and Ward, 1958.

West, Rebecca. *St. Augustine.* New York: D. Appleton, 1933.

Willis, G. G. *Saint Augustine and the Donatist Controversy.* London: SPCK, 1950.

Windass, Stanley. *Christianity versus Violence: A Social and Historical Study of War and Christianity.* London: Sheed and Ward, 1964.

Woelfel, James W. *Augustinian Humanism: Studies in Human Bondage and Earthly Grace.* Washington DC: University Press of America, 1979.

AUGUSTINE—SECONDARY SOURCES: ARTICLES

Barker, Ernest. Introduction to *The City of God,* by St. Augustine, translated by John Healey. London: J. M. Dent and Sons, 1931.

Battenhouse, Roy W. "The Life of St. Augustine." In *A Companion to the Study of St. Augustine,* edited by Roy W. Battenhouse, 15-56. New York: Oxford University Press, 1955.

Baynes, Norman H. "The Political Ideas of St. Augustine's *De Civitate Dei.*" In *Byzantine Studies and Other Essays,* edited by Norman H. Baynes, 288-306. London: University of London, 1955.

Bigongiari, Dino. "The Political Ideas of St. Augustine." In *The Political Writings of St. Augustine,* edited by Henry Paolucci, 343-58. South Bend IN: Gateway, 1962.

Bourke, Vernon J. Introduction to *The Confessions of St. Augustine,* translated by Rex Warner. New York: Mentor-Omega, 1963.

———. "Voluntarism in Augustine's Ethico-Legal Thought."*Augustinian Studies* 1 (1970): 3-19.

Burnaby, John. "Amor in St. Augustine." In *The Philosophy and Theology of Anders Nygren,* edited by Charles W. Kegley, 174-86. Carbondale: Southern Illinois University Press, 1970.

Chroust, Anton-Hermann. "The Philosophy of Law of St. Augustine." *Philosophical Review* 53 (March 1944): 195-202.

Cranz, F. Edward. *"De civitate Dei, XV, 2,* and Augustine's Idea of the Christian Society." *Speculum* 25 (April 1950): 215-25.

————. "The Development of Augustine's Ideas on Society Before the Donatist Controversy." *Harvard Theological Review* 47 (October 1954): 255-316.

Cushman, Robert E. "Faith and Reason." In *A Companion to the Study of St. Augustine,* edited by Roy W. Battenhouse, 287-314. New York: Oxford University Press, 1955.

D'Arcy, M. C., S.J. "The Philosophy of St. Augustine." In *A Monument to St. Augustine,* compiled by Thomas F. Burns, 155-96. New York: The Dial Press, 1930.

Dawson, Christopher. "St. Augustine and His Age." In *A Monument to St. Augustine,* compiled by Thomas F. Burns, 11-78. New York: The Dial Press, 1930.

Dillistone, Frederick W. "The Anti-Donatist Writings." In *A Companion to the Study of St. Augustine,* edited by Roy W. Battenhouse, 175-200. New York: Oxford University Press, 1955.

East, John P. "The Political Significance of St. Augustine." *Modern Age* 16 (Spring 1972): 167-81.

Firth, Francis, CSB. "The Importance of Saint Augustine." *Canadian Catholic Review* 4 (September 1986): 288-94.

Fortin, Ernest L. "Augustine's *City of God* and the Modern Historical Consciousness." *Review of Politics* 41 (July 1979): 323-43.

————. "Reflections on the Proper Way to Read Augustine the Theologian." *Augustinian Studies* 2 (1971): 253-72.

————."St. Augustine." In *A History of Political Philosophy,* 2nd ed., edited by Leo Strauss and Joseph Cropsey, 151-81. Chicago: University of Chicago Press, 1972.

————. "The Patristic Sense of Community." *Augustinian Studies* 4 (1973): 179-97.

————."The Political Implications of St. Augustine's Theory of Conscience."*Augustinian Studies* 1 (1970): 133-52.

Gilson, Etienne. Foreword to *The City of God,* by St. Augustine, edited by Vernon J. Bourke, translated by Gerald G. Walsh, S.J., et al. Garden City NY: Doubleday, Image Books, 1958.

Hartigan, Richard S. "Saint Augustine on War and Killing: The Problem of the Innocent." *Journal of the History of Ideas* 27 (1966): 195-204.

Hawkins, Peter S. "Polemical Counterpoint in *De Civitate Dei.*" *Augustinian Studies* 6 (1975): 97-106.

Hopper, Stanley Romaine. "The Anti-Manichean Writings." In *A Companion to the Study of St. Augustine,* edited by Roy W. Battenhouse, 148-74. New York: Oxford University Press, 1955.

Johannesson, Rudolf. "Caritas in Augustine and Medieval Theology." In *The Philosophy and Theology of Anders Nygren,* edited by Charles W. Kegley, 187-202. Carbondale: Southern Illinois University Press, 1970.

Johnson, Penelope D. "Virtus: Transition from Classical Latin to the *De Civitate Dei.*" *Augustinian Studies* 6 (1975): 117-24.

Jolivet, Regis. "La Doctrine Augustinienne de l'Illumination." *Revue de Philosophie,* n.s. 1 (1930): 382-502.

La Bonnadriere, A. M. "Le Combat Chretien." *Revue Etudes Augustiniennes* 11 (1965): 235-38.

La Briere, Yves de. "La conception de la paix et de la querre chez Saint Augustine." *Revue de Philosophie,* n.s. 1 (1930): 557-72.

Langan, John, S.J. "The Elements of St. Augustine's Just War Theory." Paper presented at the spring meeting of the American Society of Church History, Union Theological Seminary, Richmond VA, 23 April 1982.

Levere George J. "The Political Realism of Saint Augustine." *Augustinian Studies* 11 (1980): 135-44.

MacQueen, D. J. "The Origin and Dynamics of Society and the State according to Augustine." *Augustinian Studies* 4 (1973): 73-101.

Markus, R. A. " 'Imago' and 'Similitudo' in Augustine." *Revue des Etudes Augustiniennes* 10 (1964): 125-43.

————. "Two Conceptions of Political Authority: Augustine, *De civitate Dei,* XIX, 14-15, and Some Thirteenth-Century Interpretations." *Journal of Theological Studies* 16 (April 1965): 68-100.

Martin, Rex. "The Two Cities in Augustine's Political Philosphy." *Journal of the History of Ideas* 33 (April 1972): 195-216.

Mommsen, Theodor E. "St. Augustine and the Christian Idea of Progress." *Journal of the History of Ideas* 12 (June 1951): 346-74.

Mourant, John A. "The Emergence of a Christian Philosophy in the Dialogues of Augustine." *Augustinian Studies* 1 (1970): 69-88.

O'Connell, Robert J., S.J. *"De Libero Arbitrio* I: Stoicism Revisited." *Augustinian Studies* 1 (1970): 49-68.

Outler, Albert C. Introduction to *Augustine: Confessions and Enchiridion*, edited and translated by Albert C. Outler. The Library of Christian Classics, vol. 7. Philadelphia: Westminster Press, 1955.

Pegis, Anton C. "The Mind of St. Augustine." *Medieval Studies* 6 (1944): 1-61.

Rist, John M. "Saint Augustine on the Exercise of Power." *Canadian Catholic Review* 4 (November 1986): 371-76.

Roberts, David E. "The Earliest Writings." In *A Companion to the Study of St. Augustine*, edited by Roy W. Battenhouse, 93-126. New York: Oxford University Press, 1955.

Rowe, William L. "Augustine on Foreknowledge and Free Will." *Review of Metaphysics* 18 (December 1964): 356-63.

Spicer, Malcolm. "The Conversion of Saint Augustine." *Canadian Catholic Review* 4 (October 1986): 326-32.

Swift, Louis J. "Augustine on War and Killing: Another View." *Harvard Theological Review* 66 (July 1973): 369-83.

TeSelle Eugene. "Porphyry and Augustine." *Augustinian Studies* 5 (1974): 113-47.

Verheijen, Luc M. J., O.S.A. "The Straw, the Beam, the Tusculan Disputations and the Rule of Saint Augustine." *Augustinian Studies* 2 (1971): 17-36.

Walzer, Michael. "*Exodus 32* and the Theory of Holy War: The History of a Citation." *Harvard Theological Review* 61 (January 1968): 1-14.

Williams, Daniel D. "The Significance of St. Augustine Today." In *A Companion to the Study of St. Augustine*, edited by Roy W. Battenhouse, 3-14. New York: Oxford University Press. 1955.

PAUL RAMSEY—PRIMARY SOURCES: BOOKS

Basic Christian Ethics. New York: Charles Scribner's Sons, 1950.

Christian Ethics and the Sit = in. New York: Association Press, 1961.

Deeds and Rules in Christian Ethics. New York: Charles Scribner's Sons, 1967.

Nine Modern Moralists. Englewood Cliffs NJ: Prentice-Hall, 1962.

The Just War: Force and Political Responsibility. New York: Charles Scribner's Sons, 1968.

War and the Christian Conscience: How Shall Modern War Be Conducted Justly? Durham NC: Duke University Press, 1961.

Who Speaks for the Church? Nashville: Abingdon Press, 1967.

PAUL RAMSEY—PRIMARY SOURCES: ARTICLES

"A Prophet with Honor in His Own Time and Country." *New York Times Book Review,* 19 June 1960, 6.

"Farewell to Christian Realism." *America* 114 (30 April 1966): 618-22.

"Love and Law." In *Reinhold Niebuhr: His Religious, Social, and Political Thought,* edited by Charles W. Kegley and Robert W. Bretall, 80-123. New York: Macmillan, 1956.

"The Case of the Curious Exception." In *Norm and Context in Christian Ethics,* edited by Paul Ramsey and Gene H. Outka, 67-135. New York: Charles Scribner's Sons, 1968.

PAUL RAMSEY—SECONDARY SOURCES

Curran, Charles E. *Politics, Medicine, and Christian Ethics: A Dialogue with Paul Ramsey.* Philadelphia: Fortress Press, 1973.

Johnson, James T., and Smith, David, eds. *Love and Society: Essays in the Ethics of Paul Ramsey.* Missoula MT: Scholars Press, 1974.

Ramsey, Paul, and Outka, Gene H., eds. *Norm and Context in Christian Ethics.* New York: Charles Scribner's Sons, 1968.

REINHOLD NIEBUHR—PRIMARY SOURCES: BOOKS

An Interpretation of Christian Ethics. New York: Harper and Brothers, 1935.

Beyond Tragedy. New York: Charles Scribner's Sons, 1937.

The Children of Light and the Children of Darkness. New York: Charles Scribner's Sons, 1944.

Christian Realism and Political Problems. New York: Charles Scribner's Sons, 1953.

Christianity and Power Politics. New York: Charles Scribner's Sons, 1940. Reprint. Hamden CT: Shoe String Press, Archon Books, 1969.

The Essential Reinhold Niebuhr. Edited by Robert McAfee Brown. New Haven: Yale University Press, 1986.

Faith and History. New York: Charles Scribner's Sons, 1949.

Faith and Politics. Edited by Ronald H. Stone. New York: George Braziller, 1968.

The Irony of American History. New York: Charles Scribner's Sons, 1952.

Justice and Mercy. Edited by Ursula M. Niebuhr. New York: Harper & Row, 1974.

Leaves from the Notebook of a Tamed Cynic. New York: Willett, Clark and Colbey, 1929. Reprint. New York: Living Age Books, 1957.

Love and Justice. Edited by D. B. Robertson. Gloucester MA: Peter Smith, 1967.

Man's Nature and His Communities. New York: Charles Scribner's Sons, 1965.

Moral Man and Immoral Society. New York: Charles Scribner's Sons, 1932.

The Nature and Destiny of Man. 2 vols. New York: Charles Scribner's Sons, 1941-1943.

Reinhold Niebuhr on Politics: His Political Philosophy and Its Application to Our Age as Expressed in His Writings. Edited by Harry R. Davis and Robert C. Good. New York: Charles Scribner's Sons, 1960.

The Self and the Dramas of History. New York: Charles Scribner's Sons, 1955.

The Structure of Nations and Empires. New York: Charles Scribner's Sons, 1959.

REINHOLD NIEBUHR—PRIMARY SOURCES: ARTICLES

"A Christian Journal Confronts Mankind's Continuing Crisis." *Christianity and Crisis* 26 (21 February 1966): 11-13.

"Faith as the Sense of Meaning in Human Existence." *Christianity and Crisis* 26 (13 June 1966): 127-31.

"The King's Chapel and the King's Court." *Christianity and Crisis* 29 (4 August 1969): 211-12.

"Must We Do Nothing?" *Christian Century* 49 (30 March 1932): 415-17.

"Prayer and Politics." *Christianity and Crisis* 12 (27 October 1952): 138-39.

"The President on 'The Arrogance of Power.' " *Christianity and Crisis* 26 (13 June 1966): 125-26.

"The Spirit and the Body in War." *Christianity and Crisis* 2 (10 August 1942): 1-2.

"The United Nations and World Organization." *Christianity and Crisis* 2 (25 January 1943): 1-2.

"Toward Intra-Christian Endeavors." *Christian Century* 86 (31 December 1969): 1662-67.

REINHOLD NIEBUHR—SECONDARY SOURCES: BOOKS

Bingham, June. *Courage to Change: An Introduction to the Life and Thought of Reinhold Niebuhr.* New York: Charles Scribner's Sons, 1961.

Cooper, John W. *The Theology of Freedom: The Legacy of Jacques Maritain and Reinhold Niebuhr.* Macon GA: Mercer University Press, 1985.

Davis, D. R. *Reinhold Niebuhr: Prophet from America.* New York: Macmillan, 1948.

Fackre, Gabriel. *The Promise of Reinhold Niebuhr*. Philadelphia: J. B. Lippincott, 1970.

Fox, Richard W. *Reinhold Niebuhr: A Biography*. New York: Pantheon Books, 1985.

Hofmann, Hans. *The Theology of Reinhold Niebuhr*. Translated by Louise Pattibone Smith. New York: Charles Scribner's Sons, 1956.

Kegley, Charles W. *Politics, Religion and Modern Man: Essays on Reinhold Niebuhr, Paul Tillich and Rudolf Bultman*. With Expository and Critical Essays by Jovito R. Salonga, J. J. Smith, S.J., and Emerito P. Nacpil. Quezon City: University of the Philippines Press, 1969.

Kegley, Charles W., and Bretall, Robert W., eds. *Reinhold Niebuhr: His Religious, Social, and Political Thought*. New York: Macmillan, 1956.

Landon, Harold R., ed. *Reinhold Niebuhr: A Prophetic Voice in Our Time: Essays in Tribute by Paul Tillich, John C. Bennett, and Hans J. Morgenthau*. Greenwich CT: Seabury Press, 1962.

Merkley, Paul. *Reinhold Niebuhr: A Political Account*. Montreal: McGill-Queens University Press, 1975.

Patterson, Bob E. *Reinhold Niebuhr*. Waco TX: Word Books, 1977.

Robertson, D. B. *Reinhold Niebuhr's Works: A Bibliography*. Boston: G. K. Hall, 1979.

Scott, Nathan A., Jr., ed. *The Legacy of Reinhold Niebuhr*. Chicago: University of Chicago Press, 1975.

Stone, Ronald H. *Reinhold Niebuhr: Prophet to Politicians*. Nashville: Abingdon Press, 1972.

Thompson, Kenneth W. *Christian Ethics and the Dilemmas of Foreign Policy*. Durham NC: Duke University Press, 1959.

REINHOLD NIEBUHR—SECONDARY SOURCES: ARTICLES

Brown, Robert McAfee. "Reinhold Niebuhr: A Study in Humility." In *The Legacy of Reinhold Niebuhr*, edited by Nathan A. Scott, Jr., 1-7. Chicago: University of Chicago Press, 1975.

Childress, James F. "Reinhold Niebuhr's Critique of Pacifism." *Review of Politics* 36 (1974): 467-91.

Pontuso, James F. "Reinhold Niebuhr's Political Thought: Christianity and Prudence." M.A. thesis, University of Virginia, 1977.

Stone, Ronald H., and Stone, Joann M., eds. "The Writings of Reinhold Niebuhr, 1953-71." *Union Seminary Quarterly Review* 27 (Fall 1971): 9-29.

Thompson, Kenneth W. "Beyond National Interest: A Critical Evaluation of Reinhold Niebuhr's Theory of International Politics." *Review of Politics* 17 (April 1955): 167-88.

ADDITIONAL SOURCES

Arendt, Hannah. *Between Past and Future*. New York: Viking Press, 1961.

Baynes, Norman H. *Byzantine Studies and Other Essays*. London: University of London, 1955.

Bennett, John C. *Foreign Policy in Christian Perspective*. New York: Charles Scribner's Sons, 1966.

Buber, Martin. *Between Man and Man*. Translated by Ronald Gregor Smith. New York: Macmillan, 1965.

_____. *I and Thou*. Translated by Walter Kaufman. New York: Charles Scribner's Sons, 1970.

Bundy, McGeorge. "The Bishops and the Bomb." *New York Review of Books* 30 (16 June 1983): 3-8.

_____, Kennan, George F., McNamara, Robert S., and Smith, Gerald. "Nuclear Weapons and the Atlantic Alliance." *Foreign Affairs* 60 (Spring 1982): 753-68.

Butterfield, Herbert. *The Origins of History*. Edited by Adam Watson. London: Eyre Methuen, 1981.

Carlyle, A. J. *A History of Medieval Political Theory in the West*. 2nd ed. Vol. 1, *The Second Century to the Ninth*. Edinburgh-London: Blackwood, 1927.

Childress, James F. *Civil Disobedience and Political Obligation: A Study in Christian Social Ethics*. New Haven: Yale University Press, 1971.

_____. "Just-War Theories: The Bases, Interrelations, Priorities, and Functions of Their Criteria." *Theological Studies* 39 (September 1978): 427-45.

_____. Review of *Just and Unjust Wars*, by Michael Walzer. *The Bulletin of the Atomic Scientists* 34 (October 1978): 44-48.

Cicero. *De Re Publica and De Legibus*. Translated by Clinton Walker Keyes. Cambridge: Harvard University Press, 1961.

Claude, Inis L., Jr. "Just Wars: Doctrines and Institutions." *Political Science Quarterly* 95 (1980): 83-96.

_____. "The Problem of Evaluating War." In *New Dimensions of World Politics*, edited by Geoffrey L. Goodwin and Andrew Linklater, 109-26. Beckenham, Kent: Croom Helm, 1975.

Cochrane, Charles N. *Christianity and Classical Culture*. London: Oxford University Press, 1944.

Dunn, David. "War and Social Change." In *The Use of Force in International Relations*, edited by F. S. Northedge, 220-47. London: Faber and Faber, 1974.

Eppstein, John. *The Catholic Tradition of the Law of Nations*. London: Burns, Oates and Washbourne, 1935.

Ford, John C. "The Morality of Obliteration Bombing." *Theological Studies* 5 (September 1944): 261-309.

Germino, Dante. *Beyond Ideology: The Revival of Political Theory*. New York: Harper & Row, 1967. Reprint. Chicago: University of Chicago Press, 1976.

Gilson, Etienne. *The Spirit of Medieval Philosophy*. Translated by A. H. C. Downes. New York: Charles Scribner's Sons, 1940.

Gray, J. Glenn. *The Warriors: Reflections on Men in Battle*. New York: Harcourt, Brace, 1959.

Hick, John. *Evil and the God of Love*. Rev. ed. San Francisco: Harper & Row, 1977.

Holmes, Arthur F., ed. *War and Christian Ethics*. Grand Rapids MI: Baker Book House, 1975.

Inge, W. R. *Christian Mysticism*. 3rd ed. London: Methuen and Co., 1913.

Johnson, James Turner. *Can Modern War Be Just?* New Haven: Yale University Press, 1984.

————. "Just War Theory: What's the Use?" *Worldview* 19 (July-August 1976): 41-47.

————. "Toward Reconstructing the *jus ad bellum*." *Monist* 57 (1973): 461-88.

Kennan, George F. "Morality and Foreign Policy." *Foreign Affairs* 64 (Winter 1985/86): 205-18.

Keyes, Alan L. "The Morality of Deterrence." *Catholicism in Crisis* 1 (April 1983): 33-43.

Keyley, Charles W., ed. *The Philosophy and Theology of Anders Nygren*. Carbondale: Southern Illinois University Press, 1970.

Knox, Ronald. *Enthusiasm*. New York: Oxford University Press, 1961.

Lawler, Philip F. Introduction to *Justice and War in the Nuclear Age*, edited by Philip F. Lawler. New York: American Catholic Committee, 1982.

Long, Edward Leroy, Jr. *War and Conscience in America*. Philadelphia: Westminster Press, 1968.

Lowith, Karl. *Meaning in History*. Chicago: University of Chicago Press, 1949.

"Moral Clarity in the Nuclear Age: A Letter from Catholic Clergy and Laity." *Catholicism in Crisis* 1 (March 1983): 3-23.

Moss, H. St. L. B. *The Birth of the Middle Ages, 395-814*. Oxford: Oxford University Press, 1935.

National Conference of Catholic Bishops. *The Challenge of Peace: God's Promise and Our Response*. Washington DC: United States Catholic Conference, 1983.

Niebuhr, H. Richard. "The Grace of Doing Nothing." *Christian Century* 49 (23 March 1932): 378-80.

————. "The Only Way into the Kingdom of God." *Christian Century* 49 (6 April 1932): 447.

Nye, Joseph S., Jr. *Nuclear Ethics*. New York: Macmillan, 1986.

O'Brien, William V. *The Conduct of Just and Limited War*. New York: Praeger, 1981.

Outka, Gene H. *Agape: An Ethical Analysis*. New Haven: Yale University Press, 1972.

Pegis, Anton C., ed. *Basic Writings of St. Thomas Aquinas*. 2 vols. New York: Random House, 1945.

Rawls, John. *A Theory of Justice*. Cambridge: Harvard University Press, Belknap Press, 1971.

Reynolds, L. D., and Wilson, N. G. *Scribes and Scholars*. London: Oxford University Press, 1968.

Rist, John M. "Some Interpretations of Agape and Eros." In *The Philosophy and Theology of Anders Nygren*, edited by Charles W. Kegley, 156-73. Carbondale: Southern Illinois University Press, 1970.

Schall, James V., S.J. "Intellectual Origins of the Peace Movement." In *Justice and War in the Nuclear Age*, edited by Philip F. Lawler, 25-59. New York: American Catholic Committee, 1982.

Thompson, Kenneth W. *The President and the Public Philosophy*. Baton Rouge: Louisiana State University Press, 1981.

Tinder, Glenn. *Community: Reflections on a Tragic Ideal*. Baton Rouge: Louisiana State University Press, 1980.

Toynbee, Arnold J. *War and Civilization*. Selected by Albert V. Fowler. New York: Oxford University Press, 1950.

Tucker, Robert W. *Just War and Vatican II: A Critique*. With Commentary by George G. Higgins, Ralph Potter, Richard H. Cox, and Paul Ramsey. New York: Council on Religion and International Affairs, 1966.

————. *The Just War*. Baltimore: Johns Hopkins University Press, 1960. Reprint. Westport CT: Greenwood Press, 1978.

von Elbe, Joachim. "The Evolution of the Concept of the Just War in International Law." *American Journal of International Law* 33 (October 1939): 665-88.

Walters, LeRoy. "Five Classic Just War Theories: A Study in the Thought of Thomas Aquinas, Vitoria, Suarez, Gentili and Grotius." Ph.D. diss., Yale University, 1971.

Walters, LeRoy. "The Just War and the Crusade: Antitheses or Analogies?" *Monist* 57 (1973): 584-94.

Walzer, Michael. *Just and Unjust Wars.* New York: Basic Books, 1977.